FIRST
PERSON
SINGULAR

FIRST PERSON SINGULAR

Living the Good Life Alone

Dr. Stephen M. Johnson

J. B. LIPPINCOTT COMPANY
PHILADELPHIA AND NEW YORK

The quotation on page 239 is copyright by
Argus Publications.

An excerpt from this book has appeared
in *Ultra* magazine.

U.S. Library of Congress Cataloging in Publication Data

Johnson, Stephen M
    First person singular.

    Includes bibliographical references.
    1. Bereavement–Psychological aspects.
2. Divorce. 3. Autonomy (Psychology) I. Title.
BF575.G7J63   158′.1   76–51353
ISBN–0–397–01162–8

To my friends

Contents

Acknowledgments

THIS BOOK IS dedicated to my friends because they helped me write it by generously sharing their lives, their ideas, and their support. Most of them cannot be mentioned here, but I am grateful to each one for his or her special help. Perhaps more than any other, my friend and colleague Jeff Steger started this whole endeavor by smoothing my own transition to single life. This book is aimed at doing for other single people some of what Jeff and others like him have done for me. Some of those others have been directly involved in generating and refining the ideas presented here. Thanks to those who let me think out loud to them and gave freely of their ideas; especially Peter Alevizos, Judy Bancroft, Mark Condiotte, Bob Eimers, Larry King, and Susan Phillips. Many friends read portions of the manuscript and provided helpful feedback and suggestions. Special thanks are due to those few who patiently and carefully read it all and provided extensive review: Andy Christensen, Suzanne Gaughen, Peggy Cronlund, my talented copy editor, and Robert and Toni Zeiss, who also worked with me in the early development of ideas and research.

The warmest appreciation is due Beatrice Rosenfeld, my editor, who did more than anyone else to get this book from me to you. Editors do much more than edit; the best ones shepherd the books under their care. Bea has been the best of shepherds to this book and has become a treasured friend to me.

Much of this book was created while I was on sabbatical in southern California, where my friends Robert Liberman and Jim Simmons provided me the congenial environment and practical support needed to put it together. And, through it all, my friend Gwen Kingsley, who happens to work as my secretary, smoothed things out as she always has.

Background support has always been forthcoming from my mother and father and from Bette, a friend to whom I was once married.

Finally, I want to acknowledge my intellectual debt to Albert Ellis, whose ideas have made a profound impact on my life and my work. Though I barely know him, in a special way I count him a friend.

In the book of life, the answers are not in the back.
—*Charlie Brown*, Peanuts

Introduction

It is heresy in America to embrace any way of life except as one half of a couple.

—Erica Jong

THIS IS A BOOK for adults who are single. As such, it is a book about a heretical way of life full of promise, often unfulfilled. In some ways, living single has become the thing to do. The image of single independence and freedom seems even more enticing as these personal values are given heightened social support and as people try to liberate themselves from whatever bonds them. And, yet, these romantic visions of single living usually don't go very far and are only hollow approximations of anything very real—often little more than visions of the excitement of finding and falling in love with a new partner or the ephemeral joys of a superficially playful existence with continual stimulation. While these dreamy notions may certainly provide exhilarating fantasies for the quietly coupled, they seriously miss the mark for those seeking to build a constructive and meaningful life. There are plenty of incomplete images of single life, but few if any realistic or complete models.

It is overwhelmingly clear that more and more people are striking out and attempting to establish their own

13

alternative life-styles. In 1974, for instance, the divorce rate increased for the twelfth consecutive year and was up by 31 percent over 1970. During this same year, the number of marriages decreased for the first time in sixteen years. By 1975 there were 48 divorces for every 100 marriages. But those who are embracing alternative life-styles are doing it alone—without the social institutions, the customs, the legitimacy, or the support that could assist them. We are in a time of drastic social change in which the models of the past are no longer completely useful, while the models for present and future existence are only vaguely defined. We are in the distinctly uncomfortable position of living in a time when a number of possibilities are available but in which only one life-style is clearly congruent with our prior experience. That is the *coupling* which results in a closed and legal marriage. Those of us who choose or are forced to experiment with different ways of life need all the help we can get. I know because I've tried it and, as a clinical psychologist, have attempted to help countless others as they have tried it. I write this book because I think I have something to offer in the development of alternative *job descriptions* for single life.

This book is based primarily on my experience as a social scientist and clinical psychologist investigating the problems of divorce and single-life adjustment. Together with colleagues in Oregon and California, I have developed learning and treatment programs for those in the midst of readjustment to single life. And, as a divorced man, I have lived through such an adjustment in my own life. All I have learned in these pursuits is reflected in this book. You will find here the sociological statistics, the case histories from my practice, and some personal philosophies which derive from the entirety of my experience as a professional and as a human being.

One of these philosophies is reflected in Charlie Brown's lament, "In the book of life, the answers are not in the back." I chose this as the book's epigraph to tell you that I know I don't have all the answers. If you are a single person, I hope the book will provide you with some useful ideas and advice. But if anything you find here does not apply to you as an individual, let it go; just take what you can make your own and ignore the rest—at least for now. What is kept in reserve may be useful later.

The ideas presented here are directed equally to men and women, and though current differences in sex roles are acknowledged, they are not glorified or viewed as being static. Indeed, I hope that what you find here will help to further the freedom that can come from loosening the control of all kinds of fixed prescriptions for life. This book is as nonsexist as I could make it while still being honest with myself and honest about the society on which it is a commentary. But, of course, my own loosening from fixed prescriptions is still going on, and this may show in places. I hope I'll find out where those places are and that you will be able to receive what I have to convey in spite of them.

The book is divided into three parts, the sequence of which reflects what seems to be the natural course of events in the life of the single person. Part I is devoted to the problems of effecting a separation from an old relationship and life-style. Because we live in a couples culture, almost every adult now single has not long ago left the coupled state. Effecting the separation well and beginning to resolve it will be the first task of single life.

The failure to accomplish this task, practically or spiritually, is one of the most common causes for a separated person's failure to embrace a rewarding single life in all its possibilities. So, the first chapters of this book deal with the problem of separation, and one chapter contains information especially for those leaving a legal marriage or a *functional marriage* (a living-together arrangement).

If you are beyond your first adolescent romantic entanglement, you have a relationship history. So does every other single person you will meet. And you will be just a little bit ahead of the game if you realize that prior relationships are always more or less active in the lives of every single person and that they affect the ways in which singles interact with one another. Understanding the dimensions of not only your own but others' separation dilemmas will assist you no matter where you are in the process of living single.

Part II of this book is about living fully in the first person singular. Single life can be much more than a temporary way station between adolescence and marriage or between marriages. It can be a never-equaled opportunity for personal growth and development. It can provide the impetus to learn a host of new, enjoyable, and worthwhile skills for living. If lived well, it can not only be rewarding in itself, but can also serve as the best prerequisite for any other adult life-style alternative. If you can learn to live well independently, you can then embrace any other alternative by choice because of its added benefits, not because you must have it in order to survive.

Unfortunately, single life often becomes an uncomfortable trap, a lonely existence, something to be escaped rather than embraced. When single life reaches this point, it can impel you into premature and unhappy personal commitments. Living singly can deteriorate to this point for many reasons, but primary among them is the fact that there is a deficient job description for the single life; there is little legitimacy or support for this amorphous life role. As a consequence, single people often view it as a transitory and incomplete existence. Failing to work on the mastery of single life, they turn all their energies to getting out of it as quickly as possible. As a result, they fail to appreciate its advantages and escape it before experiencing it.

Part III of the book deals with the various stages involved in developing meaningful heterosexual relationships, from the problems of how to meet suitable men and women to how to define and enrich new commitments in primary relationships. Although it is hoped that what is written here will help support and legitimize alternative single life-styles, this book is not anticouple nor antimarriage. It is written with the clear recognition that the great majority of people in this country continue to view pairing in primary relationships as the most desirable life-style. The available research plainly suggests that many people who would seem to reject marriage by divorce do, in fact, remarry —usually in a relatively short time. Moreover, although functional-marriage arrangements are apparently replacing legal marriage for a significant proportion of single people, some form of marriage is still the life-style of choice for the great majority. And even those who do not endorse such commitments usually desire meaningful and comfortable relationships. For these reasons, a good deal of this book is devoted to a discussion of the initiation and maintenance of such relationships.

The focus here is on heterosexual relationships only because this represents most people's choice and reflects my own professional experiences. The book is really about living with yourself and others; the basic principles transcend sexual preference.

Because of the book's organization, it is possible that not every section will appear directly relevant to your current single situation. You may have resolved your own separation and autonomous adulthood problems and be concerned only with the pursuit of single life or of new alternatives. Or you may be in the throes of an unwanted separation or divorce crisis and see the prospects of living singly or becoming involved in other relationships as absurd and totally beyond you. But if you are a single person, you will need to deal with each of the problems discussed here, either in yourself or in the other single people who become a part of your life. And the chapters which may at first seem irrelevant can help you in looking back at the tasks that you have completed and in foreshadowing those which are to come. I hope that your adventure in single living will be a good one and that the ideas you encounter here will at least in some way make a difference.

PART I
SAYING GOOD-BYE:
HOW TO SEPARATE

1
How to Say Good-bye

The road is not the road, the road is how you walk it.

—*Juan Ramón Jiménez*

DISENGAGEMENT

TEARING AWAY from someone you have loved, saying good-bye to what is known and often still cherished, ending the familiar and beginning a journey without a destination—separating—is perhaps life's most difficult assignment. Change of every kind is hard, but the change of breaking those human attachments that give meaning to life is especially difficult. Broken dreams of love are sad, and tears are not wasted in mourning their passing.

But life *is* change. The popular myth of permanence, which suggests that commitment to love or marriage—or to anything else—means a bargain with a lifetime guarantee that no change will be required, is destructive. Like most unrealistic notions, the myth contributes heavily to people's failures and then leaves them bewildered when the failures occur. Furthermore, it prevents those who buy it from appreciating the challenge and the promise of change.

If you are in the process of effecting a separation, you are in for change. It is possible for you to postpone some of it for a while, but that very postponement will often produce other, even less welcome change. Change is inevitable, and you must begin it either within your present relationship or outside of it. This chapter is written to help you with the second alternative, whether the decision to separate is your own or one forced on you by your partner. The principles for effecting a good separation apply equally well to the termination of all primary relationships—love affairs, functional marriages, or legal marriages. Though a separation will typically be more difficult and the number of decisions greater if legal divorce and child custody are involved, the basic process is the same.

If your separation is like most others, it has been a long time in coming. We do not throw off our commitments to those we have loved carelessly. Most divorces, for example, come about only after years of unhappiness and indecision. Some couples attempt to work on their unfulfilling relationships during these years, but many others go on and on, bearing frustration but doing little, in the hope that something will happen to improve matters, until the relationship is beyond help.

Experience suggests that decisions to separate are made for three basic reasons. First, people give up hope that their relationship can ever be mended so as to fulfill their needs. Many of these people still love their partners and deeply wish that salvaging the partnership were possible but, alas, they decide it is not, and the time finally comes when they throw in the towel. Wives of loved but impossibly intransigent alcoholics are the most striking examples of this type.

Second, people simply lose the motivation to make their relationship any better. They know that many of its aspects could be enhanced with effort, but they have lost the commitment required to make the effort. Such people usually have borne the loss of that commitment for a long time and have tried to rekindle their desire, but to no avail. All too often, however, these individuals have neither communicated their long-endured pain to their partners nor attempted to improve things before making the final decision. This, of course, can be devastating to the partners who assumed that "things were fine," and their bewilderment, fear, and rage at the separation announcement are understandable. Individuals who simply lose hope can find little to say beyond "I just don't love you anymore," or "I just want out, I'm sorry." This type of separation decision is very common and usually firm. When a primary relationship is unfulfilling and one partner has no will to improve it, the prognosis is poor.

The third type of separation decision occurs in marriages in which the participants have slowly but surely grown to have little in common and in love affairs or functional marriages when couples discover serious incompatibilities in living. One can love and live with another who is so totally different that extensive accommodation is required of both partners. It is possible, but is it worth it? The time comes when it is not; and the arrival at this rational adult decision, while it may be cause for sadness at what is lost, is also a victory for good common sense.

You may be helped to understand your own or your partner's separation decision by determining which of the three basic types best fits your situation. As discussed in detail later in this chapter, working out an explanation for yourself and others concerning the reasons for your separation will be a necessary step in adjusting to it. But for now, let's assume that the separation decision has been made, let's hope wisely, perhaps foolishly, but made. Now what do you do?

If one of the partners in a relationship decides that he or she wants to end it, there is only one sensible thing to do: separate as quickly, completely, and kindly as possible. It is going to take a great deal of effort and time to build a new life after your relationship has dissolved. To grow as an individual, you must commit yourself to a new way of living. Failing to separate completely, once the end has become inevitable, simply delays that commitment and growth and usually causes further deterioration of whatever aspects of the relationship you hope to preserve.

Martha and Bill lived together for nearly a year after Bill decided he wanted to end their marriage. Their reasons for staying together were many and seemed reasonable. Martha was in school and wanted to finish. With some help from Bill, she could have finished on her own, but it would have been harder financially, and she would have had to settle for a lower standard of living. Bill wanted to help Martha finish; she had supported him during his college years by waiting on table, he still cared for her, and he would have felt guilty about leaving her now. Besides, he liked her to keep house and cook for him—he just didn't want to spend the rest of his life with her. Why couldn't they live together as roommates for a while? He would have his life and she would have hers. It would be a friendly, civilized, mature relationship.

Martha made it clear that she loved Bill and wanted to stay married to him, but would respect his wishes. She kept hoping he would change his mind—maybe it was just a phase he was going through, and perhaps if he sowed a few wild oats he'd appreciate what he had. Bill didn't like taking all the responsibility for the decision, and he hoped that in time Martha would agree it was best for them to separate and divorce.

Both were only dimly aware of these motives, however, and Martha, sometimes wanting to win Bill back, would try to be especially good to him. This would make him feel crowded and uncomfortable, and whenever he accepted her kindnesses he'd feel guilty. Soon, any kindness from her would make him at once irritable and guilty about being irritable. Besides, he didn't want to "lead her on," and so behaved in a cross or distant manner to reinforce his desire to separate. Yet from time to time he would revert to being friendly—after all, their staying friends had been fundamental to his original idea of their being temporary roommates—and Martha would wonder and be hopeful. But, of course, when Bill recognized or even suspected that, he would withdraw again.

For her part, Martha never knew how to interpret Bill's behavior or how to respond to him. Should she keep on hoping, or should she show him that she could live quite well without him? Should she avoid seeing other men so as not to confirm the impending separation, or should she show him that other men wanted her even if he didn't? As time went on, she gave up hope and began to retaliate against him. Sometimes when this happened he would remind her that he was putting her through school and was living with her only to help her out. And she, infuriated at the son of a bitch whom she'd slaved as a waitress to get through school, would rage that he owed her this and more. . . .

Retaliation led to more retaliation, and this once loving and rational couple finally needed lawyers to settle a host of petty demands and counterdemands. A year later, Bill and Martha had ruined their relationship, spent a good deal of money on their fight, and had not yet begun to work on becoming well-adjusted single people.

Many things were happening in Bill and Martha's nonmarriage to harm them both, but their most basic problem in attempting to stay under the same roof was the breakdown of *shared assumptions* for communication. Relating to those we live with is always complex, but when there is no mutual understanding of the meaning of our actions and words, it becomes nearly impossible.

Although many explanations are given for delaying an imminent separation, most boil down to three not very good reasons. The first, which can be common to both partners, is simply fear—fear of what will be demanded in separation and in beginning a new life alone. Second, the reluctant partner to the separation may hope that the one who wants to leave will somehow magically change his or her mind. Third, the partner who wants the separation is especially afraid of taking this major, honestly frightening step. He or she feels that assuming sole responsibility for this difficult decision is just too much. Sometimes, the partner who wants to separate hopes, at some level of awareness, to wear the other down so that eventually the separation decision will be a mutual one. The hope of the reluctant partner is almost always a fruitless one, and the hope of the initiating partner, although not always fruitless, is certainly destructive. If, as is almost always the case, the relationship deteriorates, there is increasingly less likelihood that the partner wanting the separation will have a change of heart. And, although the initiating partner has every right to change the other's mind by making life increasingly miserable, that's an unfortunate way to handle the situation. Making other people miserable is an unhappy occupation. So, choose whether you wish to work on your existing relationship or on your separation, and get down to business.

Although not uncommon, Bill and Martha's failure at *disengagement* was fairly extreme. Most couples have the good sense to separate when it becomes clear that that outcome is inevitable. But even these wiser couples sometimes fail to disengage in countless small but important ways and thereby retard their movement into a new life, as in the following case.

Linda and Bob separated almost immediately after coming to a more or less mutual decision to terminate their marriage. Bob moved out with only some of his clothes and checked into a very small, furnished apartment which had the appearance of a rundown motel. Bob could have afforded something larger and more homey, but surroundings had never meant much to him anyway, and he knew the divorce would be expensive.

He wanted to do right by his wife and child and felt noble in his sacrifices, which included allowing Linda to stay in their expensive home and to keep the best car and a good portion of his monthly income. Linda hadn't worked for three years, since their child, Jimmy, had come along. She knew she would have to get a job, of course, but the prospect frightened her and she wasn't sure what kind of job she wanted. Bob's generosity allowed her to delay this decision indefinitely. After six months' separation, when she finally got around to seeing a lawyer about divorce, he advised her to delay seeking employment even further. Her attorney knew from experience that if she had a job it might put him at a disadvantage in negotiating child support and alimony for her.

Bob had always been good at making and managing money, but he didn't know the first thing about taking care of himself. He stopped by the house often to see his son, to bring money, or to pick up his mail, some clothes, or other incidentals he had left behind. As he didn't know how to cook, Linda, feeling guilty about his self-sacrifice, would offer him a meal once or twice a week. And, since he was coming over anyway, he'd sometimes bring some laundry for her to do, or he'd look after the family car or check Linda's bills for her.

It seemed that all this was working out well, but Linda began to get very uneasy. She had no privacy, because Bob could drop by at almost any time. She was still fairly sentimental about their marriage, even though she knew it would never work, and the constant reminders of him in the morning mail, in the closet full of his clothes, or during the surprise visits would upset her. She began to resent not only the loss of privacy but the feeling of being used as a cook and laundress. She also resented the control Bob continued to exert over her by managing her accounts and advising her on everything from her career to her child-rearing practices. But it was hard to express the resentment, of course, because he was still supporting her, and handsomely at that.

For Bob, this arrangement was getting damned expensive, and his feelings of nobility gave way to resentment as he found that his monthly income would not stretch to support the three of them under these new circumstances. He found that he had to sell some of his stocks to make ends meet, that he didn't have the money or the apartment or the car to entertain himself or other women as he thought he should. And he didn't like finding other men in his house when he dropped by to see his child—he didn't like that one bit. The resentment changed to action when he finally consulted his lawyer, who told him flatly, "You've got an 'alimony drone' on your hands. We've got to stop that if we're going to protect your future."

Eight months after their first nonseparation separation, Bob and Linda had to separate again by really disengaging, a process made more acrimonious and difficult than it might have been had it occurred initially. Of course, it wasn't easy for Bob to begin taking care of himself and settling into a more stable single life, and it wasn't easy for Linda to look for work and give up the nice house, but the delay had only made it harder. Bob and Linda did learn something in those eight months, however: they learned how not to separate.

The failure to disengage adequately from one's

spouse during the first few months of separation is perhaps the most common and growth-retarding mistake made by separating couples. Even the simple things like Bob's failure to change his mailing address and to move out all his things provided unwanted reminders for Linda while giving Bob excuses for unnecessary contact. He also demonstrated the surprisingly common *dropping-by syndrome,* which most generally is perpetrated by men on women. These unscheduled and unannounced visits are typically upsetting because they deprive the visited ex-partner of privacy and of the control over her (or his) life which is so necessary when becoming single.

Separating couples often cling to each other after a physical separation by continuing a number of *functional dependencies.* Thus, Linda continued to cook and launder for Bob while he continued to support her completely and handled her bills and the care of her car. While some of these dependencies may seem efficient on the face of it, they tend to retard the readjustment process and to hold people in limbo between the coupled and the single state. Assuming unfamiliar responsibilities is one of the great challenges of this adjustment, and mastering them is one of its great rewards. You can buy time to avoid this endeavor, but why and at what cost?

Separating individuals often hold on to these functional dependencies in order to cover their desire to see each other, to continue their control of each other, or simply to spy on each other. All these motivations are detrimental, including the first, in part because they are all covert. They usually become obvious sooner or later and create further wedges between the people involved. If you continue to maintain these functional dependencies on your partner, what are your reasons? Are there better ways to get what you want? Or if it is information or control you want, do you really need them?

It is not uncommon for couples to break the disengagement process by getting together on special occasions such as birthdays, Thanksgiving, Christmas, or other holidays, hoping to recapture some of what they once had. To me, this represents understandable but rather magical thinking. While it is possible for distressed couples who have separated to reconcile and recapture the beauty of their relationship, it is extremely unlikely that this will occur easily. Usually, these special meetings end disastrously. They often serve the dubious purpose of reconfirming the couple's decision to separate after the unrealistic hopes of recaptured love remain unfulfilled. If you and your partner feel you must attempt this kind of meeting, go ahead, but don't be surprised if it's a total bust. A real reconciliation is a more serious and difficult matter, which is best approached with a real commitment to reach for change.

In emphasizing the need for disengagement in separation, I am *not* claiming that it is necessary for couples to close off contact. Especially when children are involved, there is a need for continued involvement and cooperation in a common endeavor. And, in any case, people can often build on the positive aspects of their relationship to form a meaningful and lasting friendship. But a disengagement of functions and a formal system for initiating and maintaining contact is advisable. Generally, a period of pulling back—a time of reduced contact and almost forced noninvolvement —is a prerequisite to the development of a friendship which differs from the preceding amative relationship.

There are some questions you may ask yourself about your current separation relationship to help you determine whether more disengagement would be advisable:

Does your involvement interfere in any way with the development of your own autonomy and the acquisition of skills required of an independent adult?

Does your interaction in any way preclude your involvement with friends or the development of love-sex relationships?

Do your meetings depress, upset, or preoccupy you?

If you can answer no to all three of these questions, fine; if you have any yeses—or even a maybe—it would probably be wise to engineer less contact, at least for a time. Disengagement as defined here is essential for a successful separation, but disengagement does not mean termination. It does mean change and it does mean loss; in a separation, both must be faced sooner or later.

What if neither partner is completely sure that separating is the best thing to do? The answer to this common problem is, in principle, rather simple, but acting on it is always most difficult. The involved individuals must do whatever they believe will help further a decision. Though it is unwise to rush this, it is in the best interest of both partners to reach a sound determination as soon as possible. Periods of living together and living apart may be necessary to achieve a sufficient degree of certainty. It is often a messy and uncomfortable process and, if drawn out too long, can often spoil the beauty of the original relationship. It is, however, a process for which I have gained increasing respect as I have endeavored to help ambivalent individuals though their separation dilemmas. A love relationship dies hard, and many people must experience their failure more than once before being sure about giving up.

Consider the relationship of Ralph and Susan, who had lived together for a year when things began to become strained. Like many of the functionally married, this couple had not discussed the *meaning* of their living-together arrangement. As I talked to them, it became clear to me that from the beginning the arrangement had had a different significance for each of them. Ralph had thrown himself into the relationship completely and thought of it as one would a legal marriage. He worked very hard to help provide for Susan and her six-year-old child and dreamed of buying a large house in the country for all of them. He became very attached to the child and, to all intents and purposes, he was married.

Susan was not. She had entered this arrangement much more casually than Ralph and made no assumptions about the future. She loved Ralph, and that was enough. But living with him became increasingly unexciting. He seemed to work all the time and was no longer spontaneous, romantic, or fun to be with. In short, Ralph became something of a dull, hardworking, responsible married man. Susan, an attractive and sociable woman open to experience, had an affair with another man and left old Ralph. That was devastating to him, and he behaved exactly as Bob had after his separation in order to keep in contact and restrict his wife. Susan didn't like such maneuvers and rejected Ralph every time he made contact, but he couldn't stop himself, and Susan never made the hard moves which would stop him.

Ralph came to our clinic and got some disengagement coaching. He stopped using covert tactics such as dropping by to see the child, and saw Susan only by appointment for pleasurable activities. As time went by, an increasing number of these "dates" were suggested by Susan, and they began to really talk and have fun together as they had in the initial stages of their relationship. They now have a much better understanding of each other and of their relationship, past and present. They both see other people, they live apart, and they're unsure of what the future may hold for them. For our purposes, it doesn't matter, because what they now have is as right as it can be in the present. They are disengaged from the former living-together unity and reengaged in a different kind of relationship. Their ability to pull this off is unusual but not superhuman. Becoming disengaged from the old ways of relating made it possible to reengage in the new.

In the introduction to this book I urged you to take whatever advice made sense to you and ignore the rest. On the point of disengagement, however, it is my experience that many ex-partners feel they can be excepted from this principle—it makes sense for others but not for them. Few if any of these people are correct in the long run. Contact with the ex-partner may be necessary and even desirable, but some form of disen-.

gagement of function and redefinition of the relationship is almost always necessary to make the contact work for those involved.

On the other hand, perhaps you never want to see your ex-partner again as long as you live, and the problems of those couples who drag their feet make no sense to you. Perhaps seeing your partner is too painful or too infuriating to tolerate. You may wish at least to avoid and at most to punish him or her severely for the pain of the past or present. You may even wish to get rid of all the material things you held in common or to move as far away as possible to avoid all contact and all those places that trigger memories. If this is the case, the first stage of physical disengagement discussed thus far will probably come very naturally to you. To separate, limit, or eliminate contact and eradicate all functional dependencies will seem the only conceivable thing to do. And this is a start. But what of your emotional disengagement? It is *time* with your ex-partner that is the antithesis of disengagement. How much time are you spending with him or her in your *head?* Disengagement, the next and last stage, involves coming to a point where your feelings for your ex-partner range somewhere from loving concern to benign indifference. With final disengagement, there is no more longing, no more blaming, no more guilt, and no more inclination to punish.

Obviously, this second level of disengagement takes time for everyone, and getting there is what much of this first section is about. But those who embrace physical disengagement the hardest, those who *must* close off all contact because they *can't stand* the pain that it brings, are often the last to effect this final disengagement. Advice on coping with this problem will be found in Chapter 2. Here, I introduce the concepts and goals of primary and secondary disengagement and request you to ask yourself honestly: How far down the disengagement road have I come? Why am I still wasting energy on a relationship that has ended? What can I start doing or stop doing to take the next step toward a more relaxed disengagement?

Even if you are the reluctant partner in the separation, it still makes sense for you to disengage and begin to live as a single person. One of two things will happen to you now. You will either reconcile or you will not. If you don't, you might as well get started on your single life right away. If you do, you won't have lost anything. Indeed, you probably will have gained at least two important things. First, you will have shown yourself that you can survive independently. You will have experienced the advantages of single life—and you may even decide you prefer it. If you reconcile, it will be with the knowledge that you can live without your partner; you merely *prefer* not to. Second, you will not have driven your loved one further away by clinging dependency. Rather, you will have given him or her a chance to miss you. Clingy, dependent people are usually not very attractive; independent, self-sufficient, confident people are. Thus, whether you reconcile or not, you will be better off to disengage and become independent. As one country-and-western song says, "How Can I Miss You When You Won't Go Away?" And you can't really decide how you feel about being single until you've tried it.

In general, it is a good idea to let your partner know if you would like to try a reconciliation, bearing in mind that this is only your *current* position, which may change with time and the experience it brings. Whether you are the reluctant partner or the one who initiated the separation, it will help you to be able to state your requirements for getting back together. Would you demand that your partner agree to counseling, for example, or would you expect some change in his or her behavior? Would you consent only to a trial reconciliation? What would your partner have to do to get you back? Knowing your own position and requirements will help you retain the feeling of being in control of your destiny. Especially if you are the reluctant partner, you will do well to formulate *your* position, so that a reconciliation, if there is one, will be the product of your decision as well as that of your partner.

If separating people who consult me wish to reconcile, I obviously don't encourage them to do anything which would preclude reconciliation, but I do advise them—for the reasons given—to act *as if* the separation were permanent. Consider the case of Hal, a forty-five-year-old devoted husband and father whose wife asked him to leave home after twenty years of marriage. His wife's discontent and desire for separation were a complete surprise to Hal, but her decision was firm, and she let him know this repeatedly and in every possible way. He wouldn't accept it—it just couldn't happen. He was convinced, despite all the evidence to the contrary, that his wife would want him back sooner or later. Instead of renting an apartment for himself, Hal moved in with his mother, since there was no sense in going to all that trouble for such a short while. He avoided seeing his friends because talking about it would "cement the separation," and he didn't want his wife to think he was speaking ill of her to others. He wouldn't even consider dating.

Hal refused to see a lawyer even though his wife was demanding most of their common property and planning to leave him with all the substantial obligations. He would see his children, but because he was so depressed they weren't very interested in seeing him. He stopped doing all the things he enjoyed because they were meaningless without someone to share them. He became a social isolate save for talking to his mother, who unfortunately supported much of his reasoning. Because of his severe depression he was referred to our clinic. Time and some confrontive therapy finally brought Hal around to acting as if his separation were permanent. He took off his wedding ring and returned to doing what gave him pleasure; he developed an active social life again, began to date, and lost his depressive symptoms. He never reconciled with his wife, and indeed, before his divorce was final he had become very doubtful whether he would want to reconcile, even if given the opportunity. By beginning to live single, Hal lost nothing but his dependency and depression.

THE RITES OF PASSAGE

There is a ritual through which every separating person must go—a ritual which most people approach reluctantly and fearfully, but which usually proves to be very reassuring. It represents the gateway to a new life, and performing it skillfully can make a great deal of difference, particularly in the first few months after separation. The ritual is simple: you must have a funeral for your relationship; you must tell your friends and family about your separation and redefine your role —not as one part of a couple, but as an individual, alone.

Even though you may be in considerable distress during this time, it is necessary for you to perform these rites, and soon, primarily because most people do not know how to behave with a separated person and particularly with someone about to be divorced. We are taught how to behave when our friends or members of our family go through other important life changes or crises. Rituals exist for birth, emergence into adulthood, graduation, engagement, marriage, and death. For these occasions, people are provided with socially sanctioned scripts—they know what they are supposed to do and say and feel. But there is no script for separation and divorce. Lacking a standard ritual, you must provide it as well as execute it. This do-it-yourself ritual will not be easy for either you or your friends and family, but for this reason it is especially necessary. Friends and family are usually very curious and concerned about a separating couple, and they would like to be helpful. But since they don't know how to ask about separation, much less how to be of help, you must tell them. Because many separating and to-be-divorced people do not understand this, or because telling is very difficult for them, they often postpone it. Unfortunately, this postponement often results in the social isolation of the separating individual at a time when he or she most desperately needs social support.

The case of Phil is typical. Phil was a very socially active professional man who left his wife after twelve years of marriage. He felt guilty about having initiated the separation, and he was reluctant to talk about it with his friends. He moved to a small apartment, stopped going to social functions, and even went to work less than usual. For several months he did not have a phone in his new apartment, where he withdrew with his books, his thoughts, and his guilt. Among the many things that bothered him during these months was his feeling that most of his friends had deserted him. Fortunately, he was to find out later that these friends were simply uncomfortable and unsure of how to approach him, and hence waited for Phil to make the first move; when he didn't, they just continued waiting. Phil's first few months of being single and the separation ritual itself would have been much easier had he taken care of it without delay.

If you are a recently separated person, the sooner you begin the rites of passage, the sooner you will be able to reconstruct a meaningful social life with continuity and promise. If you have lived with another and are now physically separated, you should have at least begun the rites of passage. If you have not lived together, your rites will be simpler and less necessary.

What do you tell people? It is best to tell every significant person in your social environment that you and your partner are separated and no longer a functioning couple. Even if everyone knows from other sources, each one should hear it directly from you, so that each of you has the experience of knowing that the other knows. For most of your associates, your statement can be extremely brief. To significant business associates with whom you don't really wish to discuss the matter at any length, you might say, "Have you heard that my husband/wife and I are separated and planning a divorce? I just wanted to let you know. I think it will be hard, but we both hope that, in the long run, it will be for the best." If the other person wishes to talk with you about it further, you can decide whether or not you want to do this. If not, it is perfectly acceptable to say something like, "All of this is kind of upsetting to me right now and, at least for the time being, I would rather not talk too much about it. It's nice to know that I could talk with you if I thought it would help. At least you know about it now, and I hope we can go on from here just as before." With more intimate friends and family you obviously will be expected to provide an explanation, and possibly a report of the sequence of events that led up to separation. Of course, some of them will probably have seen it coming anyway. It is entirely up to you to decide how much— or how much more—you want to divulge. If there are certain things you do not wish to talk about, say so. You may have to quell their inquisitiveness repeatedly, but don't hesitate to do so. Stick to the position you have worked out until you decide to change it.

Planning in advance what your general presentation of this information will be has many beneficial effects. First, it will help you figure out what went wrong in your relationship and what precipitated your separation. This appears to be one of the most important things newly separated people must do for themselves. Your story or formulation may change over time, but clarifying it in your own mind will generally help you get your feet back on the ground. In the formulation to yourself, which you may wish to censor in part for others, you should aim first to include statements of not only those things about your partner which created friction in your relationship, but those things about you which were problematic for your partner. Second, you can weigh those things to discover which caused the most serious difficulty and which precipitated the separation. Third, you can construct your own picture of the sequence of events leading to the separation. For how long was the relationship seriously distressed? When did separation become a real consideration for either one of you? What precipitated the final decision?

Once you have your *separation story* clearly in mind, it is relatively easy to derive from it an acceptable and appropriate story for others. Its length may vary considerably. In my separation counseling groups, for example, the first exercise I give is in working out "separation stories." Each member of the group is asked to tell his or her story initially in six minutes, then to condense it to two minutes, and eventually to reduce it for an inquiring friend to forty-five seconds or less. At the end of the session, an effective story told in only four seconds is offered: "Oh. You hadn't heard. It didn't work out."

Although constructing and telling the separation story does not always seem as important as some other necessary accommodations to separation, it is an essential part of the early adjustment process. To neglect it means retarding readjustment and growth, as well as risking the loss of other important relationships. It is one of the very few things that need to be done immediately after a separation occurs.

Friends, family, and associates also need to be told what it is you want them to do—otherwise they don't know. Generally, you will merely request that things go on as before—an expression of your hope that this event will not alter your relationship—but sometimes you may wish to ask for more than that. This, too, is quite appropriate and often a very good idea. You may ask one or more of your friends to be available to talk over your separation and new life. You may indicate to close friends that you get lonesome from time to time and would like to be able to call them more often than before or drop by for a visit. You may ask one or more of them to help you temporarily in some area of living alone at which you are not yet proficient, or to help you find appropriate companions of the other sex. Within reason, of course, all such requests are quite legitimate, and you should not hesitate to make them. People often wish to be helpful to others in times of serious life crises. Separation and divorce certainly qualify, and you have every right during this time to cash in some of your friendship credits.

But don't be surprised if your credit is not as good with some others as you had hoped. Friends and family do not always help out—so what else is new? You are free to ask; your friends and family are similarly free to comply with or refuse your request. While some friends may enjoy sharing your growth and growing pains, others may feel threatened by the necessary changes you will be making. Some friends and family members may welcome seeing you more, and others may see this as competing with their own needs, which are simply more important. If both you and your ex-partner are making similar demands on your friends or family, they may get overloaded with such burdens and be unable to do any more. In addition, people who want to stay on good terms with both of you are under-standably leery of listening to you sounding off about your former partner. They do not wish to take sides or even appear to be doing so for fear of losing your ex-partner's friendship; they realize that you may reconcile and that, if you do so after baring your deepest hostili-ties to them, your friendship may be strained; or they simply do not want to be put in the middle. Discussing these concerns with your friends, giving them a blanket permission not to take sides, and asking them to stop you if your talk gets out of line can often relieve them greatly, allowing them to have unencumbered contact with both you and your ex-partner.

You can see that the failure of friends or family to live up to your expectations or demands does not usually mean their rejection of you or what you have done. If such a disappointment occurs, try to accept it philo-sophically; probably it's only that your needs and the needs of the friend or family member involved do not mesh very well at the moment, and that for now you will have to rely on others.

There are, of course, situations in which family or old friends do avoid or openly reject those who seek to terminate their relationships and particularly their mar-riages. Here again, it is important to try to take a philo-sophical attitude toward this, to realize that, while these reactions may create problems for you, they are basically not your problem. You are simply not living up to someone else's expectations, and short of doing so, there may be little you can do. It is often one's parents who respond the most negatively and even hysterically to a marital breakdown. In time, however, these same parents generally accommodate to the new reality of the separation and divorce, just as they have accommodated to other deplored but unpreventable events in their children's lives.

The avoidance or rejection of friends is generally quite a bit more subtle and hence more difficult to handle. If you have initiated the rites-of-passage ritual with them and have done your best to help them develop a script in relation to you, you have done your part. If they continue to be uncomfortable with you, or even rejecting, this is fundamentally their problem. It is not the end of the world, and it most definitely does not mean that you are an unworthy, immoral, or detestable person.

While we are discussing rejection, please remember not to overinterpret the behavior of others. It is common for separating people to feel they are the center of the universe and that everyone is thinking and talking about them. If they feel the least bit guilty, they will project and assume that others condemn them. Expect others to be a little awkward with you. Don't see rejection where there is only uncertainty.

Having realized this, however, it may be useful for you to know several of the most important ways in which people who are separating, and particularly divorcing, represent a threat to the coupled majority. First, it is important to realize that separation is an issue in every relationship. As you already know, it is an uncomfortable alternative, and thoughts of separation are associated with the most negative aspects of one's love relationship. Your own separation makes the possibility a more real one for your friends and associates. Your successful adjustment to separation or divorce makes it even more viable and attractive. As a result, your separation can represent a threat to other people's way of life, and this threat is probably greatest for those married friends who have the unhappiest marriages. Current estimates indicate that many contemporary marriages are plagued by significant distress—odds that work against you. To the extent that you make the most of the many advantages of single life, you represent a very positive, conflict-producing alternative to a bad marriage. For these reasons, you would do well to be cautious in sharing the joys of single life with your married friends until you have some idea of how well they can handle such good news.

Sometimes, of course, a newly separated person is viewed as a threat in an even more direct way. Divorced women, in particular, often complain that married women view them as a real threat to their marriages, and it certainly is not unusual for newly separated women to receive sexual advances from the husband of a close friend.

What do you do about all this? You may say good riddance to these disloyal or thoughtless friends. But a more compassionate you may choose to understand their behavior and do what you can, within reason, to retain their friendship. Being aware of their human fallibility, you can realize that their behavior is a product of their own needs and their view of the world. What may seem a rejection or depreciation of you is more probably a reflection of the uncertainties, fears, and needs of those who are disappointing you. You may have to settle for putting some friendships on "hold" until your status in life becomes less threatening to them or until they work out their own problems. People have disappointed you before, no doubt, but does this make them totally unworthy? The important thing is that you avoid putting *yourself* down for their behavior. Protect yourself first by cultivating more the friends who stick by you and by looking for new ones who have more in common with you.

Concretely, here are some things you might do to protect the more fragile of your friendships:

1. Be sure you adequately observe the rites of passage with your friends and tell them what it is you want from them.

2. Invite them to share familiar recreations with you and show that *you* are comfortable in your new status with them.

3. Let them know they don't have to take sides. Tell them, if appropriate, that they should feel free to maintain a friendship with both you and your ex-partner.

4. If your friends can't handle it, refrain from sharing with them both the pain and joy of your new life.

5. If your friends find you directly threatening to their relationships and marriages, accentuate your own satisfaction with other heterosexual relationships.

6. Finally, realize that life is change; relationships that were functional at one point in your life may not be functional at another point. As you grow, you may have to say good-bye to those who cannot appreciate or share your development. That is perhaps sad, but not growing is much sadder.

2

The Emotional Turmoil of Separation and What to Do About It

To suffer one's death and to be reborn is not easy.
—*Fritz Perls*

*Sometimes it's heaven and sometimes it's hell
And sometimes I don't even know.*
—*Willie Nelson*

SEPARATION CRAZINESS

IT IS NORMAL for the newly separated to be a little crazy, and it is not uncommon for them to be a lot crazy. If you are newly separated and don't feel a little crazy, you are either just lucky or unusually rational, or perhaps still too busy to experience the myriad of emotions which occasionally threaten to overwhelm most people in your situation. This chapter is addressed to all the others—to describe and explore that kaleidoscope of emotions which generally accompany separation; to provide some handles for understanding these confusing feelings; to give reassurance that they constitute a common experience and in their way can be therapeutic; and finally, to suggest methods for losing the least to and gaining the most from your own brand of separation craziness.

Perhaps the single most therapeutic thing I do as a counselor in separation cases is to assure newly sepa-

49

rated people that intense and disturbing emotional turmoil is the common experience. The feeling of being overwhelmed by unfamiliar, unexpected, and frightening emotions is normal; the fear of being totally unable to meet new and even old responsibilities is normal; the fear of losing complete control is normal; the fear of a breakdown, of going crazy is normal. While a very few of those who experience these fears do succumb to serious emotional difficulties, the overwhelming majority do not; and in most, if not all, cases of mental breakdown, the central, precipitating cause is fear itself.

Although some separating individuals experience only the extremes of either complete elation and freedom or total despair and panic, the vast majority vacillate violently between the two extremes. At times, the newly separated person may feel only relief at leaving behind an impossible life, then suddenly be overwhelmed by feelings of helplessness and despair when he or she can form no clear vision of what the new life will hold. An appreciation of the freedom of being alone may be transformed into a devastating sense of loss, of loneliness and emptiness, for which there is no apparent cure. The list of swiftly alternating feelings is endless. Anger is replaced by guilt, elation by depression, loneliness by tranquillity. Why is this so upsetting? In part because we are incorrectly taught to think of ourselves as static, unchanging beings. This stability is what maturity and adulthood are supposed to be about. Thus, unfortunately, instability means something is wrong, and our identity is threatened.

This roller coaster of emotion, while sometimes invigorating and encouraging, can be very frightening. It is important to remember, however, that while a few people get sick on a roller coaster, falling off one is extremely unlikely. On this ride, try to hang on to whatever stabilizing rails are around and to relax, knowing that while you may not be able to get off whenever you want, the roller coaster *will* stop sooner or later. Moreover, if you can relax enough to pay attention to what is happening, you may learn a great deal. Although it may be uncomfortable, the emotional roller coaster is understandable—and normal. Understanding it should help you deal with it.

The fundamental reason for these swings between extremes is simple: change is difficult for people, especially when that change is from something very familiar to something totally unknown. The changes which accompany separation are drastic. Your relationships with friends, family, and children—if any—inevitably change. Frequently there are radical changes in your place of residence, financial status, work, and the way you spend time. The old ways of relating to life and other people are disrupted or taken away, often with no visible replacements. Unfamiliar tasks are suddenly thrust upon you. And you may have only the foggiest notion of how to begin to learn the newly required skills. Other heterosexual relationships become more possible, but as a newly single person you may have little more than a dim memory of what dating was all about and, in any case, you're vaguely aware that the rules are different now. But what those new rules are and how they can be made to fit your personality or style may initially appear to be a well-kept and potentially frightening secret. Life is change. But this much change all at once is very hard.

Recent research has established that a heightened

risk of physical or emotional illness is associated with change; and in cross-cultural studies of the stress of various life changes, separation from one's mate has been consistently ranked by thousands of people as representing the most stressful change. Thus, the changes usually faced by newly separated people clearly put them at risk for the development of physical or emotional symptoms.

More and more scientists in the health fields are accepting what may be called a cumulative stress model of mental and physical illness. Most simply, the notion is that environmental, psychological, biological, and other stressors are cumulative in their effects on the body. When the stressors in any one system or across all systems get beyond a certain finite point—different for each individual—the organism breaks at its weakest point.

"But," you may protest, "why, in this supposedly helpful book, am I being scared even further? I'm frightened enough without being told I'm 'at risk.'" I tell you this because I want you to realize that it is your situation and not you that is a little, or maybe a lot, crazy—that anyone in your situation would be stressed and vulnerable.

More important, I tell you this to motivate you to take the best possible care of yourself at a time when you are at risk. If you knew you were ten times more likely to catch a cold than other people, what would you do? If you had good sense, you'd get plenty of rest, eat properly, dress warmly, be careful to avoid close contact with others who had colds, and do whatever else would in your judgment make catching a cold less likely. Similarly, according to our cumulative stress model, any action which will reduce stress in any system will help prevent serious trouble or restore you after some special difficulty. In particular, any action which reduces stress in your own special areas of vulnerability will help protect you.

Thus your sanity is reinforced by each *little* obstacle you encounter and try to overcome. Although mistakes are inevitable, many victories are possible. Meanwhile, this time of high stress is a time to take particularly good care of yourself—to be your own best friend.

The knowledge that too much change can be dangerous to your health should also motivate you to keep the number of changes at a tolerable level. Hang on to whatever sources of stability are available to you. What you will become will certainly be different from what you have been, but a sense of continuity and rootedness is important to the adjustment of most people. Continued connectedness with friends and family, as well as occupations and absorptions that have defined you in the past, will generally help you in the present and future.

The kaleidoscope of feelings experienced by the newly separated person is further understandable from another very different point of view. Being unhappily coupled typically provides excellent training for ignoring your own feelings. Many unhappy relationships are sustained for years by sacrificing self-awareness. Closing yourself off from your feelings frees you, at a price, from having to do anything about them. And loyalty to a partner or family can cause you to be more reluctant to express the negative feelings you have to anyone else. When your relationship ends, these prohibitions are suddenly lifted, and the intensity of the negative feelings may be surprising and sometimes overwhelming.

And yet, the positive and loving feelings toward your partner may be there as well. Indeed, they may have been submerged by your preoccupation with the bad aspects of the relationship. In short, your present circumstances now allow all kinds of feelings to surface without the prohibitions and preoccupations which have kept them at bay in the past. And you may ask which set of feelings is accurate and true, the negative or the positive? Which should determine your future? The answer is that both sets are real and valid, although frequently exaggerated during the first months after separation. With practice, you will become better at listening to yourself and accepting inconsistent feelings as natural. You can become adept at using them, inconsistent as they may be, as important signposts on the new road which you will be walking. The exploding emotions which now confuse you can be the first stirrings of a new self-awareness—the beginning of a new and exciting communication with yourself, the foundation of a new identity that is more stable and secure.

Another common reaction to separation is a complex of symptoms generally known as depression. Depressive reaction may be part of the kaleidoscope or may exist alone. In my experience, depression alone is more common among reluctant ex-partners than among initiating ones. In its most pervasive form, the depressed person suffers an overwhelming sense of helplessness and hopelessness. Unable to engage in any of the simplest daily tasks and viewing everything as an insurmountable obstacle, he or she withdraws as completely

as possible from social contact and cannot seem to en-
vision a future without the lost love, remaining preoccupied with the past or mourning the lost future. All
this is frequently accompanied by disturbances of sleep
and loss of appetite. In severe depressions suicide is
often contemplated and planned—and sometimes committed.

There are good reasons to believe that some depressive reaction over a limited time may be a natural
and restorative process. Mourning and grief over the
loss of a loved one are natural, no matter what the circumstances of that loss. Even when the separation is
desired, it is usually experienced as a loss, and mourning
that loss—experiencing it rather than denying it—can be
healthy and constructive. The withdrawal and consolidation in depression can serve a restorative function pro-
tecting the individual from excessive demands with
which he or she might be unable to cope. Some people
require such a period of withdrawal and consolidation
before resumed activity makes sense to them.

Very often, however, depressive reactions are much
more than moderate in terms of either time or intensity. In these cases, the depressions are exaggerations of
what would be optimally healthy and constructive.
Withdrawal that lasts beyond a few weeks can become
self-perpetuating, establishing patterns that become increasingly difficult to break. So if depression is your
inclination in this situation, accept it as normal only
in small doses and for a brief period of time. I advise
people who come to see me with persistent depression
to be accepting of themselves but not accepting of their
depression. My attempt to help them overcome it begins with some questions. I ask, "What are you doing

this evening?" "What are you doing this weekend?" "What are you doing or planning that you enjoy?" If the answers are "Nothing," "I don't know," or "Not much," I have at least a partial diagnosis as well as a prescription for the cure. Inactivity breeds inactivity; boredom breeds more boredom; and doing nothing gives you little to think or talk about. Doing something —anything you could conceivably enjoy—is one effective treatment for depression.

In Chapter 1, I introduced you to Hal, who for a time suffered a crippling depression. Much of the initial psychotherapy for Hal was devoted simply to helping him plan his evenings and weekends, and seeing to it that he carried out these plans. He and his therapist took the time to make a list of all the things that had been or could be enjoyable for Hal. Based on this list, a schedule was planned that included contact with friends, visits with his children, attendance at club functions, ski trips, walks in the country, and eventually dates. Hal also used the list on a more ad hoc basis when he was feeling down and at a loss for what to do. He'd run down the list, pick something, even if it didn't seem overwhelmingly attractive, and do it. Sometimes he had to force himself to do it. And, especially at first, his therapist played the role of pleasant-events pusher. Depressed people can be mighty stubborn about doing anything, and psychotherapists often have to play the role of a crowbar in prying them loose from what sometimes seems to be a cherished depression. Hal kept coming to see his crowbar-therapist, and together they managed to pry him loose.

You too may need someone to get you moving again. In any case, this—the behavioral approach—is the first treatment of choice—a seemingly simple solution but not an easy or superficial one. If beginning to move does not suffice, the next step is intervention at the cognitive or thinking level. Or, when the depression is sufficiently severe and protracted, drug therapy may be employed to break it up at a biochemical level. Each type of intervention—behavioral, cognitive, biochemical —or some combination may be effective. In most cases of self-perpetuating, separation-linked depression, intervention in the first two areas—behavioral and cognitive— will be sufficient, and in either, the real work must be accomplished largely by the sufferer himself, whether or not he or she gets help with it.

The rest of this chapter tells you how to employ the cognitive approach to anything that upsets you. Though presented in the context of dealing with separation, the principles given here are general ones which will provide some consistent themes for dealing with all the dilemmas of living. So, even if your separation is way behind you, I hope you'll read this section carefully, as it will set the stage for much of what is to come.

UNDERSTANDING EMOTIONAL OVERREACTION

Michael, a thirty-year-old carpenter, came to see me because he was experiencing intense pain over a separation initiated by his wife, Janet. Six months before their separation, she had had a brief sexual encounter with another man and had told Michael about it. That was the beginning of the end. Michael just couldn't reconcile himself to that affair. He brooded for hours at a time about it; he verbally attacked his wife repeatedly and unmercifully for her immorality; he threatened divorce and seizure of their four-year-old daughter to punish her; he spent hours berating himself as a worthless, unmanly nonperson because he felt depreciated by his wife's behavior; he became alternately depressed and assaultive as each day he drove more nails into the coffin which would hold his marriage. When Janet finally left him, he was willing to do anything to get her back, but she wasn't interested—she had had it.

Michael's brooding got worse. He blamed his wife for ending the marriage, but blamed himself for driving her toward that decision. As his anger with his wife increased, so did his own feelings of worthlessness. At the same time that he blamed her for her refusal to accept any of his reconciliation proposals, he took the refusals as further evidence of his own lack of worth. To Michael, his wife was an unworthy woman; but he was even more unworthy, first because he wanted her, and second because he was rejected by her. He showed an exaggerated but common thought pattern of those rejected in love and marriage. He was in dire pain; where was the pain coming from?

I think it will be apparent to most who read this account that Michael's thinking was his worst enemy. It was not his wife's affair but the meaning he gave it that was the problem. It was not her decision to leave him but his self-destructive interpretation of it that was making him so desperately unhappy. The quotation that opens Chapter 1, "The road is not the road, the road is how you walk it," expresses a central theme of this book—it is not the events in life which give us pain; our pain we create for ourselves by the interpretation we give to events. This important insight has been re-discovered through the ages from Epictetus, in the first century A.D., who wrote, "Men are disturbed not by things but by the views they take of them," to the contemporary Pogo comic strip, in which one of the characters exclaims, "We have discovered the enemy and he is us."

A psychologist who deals directly with people's problems in living is required to perform many functions, from pleasant-events pusher to secular priest and philosopher. The role of philosopher is especially called for when, as in Michael's case, the basic problem is one involving a pain-giving thought process or philosophy. My first job as a psychotherapist, whenever I am faced with a client like Michael, is to help him discover what the pain-giving thoughts are. We work together to discover the internal *sentences* the person is telling himself, especially when he is upset or depressed. Finding the *cognitive content* of the emotion makes it operational so that it may be dealt with concretely. Giving us this handle on the pain is the first step in rational emotive therapy, a method developed by the American psychologist Albert Ellis.

Here is what we discovered Michael was saying to himself to produce his misery:

1. I don't like it that Janet had an affair and left me. She *shouldn't* have had an affair and *shouldn't* have left me. When you're married, you're supposed to be faithful, to love and protect one another. Janet violated our marriage and me and our daughter. Because of what she has done, she is an im-

moral person who deserves to be punished. I have been wronged and deserve revenge and restitution. I am justified in hurting Janet because she has hurt me. She is unworthy of having our daughter because of her immoral conduct. I will take our daughter away from Janet. I am in the right; she is in the wrong. [*This was Michael's anger sequence.*]

2. I don't like it that Janet had an affair and left me. This must mean that I didn't do what a husband should. I should have been more attentive to her. I shouldn't have gotten angry so often. I shouldn't have driven her away. I should have helped her more with the kid and listened to her and let her do more of what she wanted. I am guilty of ruining our marriage. This divorce will damage our child and it's my fault. I deserve to be punished for my guilt; the rest of my miserable life will be my punishment. [*This was Michael's guilt sequence.*]

3. I don't like it that Janet had an affair and left me. Her doing this means that she doesn't love me or find me attractive. It means that I did not meet her needs as a man should. I am less of a man because of what she did. I am unlovable and worthless because Janet does not love me. I am a failure because my marriage failed. Because I failed at one of life's important missions, I am worthless. Because I am worthless, I will never be able to succeed in another relationship or at anything else. I still love Janet

and want her back in spite of the horrible things she has done. This proves how really worthless I am. [*In case you haven't already guessed, this was Michael's worthlessness sequence.*]

4. I don't like it that Janet had an affair and left me. I want to continue our marriage and to live with Janet and our daughter. I want the future to be as I had planned it. This is unfair; it's horrible and I can't stand it. I will not accept this. I will not be reconciled to it. This cannot happen because I can't stand for it to happen. I feel angry, guilty, and worthless, and I can't stand it. I hate Janet, I hate myself, and I hate life for letting this happen. I can't stand it. I can't stand it. I *can't* stand it. [*This was Michael's "I'm not getting what I want and I can't stand it" sequence.*]

These are the four basic ways people upset themselves and make their lives miserable—by anger, guilt, self-depreciation, and "catastrophizing" (a useful word invented by Albert Ellis). Just getting these sentences out—verbalizing these emotions—helped Michael in two ways. First, it gave him a greater sense of understanding and control to know where these overwhelming emotions were coming from—to know the content of his misery. He could see that, whether the sentences were correct or not, they were making him unhappy. Second, it helped because, by simply stating these sentences, he could see how really illogical, untenable, and silly some of them were.

The insight that, at least in some measure, one's

pain is caused by what one is saying to oneself is the second step in rational emotive therapy. The third step is a philosophical one—to realize that pain-inducing sentences like Michael's are philosophically *wrong*. In the role of philosopher, I tried to help Michael by actively disputing these pain-giving notions.

The philosophical principles are simple and standard, though usually difficult for people to accept:

1. One can never prove that things "should" be any different from what they are.
2. No one is ever to blame for anything.
3. One can never prove his worthiness or worthlessness.
4. People can tolerate not getting what they want.

It is not necessary to accept each of these principles in order to employ the method, but before rejecting any of them out of hand, consider what follows.

Michael's anger and guilt were fueled first by his popular and mistaken notion that the world *should* be different in ways that he could prescribe. In this case, his prescription was that he and Janet *should* have done things differently. But he could never prove to me that things should be any different from what they were, much less that he was the exclusive holder of the prescription. He could say that he felt *it would be better if* certain things were or had been different. That's as far as he could go logically—that's all I would accept. And eventually his way of putting it changed.

But, you may protest, this is just a word game. What difference do the words make? I say they make a lot of difference! Why? Because *shoulds* and *shouldn'ts* lead to blame, anger, and guilt. *It would be better ifs* don't. When Michael said it would have been better if his wife had been more thoughtful and faithful, he wouldn't get so worked up about it all. You can try it yourself on Michael's guilt sequence by replacing all the *shoulds* with *it would be better ifs*. You will see that doing this takes most of the fire out of the guilt and the demands for self-punishment. The fact is that *shoulds* and *shouldn'ts* have been repeatedly tied to punishment by parents, religion, and society. When you violate a *should*, you are to blame, deserve punishment, and often get it. This isn't true for *it would be better ifs*.

Thus, *shoulds* and *shouldn'ts* are intimately related to the mistaken concepts of blame, guilt, and deserved punishment. No one is ever to blame for the immoral or incorrect things he does in the sense that he *deserves* to be punished for his errors or wrongdoing. Why? There are many reasons, but most essentially the concept of blame confuses the immoral or mistaken act with the person who committed it. The person is punished, degraded, and labeled as guilty when it is the act that *might* have been immoral or mistaken. Moreover, the concept of blaming assumes that people have complete free will to make unbiased decisions about everything they do. The fact is that they do not, and people's behavior is at least in large measure predetermined by past life experience. Finally, the concept of blame and guilt makes it difficult to correct mistaken or immoral behavior efficiently in oneself or others. Guilt about our own behavior makes us less able to attempt constructive change. And when we blame others, we invariably become angry and punitive toward them, thereby reducing our effectiveness in helping them to change.

The most self-destructive mistake Michael was making, however, was his continual attempt to prove himself worthless. Essentially, he was saying to himself, "I am worthless because I have made mistakes and because Janet wanted to leave me." This stupid sentence sums up much of the self-induced misery of separating men and women. To be human is to make mistakes. And to be unforgiving of those mistakes, especially when they are our own, is also distinctly human. If mistakes make people worthless, we all qualify. Fortunately, Michael grasped this quickly and also appreciated how much the self-induced feelings of worthlessness had prevented him from learning from his mistakes and correcting them. Worthlessness, like guilt, can be as incapacitating as it is unwarranted.

Michael also saw rather quickly that *his worth could never depend upon the opinion of one other person*. Even if Janet had believed him to be worthless —which, by the way, she did not—this could in no way make him so. There were, of course, many things he had done and continued to do that were beneficial and praiseworthy. To counter his feelings of worthlessness, he began to concentrate on these things instead of dwelling on his mistakes. This made him feel much better, even though attempting to prove one's worth by listing the good things one does is as impossible as to prove worthlessness by listing the bad things. Rather than listing one's faults or virtues, it is much more constructive to simply accept the principle that one's worth can never be proved. But this is a difficult life truth for people to get through their heads because most of us have been trained to believe just the opposite—and Michael never really appreciated this larger truth. But he did realize that worthlessness could not be proved by the mistakes one makes or by someone else's opinion; he did start thinking more about his assets than his liabilities and thus was in a stronger position to work on correcting his mistaken behavior. And for that, everyone around him was most grateful.

Michael was a little offended when I translated his desperation into the sentence "I'm not getting what I want and I can't stand it." It's really not my general style as a therapist to challenge or confront people because it often puts them on the defensive and they hear less of what I have to say. But in circumstances like this one, it is important to label the desperation for what it really is in order to get a handle on it. Whenever people catastrophize, as Michael did, about the unfortunate things that happen to them, they are confusing what they *want* with what they *need* in order to live a reasonably happy life. When you want something very badly and don't get it, that is hard; but it is not the end of the world unless you make it so.

Actually, Michael was handling his wife's departure rather well in several ways. By coming to the meetings with other separating and divorcing people he was able to listen to other members of the group who did not want to separate initially tell about the advantages they now had as single people. It is trite but true that almost every cloud has a silver lining—there is almost always something good to be found in any life change. The good may not outweigh the bad, but it's there if you look for it. In separation or divorce, the silver linings are generally not all visible at once and can best be appreciated and revealed by those who entered the single state reluctantly but found it to be the gateway to new awareness and life. They are excellent medicine for the newcomers who are still overwhelmed by the wrench of separation. They prove more than all the arguments anyone could ever dream up that people can not only tolerate but also benefit from not getting what they want.

After accepting intellectually the basic counters to illogical and pain-giving thought, you are ready for the more difficult and lengthier part of the treatment. It involves persistent reprogramming of your internal sentences and persistent action consistent with your new belief system. The faulty beliefs you have carried about for years are not usually changed overnight by a flash of insight.

To reprogram your thinking in an active way requires practice—the constant repetition of internal sentences that provide counters to those which give you pain. Thus, for Michael, the internal sentence "My worth is not dependent on the behavior or opinion of one other person" was particularly helpful. The proposition that one can never prove things "should" be any different from the way they are was also most useful to him. He made a concerted effort to eliminate the *shoulds* from his vocabulary and replaced them with *it would be better ifs*. He kept a record of the things he did that made him feel good in general and good about himself, and as a consequence he did more of those things. He listed the things that were advantageous about his new single status and went over them periodically. And he would tell himself repeatedly, "I don't have to have what I want."

But, of course, overt action always speaks louder than words, and a fulfilled prescription for such action is always the acid test of how the reprogramming is going. In Michael's case, the problem was his inability to get down to fixing up his new apartment to make it livable or to find even one woman to date. Like many other partners who initially resisted separation, he seemed to feel that not doing anything to confirm the new reality would prevent it from happening. This, of course, is destructive, magical thinking but awfully common nonetheless. Michael had to push himself a little to work on his apartment and to go after a date, even after he had realized it would be in his best interest to do these things and had recognized the absurdity of his wishful thinking. The reprogramming of his internal sentences helped him to act, and the action reinforced the validity of his new, self-confident internal sentences. Thus do attitudes and behaviors influence each other; to reprogram both is usually hard at first, but after a while a momentum is achieved. While a few setbacks may be encountered during periods of significant change, the idea that you do not have to have what you want can help sustain you when you don't get it.

At this point in the treatment program for Michael, I played the role of systematizer. I got him to make a list of the sane internal sentences that worked especially well for him. He carried that list around with him and agreed to go over it at least five times a day—preferably whenever he caught himself uttering the pain-giving sentences we had identified earlier. In addition, he specified the behaviors that would tell him he was getting better, and then we programmed graded assignments for him each week.

The treatment techniques I have been describing involve a combination of rational emotive therapy as developed by Albert Ellis and self-control techniques developed by behavior therapists. The following section presents these techniques in greater detail to enable you to apply them more effectively to your own specific problems.

TREATING YOUR
EMOTIONAL OVERREACTIONS

The treatment of Michael proceeded in five basic stages which may provide you with some guidelines in treating your own emotional overreactions. The stages are as follows:

Stage 1. Discover the internal sentences which trigger or occur together with your overreaction.

Stage 2. Realize that these sentences—these interpretations—are at least partly the cause of your painful emotion.

Stage 3. Discover those countersentences or arguments which provide antidotes to the pain-giving interpretations because they reveal their illogic.

Stage 4. Reindoctrinate and reprogram your thinking to include gradually more of the antidote statements and exclude more of the pain-giving statements.

Stage 5. Change your behavior so that it becomes more consistent with the antidote statements and less consistent with the pain-giving statements.

Of course, this process is not easy. Let us explore these stages one by one and in specific detail. Fortunately, Michael was directly in touch with the irrational statements that were making him miserable, and Stage 1 didn't take very long with him. With many of my more sophisticated and less outwardly emotional clients, however, this discovery process can take considerable time and effort. The central question is, "What are the internal sentences which you are telling yourself that precipitate and fuel the feelings of guilt, anger, worthlessness, or despair?" Sometimes the self-destructive sentences are so old and familiar that you may be only dimly aware of them. Theoretically, it is possible that, after years of practice, you may be able to skip over them entirely and go right on being miserable without much thought. This certainly is the way it often seems. But almost always the internal sentences are there. If you are recently separated or divorced, there probably are a few new self-injurious statements in your head which mediate your pain, and, because they are new, they will probably be easier to identify.

Let us look at some of the more common ones and see if they are familiar to you. The internal sentence which proclaims you a failure because of the breakdown of a primary relationship or marriage is probably the most popular one among the newly separated. A close second could well be the one proclaiming you a guilty louse for destroying your children through separation and divorce. Or your partner is the louse—that ties for second place. For third place, I'd pick the one that runs something like, "I'm worthless, unattractive, and unlovable because my ex-partner finds me so." And let's not forget the one that often hangs on for years to make single and divorced people miserable, "This isn't the way things were supposed to be; I've been cheated." The list is endless. To help you in this first stage of self-discovery, there are given below some common self-defeating sentences that can elicit anger, guilt, worthlessness, or catastrophizing. Pick the ones that represent your own brand of self-poisoned thinking, change the words so they are your own, and add others that come to you.

Anger

My partner should have treated me better.

My partner or spouse owes me for the years I have given him/her and the sacrifices I have made.

I shouldn't have to pay these things (settlements, alimony, child support, etc.).

My partner or spouse should pay for what he/she has done to me.

My partner is in the wrong, and is a guilty and immoral person for violating our relationship.

I have been wronged and deserve revenge and restitution.

I am justified in hurting my partner because he/she has hurt me.

I am in the right; he/she is in the wrong.

My spouse has violated the will of God and deserves to be punished.

Guilt

I should have worked harder on my relationship or marriage.

By divorcing, I am harming my children.

I shouldn't have been involved in an outside affair(s).

I shouldn't have wronged my partner as I have.

I have done some terrible things that make me feel guilty.

I am in the wrong and am a guilty and immoral person
    for violating our relationship or marriage contract.
I should have treated my partner better.
I am guilty of ruining our relationship.
I deserve to be punished for the things I have done.
Others must be condemning me for my sin.
I have violated the will of God and deserve punish-
    ment.

Worthlessness

There must be something wrong with me because I am
    single or divorced.
There must be something wrong with me because I
    don't have a steady companion.
I'm not worthy of being loved.
Because my partner doesn't love me, I am worthless;
    I am nobody.
I feel worthless because some of my friends or family
    disapprove of my actions or have rejected me.
I feel less of a man or woman because my partner was
    interested in someone else.
I feel that I am not attractive as a man or woman be-
    cause my partner didn't think so.
I am a failure because this relationship or marriage
    failed.
I am incompetent because I am unable to do well some
    of the things my partner used to do for me.
There is something wrong with me because I am alone.
I am worthless because I have done bad things.

Catastrophizing

I shouldn't have to suffer the indignation of divorce.
I can't make it alone.

I shouldn't have to work to support myself.

I shouldn't have to work at something I don't like to do.

I can't take on new responsibilities for which I have no training or interest.

I'm too afraid to get a job and support myself.

This isn't fair.

This isn't the way it's supposed to be. I have been cheated.

I'm too afraid to date other people.

I can never trust another man/woman because of what has happened.

I will never find another partner because I've already tried and failed.

I can't stand having to cook, launder, or clean for myself, or to eat and sleep alone.

No one else will ever be attracted to me.

I am degraded and ashamed to have less income than before.

I am miserable because I have no one to love.

I can't stand being alone.

I need someone else to make me feel whole again.

I am terribly afraid of doing some of the things I must do; I might fail.

I can't stand it.

Very often, the intellectual exercise of simply going over these lists and adding to them won't be as helpful to you as listening to yourself when you are upset or experiencing any kind of negative emotions. The next time this happens, try to discover just what it is you are saying to yourself. Talk to yourself, deliberately and even aloud—if you can do that comfortably—about whatever has you stirred up. It will probably help to begin this soliloquy with a moderate, rational statement about the event that seems to trigger your negative emotions. In Michael's case, this sentence was, "I don't like it that Janet had an affair and left me." Then, just as Michael did, move on to the less rational sentences that tell you what a no-good, rotten, worthless, guilty scum you really are—or your ex-partner is—or to whatever other derogatory thoughts are equally capable of inspiring outrage or despair. At first, allow yourself to become even more irrational and upset than usual, so you can discover the content of your misery. Don't hold back. And, most of all, try not to be afraid of looking foolish. You are the only one who is looking, and if you weren't a little kooky, you wouldn't be human. Far better to find out how really crazy your ideas are so that you can change them than to go on being crazy and making yourself miserable. And you may be quite surprised at how irrational your thoughts really are. If so, that's an awfully good sign. It means that you've really dug in deep and that you have already begun the next step in this sanity-building process. As the internal sentences surface, write them down—make them external—so that you can go back and analyze them when you are in a better frame of mind. When you are satisfied that you've explored the depths of your own brand of crazy thinking, you are ready for the second stage of this therapeutic process.

Stage 2 is typically the easiest, for it is merely an intellectual exercise, but it is an essential step in the treatment: you must simply accept the basic premise—that your negative internal sentences are an important factor in making you miserable. When you can see this, you will be better motivated to try to get rid of them.

Stage 3 of the process requires you to discover the *antidote* sentences that can serve to neutralize or cancel out the pain-giving thoughts and sentences. This requires you to discover the basic illogic of those thoughts and to verbalize that illogic in a way that makes sense to you. Or it may require that you express your negative feelings differently in the future so that unpleasantness is distinguished from catastrophe.

For example—to take the fourth type of negative thinking first—there are two basic errors in the sentences listed under "Catastrophizing." First is the error of failing to distinguish what you would prefer to have from what you *must* have in order to live. It is, of course, uncomfortable to be alone when you would rather have company. It is in some ways unfortunate when you would very much like to have someone to love and you have not. It is hard when you have to live apart from your children and are forced to be an absentee parent, and hard when you must live with them all the time and care for their every need with little money. But none of these things are catastrophic; none represent the end of the world or the end of a potentially rewarding life. Needlessly translating unfortunate events into catastrophic tragedy does not hold up to cold inspection. People may generally be better off with a loving, intact family; but no one *must* live in this condition to survive or thrive in life. In fact, some people do far better without the social supports and constraints which are such a comfort to others. Making tragedy of discomfort also has the effect of leading to emotional upset, which hampers the achievement of reasonable goals. Time spent feeling sorry for yourself is time taken away from living and solving those problems which bring your discomfort. Catastrophizing doesn't make sense in the first place and is inefficient in the second.

The second basic error in catastrophizing is overgeneralization. How often have I heard my clients write off love, marriage, men, or women because one love, one marriage, one man or woman has disappointed them. The disappointment is first made catastrophic and then overgeneralized. What people are really saying in their overgeneralizing is that they have been catastrophically disappointed once and they will not risk such disappointment again. The catastrophic hurt is self-made, however, and one pays dearly for closing off life to avoid the possibility of pain. Everyone has the right to do this, of course. My job as a psychotherapist is to label that option exactly for what it is and to call attention to the cost of that decision.

The antidotes to catastrophizing follow from its basic errors. The first basic antidote is, "I do not have to have what I want." This leads to a restatement of the *shoulds*, the *musts*, and the *needs*, and to statements of preference rather than of demands. It leads to changing the intolerable to the undesirable.

Once again, let me remind you that this is more than a word game. With the practice involved in this stage of the treatment, the changing of internal sentences can have a profound and lasting effect on the way you think about life and the way you live it.

The second basic antidote to catastrophizing is to challenge all overgeneralizations. One disappointment is just one disappointment; no more. That constant self-reminder can save you from a lot of stupid thinking and thereby a lot of grief. You are not necessarily bad marriage material because your marriage terminated. All men or women are not untrustworthy because you mistakenly trusted one. You are not inherently unattractive or unlovable because one person now finds you so. And, for that matter, your relationship is not a failure because it has come to an end. Relationships and marriages do not fail; they often stop working for their participants, that's all. As Alex Craig tells us, "To judge a love affair by its length is as absurd as to judge a picture by its size."

The internal sentences which proclaim your worthlessness are fallacious for one basic reason. You cannot prove your worth or worthlessness in life by any criteria, and certainly mistakes in *one* or even a few areas are patently insufficient proof of anything. The basic error in statements of worthlessness involves the confusion of what you do or do not do with what you are. You are not an incompetent person because you are unskilled in some things. You are not a failure as a person because you fail at some tasks. You are not one big mistake because you have made some mistakes. You merely are; that's all. And, you are certainly not worthless because somebody else may think so. Your worth does not depend on the opinion of other people. Most especially, it does not depend on the opinion of one other person. To be mistaken, inept, and even immoral is part of the human condition. Acceptance of life and yourself requires acceptance of this truth. To become less mistaken, inept, and immoral is a fine goal and a more attainable one as it becomes an end in itself.

Feelings of worthlessness and guilt are natural companions, but I have distinguished between them because guilt implies deserved punishment. No one ever *deserves* punishment for anything. As discussed earlier, the concept of guilt presumes perfect free will, it confuses the actor with the act, and it prevents people from intelligently correcting their mistaken or immoral behavior. The antidotes for self-destructive guilt sentences involve a restatement of the self-accusation, such as, "I have made a mistake or taken an immoral action. That's unfortunate, but human. I am not my mistake. What can I do now to rectify the mistake? What can I do to avoid making that mistake again?" And that's it.

The basic antidotes to guilt are: (1) restate your self-accusation to eliminate the *shoulds*; label your mistake as a mistake or your immoral behavior as simply immoral; (2) state that you are not your mistake; and (3) state that no one, including you, *deserves* punishment for anything.

Anger, like guilt, springs from the arrogance of thinking that one knows how other people "should" behave. When others violate *our* rules for *their* behavior, we become angry. In anger, we blame others and feel they deserve punishment for violating our standards. The logical errors in the internal sentences which constitute anger are the same as those involved in guilt. A recognition of those errors will prompt a restatement of the problem. The restatements are similar to those given for guilt—people do mistaken and immoral things which harm others. Punishment may be necessary or wise if it can serve to stop or deter mistaken or immoral behavior, but it is in no sense deserved. It is the height of arrogance for us to claim we know exactly how others

should behave, and higher arrogance still to set ourselves up as the authority on the punishment they deserve for transgressing our code. Moreover, as do all
disturbing emotions, anger interferes with our efficiency, making us far less able to influence people to
change.

The antidote sentences for anger are the same as
those for guilt—only the target differs. The steps in developing antidote sentences to anger are: first, restate
the accusation to eliminate the *shoulds* and the labeling
of others' behavior as mistaken or immoral; next, state
that a person is not his mistake or his immoral behavior
and that much of what one does one must do; and last,
state that no one deserves punishment for anything. Once
again, punishment may be *warranted* but never *deserved*.

It is generally a good idea to write down the countersentences which you develop for anger, guilt, worthlessness, or catastrophizing to help in the reindoctrination process of the next stage. Before outlining the reindoctrination process, though, one word of caution is in
order. The philosophies presented here can be misused
to provide you with a whole new list of *shoulds*. As you
go along trying to change your more irrational thinking,
you will find that old habits die very hard and that you
will continue to blame yourself and others, to feel worthless, and to catastrophize about life. And, you may find
yourself perfectionistically demanding that you "should"
stop all that. When this happens, just remember *it
would be better if* you didn't say *should*, and go about
your business.

Reindoctrination requires practice. The antidote
sentences have to be repeated frequently and on a more

or less daily basis in order to take. This repetition is most effective at those times when the more irrational sentences surface to make you miserable, but repetition at any time can be useful. Stage 4, then, merely involves the practice and repetition of more sane and constructive thoughts. That sounds easy, and for a few people it is. But, for most, a more systematic programming of reindoctrination is required. The same principles that are often used by psychotherapists to help people change more overt behavior can be employed to change internal thinking. In Michael's case, for example, we employed three basic behavior-change principles: goal setting, systematic self-observation, and contingencies. Michael agreed to set a goal of five reprogramming sessions per day in which he would deliberately repeat the antidote sentences to himself and think about them. He agreed to record the times he did this, and to forfeit part of an advance deposit he had given me to be donated to charity if he failed to meet these goals.

These behavior-change methods for altering thinking may seem strange and distasteful to you. But, if you decide to try to accomplish your own reindoctrination and the wanted changes do not come quickly or spontaneously enough, give these more systematic procedures a try. Set your own goals, establish your own method of self-recording, and establish your own self-determined contingencies. A more detailed presentation of these principles of behavior change will be presented in Chapter 5, and additional examples of possible methods of self-recording and contingencies are outlined there. Irrational and hurtful thinking is just another bad habit and, like all bad habits, can be exceedingly resistant to change. Systematic reprogramming has worked for others and can work for you.

Finally, Stage 5 is to begin changing any behavior which is inconsistent with sane thinking. Michael was doing three specific things which reflected his irrational thoughts: he continued to live out of packing boxes in his new apartment, ate exclusively in restaurants, and failed to begin friendships with women because of his feelings of worthlessness and his irrational belief that he could never trust another woman. As Michael began to see the errors in his thinking, he saw the need to change his behavior. He began fixing up his apartment, started cooking, and slowly but surely began new friendships. Only then did he know that his rational thinking had the upper hand. Whenever I am faced with a person who is suffering from any type of emotional overreaction, I do everything in my power to reinvolve the person in living. I become a promoter of the good things of life even when my client thinks the good things aren't all that good. I take on the inglorious role of recreation director and push social contact and exercise, helping my client to plan his evenings and weekends. Usually, I set up rewards and forfeits for my client to ensure that the schedule will be adhered to. Now, this may seem superficial therapy to some, but to become uninvolved with the emotional turmoil, it is necessary to become reinvolved with life. You can do this by setting up a planning session with yourself at least once a week. Schedule a time when you sit down to plan your weekly recreation and social engagements. Do it regularly, at the same time each week. If you need extra help, set goals for yourself, monitor your progress, and reward your own efforts in line with the specific suggestions on how to do this that you will find in Chapter 5.

Learning to think rationally and to stop upsetting yourself is really a lifetime task which is probably never completely mastered. But an extremely traumatic experience like separation or divorce can provide the necessary shock and pain required to force a reexamination of the truly irrational way most of us look at life. To experience that rebirth is a promise you can fulfill.

3
Negotiating the Future

*In the midst of winter, I finally learned that
there was in me an invincible summer.*
—*Albert Camus*

IF YOU ARE NOT facing a current separation from a legal
or functional marriage, you may wish to skip this chapter. It is devoted to the dilemmas and necessary decisions of that difficult and important time and thus will
not be directly relevant to all single people. But those
who need the information and guidelines of this chapter often need them very badly. If you do, this chapter
was done for you. If you don't, just skip it.

In the typical separation crisis, the sheer number
of decisions and steps which confront you are overwhelming. The most essential principle to understand as
you begin separation is this: NOT EVERYTHING HAS TO
BE DONE AT ONCE. While some decisions must be made
immediately, all critical decisions can and should be
postponed. Furthermore, none of the decisions which
need to be made early are irrevocable. Below is a list
of all the major decisions and steps involved in separa-

tion and divorce, grouped in three categories—immediate, interim, and final.

This list has been prepared as a tool to help you organize your thinking. The order in which these steps are presented will correspond, in most cases, to the order in which they may best be undertaken. Obviously, no one can make these difficult decisions for you, but I believe I can offer you some useful handles for thinking about each one. I can tell you the kinds of mistakes others have made in the hope that you can learn from them. And I can identify the kinds of reasons for decisions that have been valid for others and have stood up with time, and those that have not. The Decision Table and the accompanying discussion can provide you with anchor points for your own dilemmas. So, let's begin by considering each item in the Decision Table.

Decision Table for
Separation and Divorce

Immediate Decisions

1. Determining the Need for Legal Counsel
2. Temporary Residence: Who Will Move and Where?
3. Temporary Child Custody

Interim Decisions

4. Temporary Division of Family Income
5. Temporary Division of Household Goods
6. Arrangements for Contacting and Meeting Spouse
7. Temporary Child-Visitation Program

8. Temporary Division of Family Property (if Necessary)

Final Decisions

9. Establishing Grounds for Divorce and Who Will File
10. Division of Family Property
11. Child Custody and Visitation
12. Child Support
13. Alimony
14. Permanent Residence Arrangements
15. Occupational-Educational Change

THE NEED FOR LEGAL COUNSEL

The first issue involves determining whether you need to consult an attorney, and when to do so. In many cases, consulting an attorney early is advisable to avoid making errors that could prove to be costly later on, but the optimal time varies widely. Under certain circumstances, a divorce can be obtained rather easily in no-fault states without benefit of legal counsel. But you had better consider the option of legal counsel and its timing before you do anything else.

You can start your deliberation of this issue by considering what an attorney can offer you and how much you need it.

In the initial stages of separation, an attorney can be helpful by informing you of your legal rights and obligations at each stage, especially in avoiding possible legal pitfalls which could jeopardize your case. Given your circumstances, he or she can inform you of the norms in your community for grounds for divorce; property division; child custody, visitation, and support; and alimony. He or she can tell you roughly what your divorce will cost if it does not involve extensive legal negotiations or a court test, and how much it will cost if it does. Moreover, an attorney can act as your advocate at each stage. Initially, he or she can be your advocate against any tendency you may have to give everything away. Next, he or she can act as your advocate and negotiator with your spouse and his or her attorney, eliminating the need for your participation if this is painful. Finally, of course, an attorney can act as your advocate in court if that becomes necessary.

It is also useful to look at this decision and its timing in the light of what you have to lose that an attorney can help you protect. Basically, people lose three things in divorce: currently held property, child custody, and future income in the form of alimony, child support, and the responsibility for outstanding obligations. The more you have to lose, the more you need legal assistance.

The immediate need for legal counsel also increases if the divorce is an adversary contest or if it is bound to become acrimonious. It is generally more crucial to have legal advice early in states with archaic, adversary divorce laws than it is in no-fault states. And, of course, the more acrimonious the separation, the greater the need for a buffer, negotiator, and advocate. There is also the advantage of moving your separation and divorce along to completion. This can expedite your necessary disengagement and the redefinition of your status.

The most obvious drawback is cost—and, of course, if one spouse retains an attorney, the other will usually need to do the same. But if you intend to retain counsel to handle your case at any time during the divorce process, it will usually not cost you any more to initiate contact early, provided your getting an attorney does not precipitate early freezing of a position or intensify the adversary, combative nature of the process when a more cooperative climate could have prevailed. But these are distinctly avoidable problems. You can avoid them by making your early consultation solely an information- and advice-gathering venture. You have time to decide on all the major decisions that will shape the rest of your life—don't let anyone, including your spouse or your attorney, rush you into a premature settlement. And beware of an attorney who promises you an unreasonably high settlement or who seeks to rush you to judgment. If you feel the attorney you have chosen is not performing his or her functions adequately, find another.

Finally, you should know that you can *consult* an attorney (at an hourly rate) to obtain legal information, advice, or assistance with specific application to your own divorce. You need not be shy about shopping for such consultation by telephone and asking about the hourly fee involved and the attorney's willingness to assist you in the way you want to be assisted. In addition, there probably are legal-aid services in your community for low-income individuals. In some states there are very good aids for those wishing to handle their own dissolutions, including manuals with explicit do-it-yourself instructions, and organizations that provide low-cost consultation.

HOW TO NEGOTIATE

Almost every other decision in the Decision Table will involve negotiation with your partner. Before considering each one individually, you would do well to develop a general format for such deliberations. A set of guidelines for such a format is offered here.

First, it is critical to realize that these "mutual" decisions will be a product of negotiations between *two separate individuals*. Now that you are, and presumably will continue to be, separate, it is best if you can begin to think as *a separate individual* rather than as a part of a couple. Because this may be new to you, it will require some practice. In considering each decision, formulate a position which primarily reflects *your own best interests*. While you will not want to neglect your responsibilities and the needs of others in your family, it is best to begin by determining what *you* want. Now is the time to trade in your couple-think for a new single-think more appropriate to your single status.

The decision on where you will live is a good example of where single-think must predominate. You are free to live where you wish and, in the final analysis, what your partner wants is comparatively unimportant. If you are a woman with children, for example, you may feel considerable pressure from both them and their father to remain in an area where he resides. While your children's welfare will be a factor in any move you make, and while their ability to see their father may be an important consideration for you, it is *only one* consideration to be weighed in deciding where you will live. With this and every other decision, the central question must be, WHAT IS BEST FOR YOU AS AN INDIVIDUAL? Listen to yourself and pay attention. Allow yourself to want what you want. *Your* time has come.

Nevertheless, what you want and what you must have may be different. What you want and what you can get may also differ. Expect your first proposal, which reflects your best position, to be scrutinized and challenged. Begin by challenging it yourself. Is your position reasonable? How does it stack up in relation to the guidelines given in this chapter? How does it measure up to the standards in your community as provided by your lawyer or other informed sources? What are your realistic chances of winning what you want if it should come to a court test?

In the first weeks of separation and preparation for divorce, it is generally best not to commit yourself in any way to a final agreement on any important decision. These weeks may be fraught with upset, hostility, and guilt, rendering you unable to arrive at sound decisions about your future. This is especially true if you feel overwhelming depression about what has happened. In this condition, you are less likely to appreciate the fact that there is a future, let alone protect it. I personally know many people who are paying large and unjustified installments on a now-forgotten guilt. If you are incapable of looking out for your own best interests, start consulting people who are capable and listen to them. If you are divorcing and even suspect that you are in this position, get yourself a lawyer.

In line with these considerations and the information you have received, scale your demands up or down. Finally, determine what you can give up in negotiations. When you have determined your best position and your points of compromise, it is time to attempt negotiation. If there is a chance it will work, contact your partner and propose a negotiation session. Offer to inform your partner, preferably in writing before the face-to-face contact, of what you want. Obviously, since all interim and permanent decisions are integral parts of a whole, your position at each stage should contain all elements. Make it clear whether you are proposing a temporary or permanent package. Then get together and try your best to negotiate responsibly. If you think it would help, propose such a meeting in a neutral, perhaps public, place where neither of you has an advantage and where yelling or open fighting is less likely to occur. If such meetings are particularly stressful or liable to get out of hand in any way, it is often helpful to put a strict time limit on them. Attempt to keep to the topic at hand, to present but not argue rationale, and to avoid bringing up the history of your relationship. If you come to a point of irreconcilable difference, recognize it as such for the time being. Propose that each of you retreat for a week or more to consider whether there are any potential compromises. Then move on to other points to see if you can resolve remaining issues. At the end of your meeting, summarize and write out your points of agreement and disagreement and plan for your next meeting. If you and your partner have gotten this far without much hostility or hysteria, you both are to be congratulated. Congratulate one another and split.

If you can't get this far, you're not unusual. If the negotiation session cannot be arranged when first suggested, ask yourself whether one or both of you merely need more time, or is this kind of rational, face-to-face discourse beyond you or your partner? If your meeting becomes destructive, stop it immediately. Then ask, "Did we accomplish anything? Is there a reasonable chance that another conference could accomplish anything?" If so, give it another go, but stop it once more if it again becomes harmful. If negotiations break down unproductively or destructively more than once, it is time to consult a professional. A lawyer or possibly a separation-divorce counselor can facilitate a negotiation session by assisting both of you to follow the rules of decent discourse.

But, of course, you may not be able to find such a counselor, or you may feel that face-to-face negotiation will not be productive under any circumstances, or is simply not worth the trouble. In such cases, consult a divorce attorney, if you have not done so already, and instruct him to negotiate for you. Once negotiation has been turned over to your attorney, leave it wholly in his or her hands, unless there is some clear sign that direct consultation with your spouse would be productive. If necessary, simply refuse to discuss these matters directly, as this can make things progressively worse and can significantly retard disengagement. There is nothing quite as engaging as perennial battle.

But whether negotiations are done directly or delegated, the process remains the same. You and your partner make an opening bid, note points of agreement and disagreement, and attempt compromise. This negotiation process may take some time and may be quite difficult for you. But the costs of a court battle, both economically and psychologically, can be high, and you will be well served to conscientiously attempt compromise and accommodation. You will be ill served by fighting a court battle simply to punish your spouse for the wrongs that he or she has committed. If, on the other hand, you try and are unable to come to a compromise which meets your needs, do not hesitate to stand up for your rights and fight out these matters in court. The outcome of these decisions will seriously influence the nature and quality of the rest of your life. Giving away your future because you are afraid of conflict is one of the most damaging things you can do to yourself.

THE MOVE AND
TEMPORARY CHILD CUSTODY

Apart from making an early determination on the need for legal counsel, only one decision must be made at the time of physical separation or very shortly thereafter—who will move and where. In many instances, this first decision is obvious to both parties and not contested. Considerations which influence the decision include: Who wants to move and who does not? Who requires greater space? Who will have custody of the children, if any? What will be the temporary means of making rent or mortgage payments? You can see that the major problems—residence, child custody, and division of income—form an interrelated complex. Fairly often, however, couples agree on who will retain custody of the children, and therefore who needs greater space and who will move, but still are in no condition emotionally to discuss the temporary division of income. With most divorces in this country, the woman takes temporary and eventually permanent custody of the children, and in line with her greater need for space and the children's need for stability, she more frequently remains in the family home. This reasoning makes sense and would, of course, apply to whichever parent retained temporary custody. If this situation applies, you can come to immediate agreement on the first two major issues and postpone, for a short period, a determination of the division of income.

You should be aware that, if you are married, the particular circumstances of your move may in some states involve legal desertion, thereby affecting the issues of child custody and alimony. If you don't know the law on this point, find out and proceed accordingly. What makes sense and what the law says often conflict.

The decision concerning who is to move should be affected very little, if at all, by who initiated the separation. The other considerations mentioned earlier are far more relevant than this technicality, but it does have slight relevance in that it is often perceived as more just for the one who is moving out of the relationship to move out of the house. Furthermore, the initiating partner may be more mobilized for a move and more able to carry it off successfully. On the other hand, there are many advantages to moving out, and if you are the reluctant partner to a separation, the sooner you get over feeling sorry for yourself for being "kicked out of your own home," the sooner you can begin to appreciate the pluses. First, it is often easier to begin moving to a new life by moving to a new home devoid of memories, pleasant and unpleasant. Second, both partners frequently have to move from the common residence sooner or later anyway, and to get this step out of the way early while establishing a more permanent residence is a definite advantage. Third, a move can afford you the opportunity for making many new contacts more appropriate to your new single status. The social and recreational opportunities available to a single person living in a small apartment in the city are generally greater than for one living in a big house in the suburbs, and the burdens of home maintenance are usually less. Furthermore, dating and entertaining new friends may be much more comfortable in a new residence with a new set of neighbors. Remaining in the home has the advantage of providing greater stability during a time of great change, and it will generally be a more substantial residence. But these advantages are bought at a price.

If you cannot come to an agreement on this first decision in a relatively short time, it may be necessary for you to seek legal aid in obtaining some form of legal separation which will include a temporary resolution of this issue.

While it would naturally be better if the arrangements for temporary child custody were similar to the permanent arrangements, this is not essential. If child custody is an issue at all, you may have to separate out short-term and long-term planning. One or both of you may have a change of heart on this issue before your divorce is final, and sensible temporary arrangements may assist you in making a rational and informed decision. Current estimates indicate that women retain custody of the children in approximately 90 percent of the cases, and usually this disposition is made by mutual agreement. It is likely that this will change with changes in the sex-role expectations of men and women, and there are movements in several states to remove the custody clauses differentially favorable to women.

I have witnessed a number of divorces involving young couples in which all economic issues were readily resolved but child custody was a serious problem because both parents genuinely wanted custody of some or all of the children. Both parents were similarly unwilling to give up temporary custody in these cases because they wanted to be with their children, and they were afraid of establishing a precedent which might harm their claims in court. In several of these cases, I have been able to get these parents to share the custody of their children temporarily, rather than immediately fight this issue out in court. More than once, this interim solution was helpful in that one parent eventually decided that he or she did not want custody after all, and so there was no need for a court fight. It is not uncommon for parents to assert a desire for custody initially and then realize that they don't really want the great responsibility it entails. Women in particular may feel obligated by custom to take children when they don't really want them. Men are more prone to use child custody as a weapon to retaliate against their errant wives. In no-fault states, custody may be the only issue on which the "moral" character of the divorcing person will be seen as relevant, and this, of course, enables one to use the issue aggressively. But with some form of trial-custody arrangements in which both parents participate with relative equality, they can begin to sort out their good and bad reasons for demanding custody. They can experience the total responsibility of what they say they want and have time to reevaluate their position. Typically, the desire to punish the spouse will wane with time, along with the child-custody claims that are based on this motive.

Trial child custody, like trial marriage, is a somewhat unconventional idea, but no less beneficial when called for. It is better, of course, to avoid shifting children back and forth rapidly, on a day-to-day or even week-to-week basis. But to have a child spend a month with one parent with some visitation from the other and then to shift this arrangement for a month can provide a meaningful trial. But, you may ask, isn't this kind of unstable situation damaging to the child? Of course, it isn't the best of all possible solutions, but it is less damaging than awarding custody to a parent who really doesn't want the child. And how much more damaging is a raging child-custody battle to everyone involved. I cannot guarantee that trial child custody will eliminate either of these unfortunate outcomes, but my experience suggests that such temporary arrangements could reduce their occurrence.

Of course, if you feel that your spouse will not provide adequate care for your children even on a trial basis, and you desire custody, you will feel obliged to do whatever you can to secure that custody as soon as possible. Again the court will be your last resort. Between the time of your separation and the time of the court proceeding, and even thereafter, either you or your spouse may change your mind on this question. During this time, ask yourself honestly and repeatedly these simple and obvious questions: Which parent wants the children more? Which parent will be more able to provide for their needs? If the child is old enough to make an informed choice, what is it? If you consistently and honestly come to the conclusion that you want the children

more and are better able to care for them than your
spouse, who, for whatever reasons, disagrees, then pursue negotiation with a counselor or a lawyer, and eventually the court. Although it is not common, this is one
area in which mutual accommodation is sometimes impossible and therefore the ruling of the court must be
pursued. But where there is time, that time may help
resolve the issue, particularly if it is filled with a real
child-custody trial.

TEMPORARY DIVISION OF INCOME
AND OBLIGATIONS

The issue of the temporary division of income and
obligations is a tough one, and it may take you a while to
come to a workable solution that will apply between the
time of your physical separation and the time of your
final divorce settlement. You may have more than one
such agreement over this period, since it may last for a
year or more, depending on the circumstances. Initially,
you will need to see that the bills get paid and that both
of you have enough money to get by on. If you can't
discuss this at the time of physical separation, it would
be helpful to indicate that such a discussion is needed
and that you will be reasonable in pursuing it. As soon
as possible, make some temporary but formal arrangement so that each of you knows what to expect for the
immediate future. As your final decisions are made concerning child custody, child support, and alimony, you
can revise your division of income to more accurately
reflect your eventual settlement. For help in determining

this division of income, I refer you to the guidelines in the later sections of this chapter, "Child Support" and "Alimony." Your attorney can also provide assistance with this question. If necessary, you can usually obtain rather quickly a legal separation agreement that will enforce a division of family income until the final divorce is granted.

When these temporary financial arrangements have been made, it is best if the money changes hands through the mail. This procedure is less demeaning to the person who receives the money—to which he or she is presumably entitled. Furthermore, this aids disengagement by canceling another unnecessary opportunity for contact in the context of a functional dependency.

DIVISION OF HOUSEHOLD GOODS

You will need some interim decision on the division of household goods. If, as is usually the case, one partner moves out of the shared residence, it is important that he or she take along some of the common household property. This is important both from a practical and psychological point of view. Practically, setting up a completely new household is expensive, and it is better if the burden of doing this does not fall solely on one person's shoulders. Psychologically, it is important to people, particularly during periods of stress and dislocation, to maintain some identity props around them. Our possessions help to define who we are; continuity in possessions helps maintain the continuity of our identity. If you are the one who leaves, attempt to take with you those things which will help provide you with this continuity. It is generally a mistake to move without taking a good deal of baggage.

GETTING TOGETHER

Although your living together may be ending, your relationship may never end, and at least for a while you will have things to discuss. For this reason, it is best to have some formal understanding about the arrangements for contacting and meeting each other. This should eliminate the dropping-by syndrome discussed earlier and will make your contacts more efficient and constructive. It is also best to arrange your meetings in advance with some stated purpose. It may seem like a small point, but a system for contacting and meeting each other can save you a good deal of grief.

CHILD VISITATION

Arrangements generally need to be made for visitation of the children by the parent who does not have custody. Many couples create a great deal of trouble for themselves by leaving this issue open and resolving it on a day-to-day or week-to-week basis. This, of course, creates the need for continuing contact which is largely unnecessary and frequently disruptive. It creates a rationale for the dropping-by syndrome, provides the opportunity for unsystematic, unproductive discussion of issues, and sets the stage for employing the children as weapons in the separation battle.

It is essential that a formal child-visitation program be established as soon as possible, so that each parent knows what the schedule is and what his or her responsibilities are. In this way, communication and contact can be minimized. If, as is sometimes the case, contact with your spouse is particularly upsetting or unproductive, you should consider child-exchange programs which relieve you of contact. For example, arrangements can be made whereby parents leave or pick up children at school or involve some intermediary in their exchange.

TEMPORARY DIVISION OF PROPERTY

Occasionally, it will be necessary to effect, for the interim period, a temporary division of property such as real estate, stocks, and bonds. Such a division is usually required only with larger estates. Legal advice on division of this kind is obviously called for.

SOME FRIENDLY ADVICE

Thus far, we have covered all the immediate and interim decisions in the Decision Table. Before tackling the remaining issues, here are a few suggestions for making the early period of your separation more constructive:

1. If you move out, move into a place you like. Within the restraints of your income, try to find a place in which you're comfortable. If possible, find a place to live which in some way symbolizes *you*. Try to avoid, at almost all costs, very temporary-looking, temporary-

feeling places. Motels and hotels may be all right for traveling, but they are no place to begin a new life. Make your new residence a home.

2. If you do not move out, *change* the place you live to symbolize the change in your life. Rearrange the furniture, buy new curtains, add plants, or whatever else makes sense to you.

3. Come to some temporary agreement on the division of household goods and furniture in which both of you share. Attempt to keep with you any things which have meaning especially for you and provide continuity with the past—a favorite chair, a piece of art, a plant. Keep these things, whatever the inconvenience.

4. Do something for yourself. Better yet, do lots of things for yourself. You are beginning a period in which you will need to be your own best friend. Begin by being nice to yourself in significant ways—if possible, in ways that symbolize your change to a new life. Things that bolster your self-image and self-confidence are particularly good. So, if you can, buy yourself some new clothes, treat yourself to a special trip, do anything which will help you feel vibrant, alive, and sexy.

5. Disengage from your partner as much as possible. If you move out, do the simple things that are always involved in moving: change your mailing address, get a telephone, take with you all the things you need. But relinquish your old house keys. See your spouse only at prearranged times to discuss prearranged topics. Do not drop by your former partner's home unannounced. Decide on a formal arrangement for the division of family income, and handle these transactions by mail. Establish a formal arrangement for child visitation and

stick to it. Assume responsibility for yourself in every area, and begin living as a single person.

LEGAL DIVORCE

The remaining issues to be negotiated involve legal divorce issues: the permanent division of income and property, custody of the children, and grounds for divorce. Considerable negotiation on these points may be necessary, and their settlement may require the involvement of counselors, attorneys, and even the court. Current estimates indicate that approximately 85 percent of divorce cases are uncontested and settled by out-of-court negotiation. There are very few guidelines, however, to help you determine equitable solutions to any of the questions at issue. Even the statutory rules which are supposed to give guidelines to the court are frequently inconsistent. The laws, especially on property division and alimony, vary widely from state to state, and the application of legal principles varies widely within the same state depending on the circumstances of the case, the attorneys and judge involved, and a host of other uncontrollable factors.

The divorce laws in many states are inhumane and absurd, based as they are on archaic legal and moral principles. In these states, a suing party must prove that his or her spouse has violated the marriage contract in some way in order to be awarded a divorce. If this cannot be proved, the divorce is not granted. It has long been recognized that these archaic laws often result in collusion between the divorcing husband and wife and a rigged case based on the least reprehensible grounds. However, when one party has real proof of contract violations on the part of the other, he or she is usually in a much better position in the contest for the property, the money, and the children. In general, this is true whether the case ends up in a real court fight or not. Some of the unnecessary pain and absurdity of divorce has been reduced by the no-fault divorce laws in such states as California, Oregon, and Iowa—where divorce is commonly obtained through a "dissolution of marriage." Grounds, in the traditional sense, are unnecessary, and the property settlement, child support, and alimony are based on more valid economic considerations, and at least theoretically have nothing to do with the fault of either party in bringing about the dissolution. In these states, the same sordid court proceedings *can* occur around the issue of child custody, and on this issue the circumstances of the dissolution can be considered relevant. While it is true that child-custody proceedings are occasionally used by vindictive spouses for this very purpose, it is not common. So, if you are fortunate enough to live in a state with a humane divorce law, you can be very grateful. If not, you will have to do the best you can with what you've got. In many cases, the grounds for divorce will be the subject of negotiation and collusion between divorcing parties.

Since wherever you live you will find few formulas for fair and equitable decisions on division of property, alimony, and child support, I shall take the bold step of offering you some guidelines for thinking about these questions. Again, there will be exceptions and special circumstances that will affect your deliberations, but the following guidelines may provide an anchor point for you.

CHILD SUPPORT

Constructing initial guidelines for child support from the parent who does not have custody is not difficult. Most lawyers who handle divorce cases can give you some estimate of the norms in your community for child support, given your own and your spouse's income and circumstances. These estimates may have a wide range, however, and other methods of making a decision on this question are available to you. Child support should be considered exactly that—financial support for the children. Thus, if you can determine the amount that it costs to support your children, you have a basis on which to begin an intelligent determination. In general, the child support provided by the noncustodial parent should be somewhere between 50 and 100 percent of the cost of maintaining them. This cost should include all expenses of housing, food, clothing, child care, education, and entertainment. Whether this amount is closer to 50 percent or 100 percent would depend on various factors, including the noncustodial parent's ability to pay and the income of the custodial parent.

Should the level of support be judged on the basis of the past standard of living to which the children have become accustomed? Or should a reduced standard be adopted, reflecting the reality that people cannot live as handsomely apart on a fixed income as they can together? Should everyone in the family share the reduced

standard of living or should the children be "spared"?
This issue, of course, can arm the custodial parent with a
tremendously powerful guilt-inducing argument. The
fact of the matter is, however, that if the children are
spared any sacrifice, the *financial* sacrifice may fall very
heavily on the noncustodial parent. Divorce usually involves a decline in the living standard of the family as a
whole. That's unfortunate but true, and the norms for
child support in your community will probably reflect
that fact. If you are the custodial parent, you may have
to accept this as one of several unpleasant facts of divorce. Allowing yourself to feel cheated on this point
can often fuel much unhappiness. Making your noncustodial spouse feel guilty about this may work if he or
she is particularly susceptible or not well represented by
an attorney. Otherwise, it will not. If you are the noncustodial parent, it may be necessary for you to resist
guilt-inducing tactics of this kind, but resist them you
can. On the other hand, be careful not to use such tactics
yourself—promoting guilt in your ex-partner for taking
money to help raise your children. The cost of maintaining the children should be based on a realistic and
probably reduced estimate based on the new circumstances.

Of course, there is considerable latitude in the
guidelines given here, but that latitude reflects reality.
You should at least be able to determine the range of
child-support payments by using this procedure. And the
rationale of the procedure can be particularly important
to the custodial parent in developing the realization that
these monthly payments are for the support of the children. The custodial parent should no more feel guilty
about accepting this child subsidy than the spouse

should about the amount, which usually will provide considerably less than 100 percent of what it costs to house, feed, clothe, care for, educate, and entertain the children, not to mention the incalculable cost of the labor involved in this endeavor. Child support is sustenance for the children—nothing more or less. It is important that both parents think of it that way.

PROPERTY SETTLEMENTS

In considering the property-settlement issue, determine what property you believe belongs solely to you, what belongs solely to your partner, and what you hold in common. There may be assets or property which you brought into the relationship and which you consider to be your own for that reason. This is a legitimate way of viewing the situation and a legitimate consideration in constructing a solution. It is a common consideration employed in many state statutes. Your spouse, lawyers, and the courts may, of course, disagree with your determination, but that does not mean that their solutions are necessarily more rational or fairer than your own. Are there assets or property which your partner can legitimately claim as his or her own because they were brought into the relationship at its inception? Generally, people tend to view the income and assets acquired during the period of marriage as common property to be divided more or less equally on divorce. In community-property states, such commonality will generally be favored unless the legal title to the property is in only one name. If there are very special circumstances in your case, however, where this guideline does not seem appropriate or applicable, this may again be considered in developing your position. You may, for example, feel that you are solely responsible for the acquisition of certain special savings or property, and wish to claim them as your own for this reason. The fact that others may not readily agree with you on this determination should not hold you back at this point. Remember, your first position is your best position. Once you arrive at these decisions, your division-of-property proposal is complete. You allocate to yourself that property which you view as your own by virtue of your bringing it into the relationship or your being especially responsible for its accumulation. You allocate to your partner the property he or she brought in or accumulated. You then divide the rest equally. If you are realistic about that property which you allocate to yourself and your partner respectively, the proposal should be rather close to a reasonable property settlement which your spouse or a court would develop if such a decision were made without reference to fault. In general, such a settlement should correspond rather well to the guidelines developed in no-fault states.

ALIMONY

And what of alimony? It is in this area that the laws are clearly the most confusing and the guidelines most difficult. I would be untrue to the mission of this book, which has autonomous adulthood as one of its central themes, if I did not forthrightly say that I consider the receipt of large and long-term alimony as completely inconsistent with that goal. Temporary or transitional alimony is frequently necessary and desirable in circumstances where the receiving spouse will be required to make an occupational or educational readjustment. It is particularly necessary where the employment record of that spouse is poor and he or she requires some retraining in order to be employable. It may also be especially justifiable in cases in which, for example, a wife worked to support her husband's education with a reasonable expectation that the support would later be reciprocated.

Although the concept of alimony is rapidly losing favor, particularly in those states with more progressive divorce laws, I generally advise wives who have not worked in the recent past or who require additional training in order to do the kind of work they would like to do to make a temporary-alimony demand. Once again, these decisions are best based on what is equitable and fair, given the circumstances and irrespective of any considerations having to do with guilt or fault in bringing about the dissolution of the marriage.

SPECIAL LEGAL CONSIDERATIONS

Before leaving the issues involved in legal divorce, let me briefly call your attention to some often-overlooked settlement points which may be very important to you.

I. *Disposition of Life Insurance Policies*

You and your spouse may wish to stipulate the disposition and/or beneficiaries of any life insurance policies which you currently hold. This determination can be written in as part of the divorce decree.

II. *Division of Pension and Profit-Sharing Plans*

If either spouse is involved in pension or profit-sharing plans, these future assets can be subject to court-ordered division.

III. *Income-Tax Dependency Deduction for Children*

It is well to stipulate in the divorce decree who will take the children as income-tax deductions. The guideline on this point from the Internal Revenue Service suggests that the parent who provides more than 50 percent of the financial support is entitled to the deduction. However, deductions can be given to either parent by agreement if some minimal level of support is provided by each. There is one very important consideration here that is often overlooked. The custodial parent cannot claim any child-care deductions for children unless he or she can list them as dependents. Whatever the decision on this question, it is best to consider it carefully and stipulate it in the divorce decree.

IV. *Tax and Other Implications of Financial Settlements*

Regular court-ordered alimony payments are tax deductible for the one who pays such support but counted as taxable income for the recipient. Such regular alimony payments normally terminate on the remarriage of the recipient. Child-support payments are not tax deductible for the one who pays, nor are they taxable income for the recipient. They do not terminate on the remarriage of the custodial parent. The tax responsibilities of lump-sum settlements are complex and depend on several factors including the period of time over which the amount is payable and the presence or absence of contingencies for future payment.

V. *Provision for Open Alimony*

In some states, it is possible to leave the question of future alimony open by providing alimony in the amount of some nominal sum (e.g., one dollar per year). This is a kind of insurance providing that a substantial alimony may be awarded at some future time if circumstances warrant. If no such provision is made, the possibility of future alimony is permanently closed.

VI. *Medical Care and Insurance for Children*

It is not uncommon for this issue to be settled separately from child support. This is the time to determine how such medical expenses will be handled. If the non-custodial parent is to provide such care, this should be stipulated in the decree.

There may be many other special considerations in your particular case, but these represent the most commonly overlooked ones which you would do well to consider.

NEXT STEPS

As you begin considering your position, based on the guidelines provided, you may find it helpful to follow the list of assignments I frequently give to people who consult me. Each assignment requires paper, a pencil, and some hard work.

I. *Temporary–Interim Decision Package*

Write out your proposal reflecting your best position for temporary arrangements in each of the following areas:

1. Temporary residence for you.
2. Child custody.
3. Division of income and obligations.
4. Division of household goods.
5. Arrangements for contacting partner.
6. Child-visitation program.
7. Division of property (if necessary).

II. *Child Support* (especially if you are the custodial parent)

Estimate the reasonable future cost of providing for your children in

1. Housing, including the increment required for rent or mortgage payments and all utilities.
2. Clothing.
3. Food.
4. Medical care.
5. Education.
6. Child care, including baby-sitters, summer camps, etc.
7. Recreation.

III. *Division of Property and Household Goods*

List the property or household goods you consider your own, estimate the value of each item of significance, and determine the total. Do the same for the property of your partner. List all of the property you hold in common and estimate the cost of each item of significance. Propose a division of this property. Determine the total value of the property you assign to your spouse and the value of the property assigned to you.

IV. *Deciding on Child Custody*

Take a piece of paper and make a decision diagram divided into quadrants as shown below.

Retaining Custody

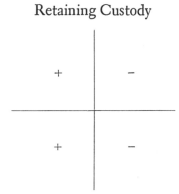

Foregoing Custody

In the upper left quadrant, list all the advantages *for you* in retaining custody. List all the disadvantages in the upper right quadrant. Repeat this in the lower quadrants, listing all the positive aspects *for you* of forgoing custody and all the negative aspects. Now make another diagram and repeat this procedure from the point of view of your children. In their upper quadrants, list the advantages and disadvantages to them of *your* having custody; in their lower, similarly treat their *other parent's* having custody. Review, revise, and deliberate every list.

V. *Deciding on Who Will Move*

Make another pair of decision diagrams and list all the advantages and disadvantages of moving or staying for you and for your children.

VI. *Deciding on Reconciliation*

Make another decision diagram and list the advantages and disadvantages *for you* of retaining (top quadrants) or terminating (bottom quadrants) your marriage.

VII. *Final Decisions on Alimony, Child Custody, Visitation, and Child Support*

Combine with your written proposal on division of property a written proposal on each of these issues. In considering alimony, stipulate the amount and indicate for how long it will be paid and under what circumstances it would be reduced or stopped. On child visitation, indicate both the minimum and maximum amount of visitation you would desire or allow. Specify the procedures you want to follow in arranging and carrying out visitation. Determine the points on which you would compromise in each area and write them down.

VIII. *Establishing Your Position Regarding Reconciliation*

Develop your stand on reconciliation: whether you are generally in favor of, opposed to, or undecided about it; under what circumstances you would reconcile or consider reconciliation; whether your spouse would have to agree to do anything before you would consider reconciliation, and if so, what.

Each of the foregoing assignments is difficult, involving decisions that are agonizing at best. Facing them is certainly one of the most noxious parts of beginning a new life, and it is natural to want to put them off. Of course, many of your decisions can be only provisional at first, but I think you will find it helpful to have your working position developed on each important issue. You *are* beginning a new life, and you must travel this hard part of the journey first in order to say good-bye to your old life and embrace the new. As you finish these uncomfortable chores, you are entering autonomous adulthood. Welcome!

PART II

LIVING IN THE FIRST PERSON SINGULAR

4

Autonomous Adulthood: A Job Description for the Single Adult

> For every thing you have missed, you have gained
> something else; and for every thing you gain, you
> lose something.
>
> —Ralph Waldo Emerson

WHO AM I?

I AM CONVINCED that one of the primary reasons people have such difficulty in living single is that they are simply unaware of what they need to do in order to live a reasonably fulfilling life alone. Most individuals are simply unskilled or out of practice when it comes to many of the necessary tasks of single life. To do any job well, one needs a job description, a feeling that the job is worthy, and practice in carrying out the required tasks. The object of this chapter is to provide you with a job description for single life and to assist you in beginning the practice of the skills it requires.

The overwhelmingly dominant job description for adult life in America is threefold: to be part of a functioning couple, to get married, and to stay married. And, of course, most people in our society are fulfilling the first two elements. In this country, 70 percent of the adult population are married at any given point in time, and a very large but unknown proportion of adults who are legally single are, for all practical purposes, paired off in more or less monogamous bonds in the fulfillment of element number 1. The separated single, the divorced, the widowed, and those who terminate their functional marriages typically move on quickly to establish other primary coupling arrangements which may or may not involve legal marriages.

Truly, this is a couples culture. Couples are usually formed early in life, with men marrying at a median age of twenty-three and women at a median age of twenty-one. For most of us, fully independent living has been either totally nonexistent or very short-lived. Young adults in high school or college generally live with parents or roommates in a mostly single condition of high social support. An independent existence, if it occurs at all, is usually of short duration and viewed as a temporary transition between young adulthood and the true maturity that involves monogamous coupling, marriage, and the creation of a family. Although we read a great deal about dramatic social changes in recent years, to be grown up in this society still means to be married. In the most recent Roper poll on the attitudes of American women, for example, it was found that 97 percent reported that marriage represented the most desirable personal life-style.

What is the point of this rather academic and statistic-laden discussion? It is this: mastering those roles in life for which there is little training, legitimacy, or support is tough. It is hard to do a job for which one has not been trained, for which there is a deficient job description, and for which little social support or legitimacy is offered. Most of the available research on the adjustment to divorce, for example, indicates that the older the individual is, the longer he or she has been married, the harder is the adjustment. For such people, the job description of autonomous adulthood must certainly be more obscure, more difficult to realize, and certainly less legitimate in the context of their upbringing and life experience. And irrespective of our age, most of us have been taught to think about our adult development in terms of our position in a functioning, two-parent family.

But if you're not in one, you may have to change your thinking. Consider autonomous adulthood. To achieve it, you must master two basic sets of skills. First, you must perform the social tasks involved in the acquisition and maintenance of a well-operating social-support group. Second, you must be able to live autonomously as never before and to perform all self-care functions that have been previously shared or delegated. The more unfamiliar these tasks are, the more difficult you will find learning how to perform them. The more division of labor and mutual dependency in the previous relationship, the more difficulty there will be in getting along alone.

One initially curious but overwhelmingly consistent finding that continues to crop up in the research on adapting to single life supports this line of reasoning: in general, men have a far more difficult emotional adjustment to separation, divorce, widowhood, and single life than do women. At first, this finding seems curious because it runs counter to the popular myth that characterizes the man as the more reluctant and constricted partner in marriage and the woman as more dependent and contented. We are wont to see the single man as being free of family obligations to pursue an exciting and unencumbered bachelor life, while a woman alone is more often viewed as a pathetic, unfulfilled person. But the fact is that, compared to their married counterparts, single, divorced, and widowed men experience far higher rates of suicide, mental illness, and hospitalization for psychiatric problems than do single, divorced, or widowed women. One of the most striking and powerful findings in our research on divorce adjustment is that divorced men report much poorer adjustment after their separation than do women. It may well be that men marry more reluctantly than do women, but the evidence is clear that men benefit from marriage more than women and suffer more as a consequence of separation, divorce, or the death of their mate.

Why is this truth so discrepant from the myth? No one knows the answer for sure, but my educated guess is that women in this society are simply better equipped to fulfill the requirements of *autonomous adulthood* than are men. This is not to say, of course, that adjustment to single life, especially when prompted by separation, divorce, or the death of a mate, is not very difficult for women; but a woman, especially if she has a good occupation and resources, is generally better trained in autonomous-adulthood skills and more psychologically prepared to see the accomplishment of these skills as rewarding and legitimate to her sex and her role in life. A man coming out of a traditional marriage, for example, may be quite able to earn a living, but extraordinarily inept in performing the necessary tasks required to keep himself reasonably well fed, clothed, and housed. More serious may be his reluctance to take on these tasks for which he has had no prior training, for which he thinks he has no aptitude, and which he may have grown up believing are not even manly.

I first came up with the concept of autonomous adulthood to assist people who were going through separation and divorce. Yet, as I have developed the concept further, it has become increasingly apparent that it may very well be the emerging job description for all adults living in the last quarter of the twentieth century, irrespective of their marital or relationship status. Certainly, being able to live autonomously should improve the basis from which one decides to pair off or marry. If you are able to live happily and comfortably as a single person, you are going to actively choose to become part of a pair, not because you *have* to, but because you *want* to; because you find important added benefits in the person and the relationship you choose. In discussing marriage in their book, *Mirages of Marriage*, William Lederer and Don Jackson have pointed out that, in any relatively monogamous relationship, one constant issue is whether both partners are in the relationship because they want to be or because they have to be. When a person knows that he or she can survive and thrive as a single, autonomous adult, he or she is in a relationship by choice.

Autonomous adulthood, then, is viewed not only as a desirable and viable life-style for the single person, but it is recommended as the best precursor to any primary relationship. Particularly today, when the job description for married life is changing to one involving more openness, independence, and fluctuation of responsibility, both partners need to possess autonomous-adulthood skills. A recent Roper survey, for instance, showed that half of all college-educated women in this country and 61 percent of all women under thirty desire a marriage characterized by equal partnership, where both partners share equally in the responsibilities involved in home management and children. This same survey showed that younger women especially are now attempting to teach all their children—boys as well as girls—the autonomous maintenance skills that many single adults must now learn more or less from scratch.

THE JOB DESCRIPTION

What do you think would happen if you could commit yourself to living well alone as completely as you might to a really good career, relationship, marriage, or family? What if you committed yourself to learning autonomy skills with the same enthusiasm you might muster for learning a new sport? What if you spent as much energy in developing yourself as a functioning single adult as you have spent on your education, career, or family? What if you viewed single life as an exciting challenge in which much could be learned rather than as a temporary discomfort to be endured? What could you do then?

If you are ready to take on the challenge of living the good life alone, the best way for you to begin is to take inventory of your ability to perform the needed tasks. I hope you will take the time to rate yourself honestly on the inventory outlined below. Having the entire record before you at once will help you to establish priorities and plan the work ahead.

In rating yourself, remember that this is an inventory of your *current* ability to meet your *current* needs.

Don't be too hard on yourself. You don't have to be a gourmet cook to feed yourself adequately or an automobile mechanic to keep your car running. You merely need the skills and attributes that will enable you to live comfortably as an independent person. These are grouped into three categories. The first, Autonomous Functioning Skills, represents those abilities necessary for independent living. The second and third represent those special skills that are particularly important for singles in developing and maintaining a functioning friendship system and in mastering the intricacies of dating, sex, and love relationships.

To take this inventory, you need a large sheet of paper (standard typewriter or legal size) and a pen or pencil. Using the longest side of the sheet as the top, start five columns across it with headings under which you will rate your own competence. The headings are:

Excellent   Good   Adequate   Fair   Poor

Now, consider each item on the list and enter it in the appropriate column. If, for example, your cooking skills are excellent, enter "Cooking" under that heading. Or, if you are unable to enjoy being alone, you'd enter two items under *Poor:* "Tolerating/enjoying aloneness" and "Enjoying solitary activities."

Skills and Attributes for Autonomous
Adulthood

1. Autonomous Functioning Skills

     Cooking
     Housekeeping
     Providing own transportation
     Automobile maintenance

Money management
Wardrobe management
Caring for children (if applicable)
Tolerating/enjoying aloneness
Enjoying solitary activities
Providing adequate income
Pursuing satisfying career
Pursuing satisfying interests or hobbies

2. Social Attributes and Skills for Friendship Maintenance

Making and keeping same-sex friends
Making and keeping other-sex friends
Developing depth of friendships
Ability to communicate with friends
Being with friends regularly
Initiating outside activities with friends
Entertaining friends at home
Finding ways to meet new friends

3. Social Attributes and Skills for Dating, Sex, and Amative Relationships

Initiating conversation with other sex
Finding ways to meet other sex
Ability to attract members of other sex
Ease in asking for dates
Ease in refusing dates
Dating regularly or often
Knowledge of and comfort with dating
   etiquette
Ease in communicating with other sex in
   early contacts or dating
General ease in dating
Ease in being affectionate
Ease in receiving and reciprocating affection

      Ease in rejecting affection
      Ease in making sexual advances
      Ease in receiving and reciprocating sexual
         advances
      Ease in rejecting sexual advances
      General sexual ability
      Ease in sexual interaction
      Ability to communicate about affectionate
         and sexual behavior
      Ability to communicate in love-sex relation-
         ships
      Quality of love-sex relationships

To take the next step, get another sheet of paper, divide it in half, and list at the top those skills or attributes you have entered under *Fair*; list on the lower half those you entered under *Poor*. Then classify each item on the list according to its *importance* to you. Give an A priority to those problems you see as most critical for you in attaining autonomous adulthood, a B to those of moderate importance, and a C to those of less importance. Also rate each item as to how easy it would be to remedy the problem. Thus, give an A priority to the things that would be easiest to improve or learn, a B to more difficult items, and a C to the really difficult items. Here is an example of one such list made out by a male client.

Autonomous-Adulthood Learning Priorities

Fair

Item	Importance	Ease
Cooking	A	A
Housekeeping	C	A
Wardrobe management	B	B

Item	Importance	Ease
Ease in asking for dates	A	B
Making other sex-friends	B	A

Poor		
	Importance	Ease
Initiating conversation with other sex	B	C
Tolerating/enjoying aloneness	A	C

It may be useful now to think about your list and the priorities you have attached to each item and then lay it to one side as you continue to read. You may change your priority ratings as you go along, or you may add items. You may wish to use this list to choose the first things to work on. More guidelines will be given on how to do this as we go along. Obviously, those skills you have rated high in both categories would give you the best starting points for your self-change program. In the sample list, "Cooking" averages highest, followed closely by "Ease in asking for dates." Other things being equal, one of these would be the best initial target for this person.

PRISONERS OF
NONAUTONOMOUS LIVING

For many, single life is merely a temporary way station between adolescence and marriage, or between marriages. As such, no commitment is made to it; it is not something to be mastered but something to be endured and finished with as quickly as possible. Only the very fortunate do not have some serious deficits in autonomous-adulthood skills, and these deficits, if not overcome, can become prisons. I am convinced that one of the reasons people prematurely settle for and stick with an unsatisfying relationship is that at least it provides an escape from the discomfort of such a single prison. Let us consider what some of these jail cells look like.

Karen's Prison

Some women develop a talent for getting ripped off by men, but Karen had become an expert. When she first walked into my office, she reminded me of one of those sad women I had seen in bars night after night during my own postmarriage barhopping. I was right; she probably had been. But now it was several years later, and Karen was still spending most of her evenings in bars. She was basically an attractive woman, but she appeared drawn and burned out. This was her story.

After graduating from secretarial school five years before, she had moved away from home and almost immediately moved in with a man. He was the exciting, irresponsible sort who had made her life alternately ecstatic and miserable. She described him as a very intelligent, interesting, and masculine man who could turn her on by almost anything he did but who could also cause her incredible pain. He made her miserable by staying away from home overnight and refusing to tell her where he had been, and from time to time he would become depressed, withdrawn, and abusive. She knew he was seeing other women; he did nothing to conceal his affairs and would occasionally flaunt them to her. But just as she would begin to get fed up with this situation, he would change to his more charming, considerate, and brilliant self. He would protest his love and promise to change his ways, and thus win Karen back.

Eventually, he left her for another woman, returned for a while, left again, and tried to return a second time. But at last she had had enough. That had been three years ago, and her situation had become even more distressed since then. Her love life had been unrewarding, to say the least. She had had four affairs that started out very intensely, but for reasons she could not understand, each one ended abruptly after a few weeks. In each affair, the man simply stopped calling, leaving her depressed and nearly suicidal for a time. Besides these affairs, she had only periodic "one-night stands" with men she would never see again. She hated this way of living and the self-image it imparted to her, yet she had to keep looking. To Karen, finding a man was the most important thing in the world because only if she could find him would her existence begin to take on form and meaning.

I asked Karen to tell me about her daily life. She worked in a law office and found her work moderately interesting. It was after work that her problems began. Usually she would go out for a couple of drinks with a friend after work. Then she'd go home, throw something unsubstantial together for dinner, and after watching television for a while, go out again until the bars closed. She was unable to get to sleep until two or three in the morning anyway, she said, and she absolutely detested being alone at night. If she tried to stay home, she would get panicky from loneliness and finally run out of her apartment to a familiar bar. On weekends she would catch up on lost sleep during the days, but her evening schedule was the same.

The brief love affairs she had had provided a much-needed escape from this hectic and depressing schedule. During these times she was better able to stay home alone, knowing there was someone meaningful in her life. But, as she said, these tranquil periods were few and far too brief. She concluded her story with the pathetic statement, "I just seem to have a talent for getting ripped off. I'm beginning to think I'm just a loser."

By most people's definition, Karen was right. She was a loser. But she was not losing simply because of her failure to find a good man. There were many locks to her single prison cell—so many that it took some time and a lot of work to spring her—but this was a strategic lock— the idea that her life was without meaning unless it included a man. Women, even though they typically possess more and better-developed skills for attaining autonomous adulthood, are frequently imprisoned by this psychological barrier. Indoctrinated by our culture with the idea that having a man is all-important, they will sacrifice a great deal for men and can easily become experts at being beaten down by them.

A second lock on Karen's single prison was, in a way, related to the first: she simply had very little going on in her life. She had no absorbing interests, hobbies, or involvements of any kind. Clearly, one of the reasons she was so taken with her old boyfriend was his stimulation value. He brought the kind of excitement and interest to her life that she could not provide for herself. She could be an extremely loving and caring person, but she had little else to offer. She couldn't have been interesting to talk with for any length of time because she didn't have anything much to talk about. This deficit was undoubtedly partly responsible for the fact that she could sustain little more than brief affairs or one-night stands. A third lock on her prison door was her fear of being alone. This is what drove her out to bars every night into an exhausting and demoralizing existence.

The final lock was a product of the first three: she was thoroughly demoralized. She looked the part of a loser. Her clothes fitted poorly and were not coordinated well, her posture was bent, and her facial expression reflected her beaten attitude. Although basically an attractive woman, she wasn't at this point in her life attractive at all. And people treated her like the chronic barfly she was.

One by one, we found and used the keys to Karen's dreary cell. Without going into the details of the therapeutics used in this and similar cases, let us review in a general way what had to be done.

It was most important to get Karen out of the bars and into some other activities. I found that she had once been interested in tennis but had never learned to play it well. Similarly, she had once tried to learn the guitar and still owned one. In a matter of two weeks I had persuaded her to participate in a tennis class and to begin guitar lessons. Both of these pursuits are creative and active, and can begin to give a person sources of self-esteem and a repertoire of meaningful activity upon which to build an identity.

I have labeled this kind of activity a *creative operant*. "Operant" is a psychologist's word for an active response. In a general way it refers to any behavior which operates on or changes the environment. Such abilities are critical for everyone and are especially important for individuals who need a greater sense of personal identity. By my definition, playing the guitar, tennis, cooking, and skiing are creative operants; eating, watching a play, or watching television are usually not, unless one is a serious gourmet, a theater buff, or a television critic.

Karen also needed more and better friends and had to learn to stick up for herself. To deal with these things, I arranged for her to enroll in a special group designed to teach women to be more assertive. As I had hoped, once she began to become active in all these pursuits, her visits to the bars became fewer and shorter. She made new friends in the group and found one really close friend while playing tennis. She began to get invited to a few parties and to weekend activities with a woman friend and her husband. Interestingly, as Karen's social and recreational life began to take on better form, she gradually changed in other ways. She began to go to bed earlier, and she looked and dressed better.

Meanwhile, she and I spent most of our time together working on her two other problems—fear of loneliness and an excessive need for a man. She followed a prescribed routine at home designed to help increase her tolerance for being alone. This regime involved exposing herself to increasing doses of solitude, at times of her own choice.

Finally, we talked about her crippling idea that she was nothing without a man. We examined the logic of this poisoned notion with the same procedures and guidelines outlined in Chapter 2. As she developed her music, tennis, friendships, and tolerance for aloneness, she did, in fact, need men a lot less, and that helped. We talked about her relationships with men. She thought she was unattractive to men because of her figure—she thought she was too thin and that her breasts were too large. She was a bit thin, but not excessively so, and I assured her that I thought her breasts were nice.

It is not at all uncommon, of course, for all of us to have serious hang-ups about the inadequacy of our bodies or to attribute our relationship problems to them. Often these body-image concerns are about some characteristic which to others would be unnoticeable, unimportant, or even attractive. The advertising industry, among other influences, has succeeded remarkably well in getting us to feel insecure about our bodies. I boldly and honestly told Karen that many men would find her kind of body exceedingly attractive; and I used this opportunity to add that, while her body was indeed an asset in attracting men, she would do well to ask herself what she could offer to *sustain* a relationship with a man besides good looks, sex, and fair cooking. I suggested that, although she was certainly not worthless without a man, she would do better in getting and keeping one if she had some activities, interests, and friends to bring to the relationship. These talks eventually resulted in her enrolling in some community college courses which provided still more opportunities for her expanding spiral of life contacts.

Now, all this sounds too easy, I know. It wasn't. As with most people who get themselves badly messed up, Karen had to work hard to effect changes and learn new skills, and much of it was very slow. Sometimes she would feel that what I had asked her to do was superficial, unnecessary, or, more often, a good idea that was just too hard to accomplish. But these reactions are par for the course. Human habits are stubborn, but Karen and I were stubborn, too; and each little opening in the single prison cell seemed to lead to other openings.

Note that there was no need to view Karen as a victim of childhood traumas that only long-drawn-out analytic treatment could and should uncover before we could get her life in order. She was the victim of her own deficits in living and her own kooky ideas. Of course, both were the product of her life experiences, but both were remedied by directed work and learning. Karen escaped from her single prison cell by unlocking the locks, not by digging up the floor.

Frank's Prison

Frank was thirty-four when he finally decided to seek help with his problems. He had been married four times and was currently in a monogamous and unhappy relationship with a much younger woman. According to Frank, his current relationship was much like what he had experienced in his marriages. He had met Cheryl only a week after his separation from his fourth wife. They went out together a few times and seemed to enjoy each other's company. She told him later what other women had told him in the past, that she was impressed and pleased by his gentlemanliness and the fact that he never "pushed her" sexually. In our therapy sessions, he indicated that he had always been successful with this type of shy and inhibited woman, and, as he saw it, the secret of his success was his polite reticence concerning sex. As with the other women before her, he waited for Cheryl to make sexual advances to him. But once Frank slept with a woman, he felt obligated to her and responsible for her. According to him, it was not love that had prompted commitment and marriage in the past, but rather a sense of duty to those who had become dependent upon him. In each of his four marriages, the idea of legal union had come from the woman, and Frank had just gone along, thinking he was doing the right thing.

His current relationship was becoming repetitive and boring, just like all the others. Cheryl would come to his apartment every night at about six o'clock; she would cook dinner for the two of them, and they would then watch television until eleven, when she would go home; she still lived with her parents. Frank would then stay up late watching more television, get up late the next morning, and often arrive late for work. Sometimes, when Cheryl initiated it, they would have sex together, but that too was becoming boring for him, and as often as not he was unable to get or maintain an erection. This appeared to puzzle and distress Cheryl, but they never really talked about it. Frank said that this rigid and boring pattern was rarely broken up by other activities, but that he now wanted to become involved in other things, such as engaging in an evening sports activity and seeing other women. But he was afraid that, if he tried to be more independent, he might lose Cheryl. So he continued to settle, as he had so often before, for a dull, constricted relationship. There was only one difference, this fifth time around: he had begun to suspect that something was basically wrong.

At first it wasn't clear what had perpetuated this series of compromising relationships. Frank was a relatively attractive and intelligent man who presumably had the skills for developing and maintaining relationships far more rewarding than the ones he had had. Certainly, there was more going on here than a simple case of an exaggerated sense of obligation. What was in this for Frank? From patient and detailed history taking, his therapist learned that Frank had never really lived on his own as an adult. The pattern he described as typical had begun almost immediately after he left high school and had continued until the day he sought professional assistance. He had never learned to cook, keep house, attend to his clothes, or do a myriad of other things that his mother, and then other women, had seen to for him.

Moreover, he had a recurring ulcer condition that would act up from time to time, particularly when he did not take proper care of himself. If he drank, failed to get enough rest, or became overly stressed, his ulcer symptoms would flare up and he would be ill for several days. And, as you might expect, he was not very good at disciplining his diet or other living patterns. During those brief times on his own, his health would deteriorate markedly. In his current relationship, his sleeping habits were worse because Cheryl had to sleep at home.

Finally, he had learned to be a good boy; and he had learned that there were certain expectations in life that you had to live up to. If another took care of you and expected you to stay home, be faithful, and live locked into a tedious relationship, that was what you did—up to a point. In each of his four marriages, Frank had finally broken out. In each marriage, he had resented the mothering, the restriction, the boredom, and —perhaps most of all—his own weakness. When all these things became intolerable, he would slowly and painfully leave the relationship, first through his impotence and then through other forms of polite but deadly withdrawal. Some men and women settle for this kind of infantile and depressing life until they die. Frank was a little bit ahead of these people, for he would settle, then rebel, then resettle and rebel. Although he was only dimly aware of it at the time, his coming for assistance marked the beginning of his breaking away from this pattern that was so destructive to him and to the women who played out the other half of his script.

The solution for Frank was a difficult one. As with Karen, there were many complex locks on his prison door. Frank has had to learn a greater level of self-discipline in controlling his diet, sleep, and work habits. He has had to learn self-care skills in order to get by without a doting mother. He has had to work through his exaggerated sense of obligation, to learn to say no when he wants to, and to say yes to his own desires. In short, he has had to fill in the gaps in himself in order to live well alone or to hope for a mature and fulfilling relationship with another. At this writing, he is still working but is in touch with what he needs to do and is proud of the person he is becoming.

Mary's Prison

In many respects, at twenty-nine my friend Mary was a model of the autonomous adult. She could take care of herself in every way. She was successful and respected in her career as a school counselor in the primary grades. She was happy being alone to read, cook, sew, listen to music, or just go for a long walk. She had a good friendship group made up of other women, and, through them, she always had companionship when she wanted it. She had a long list of creative operants, including swimming, gardening, skiing, and sailing. She was financially comfortable. She was buying her own small house, owned a new car, and took a vacation to Hawaii or Europe every other year. But, she told me, something just seemed to be missing.

"And if you are like the rest of my friends," she said, "you will tell me I need a man. I don't know, maybe I do, but I treasure my freedom and independence and certainly don't envy those women whose very existence depends on a man. Besides, I've never really met a man who could do as much for me as I can do for myself. I'm not ecstatically happy living as I do, but I am quite happy enough, and it would take quite a person to make things all that much better. And what good has love and marriage done most of my friends who married in their early twenties, had some kids, and are now going through divorces? They're so far behind me it's not even funny. I never want to be dependent on someone else as they are and be crushed by separation or, worse yet, be trapped in an unhappy relationship I can't get out of. My life does feel a little hollow sometimes, but you see, it's just not that bad a compromise, and it's better than a lot of others I see. And yet, I can't help but feel that I'm missing something. I don't want what my friends have, but I do want more than I've got, and I honestly don't know what it is."

Perhaps I was jumping the gun a bit, but as I heard Mary talk I remembered some important wisdom written by Milton Mayeroff in his book *On Caring*. I looked up the lines later that evening. Here they are:

> In the context of a man's life caring has a way of ordering his other values and activities around it. When this ordering is comprehen-

sive because of the inclusiveness of his caring,
there is a basic stability in his life; he is "in
place" in the world, instead of being out of
place, or merely drifting or endlessly seeking
his place. Through caring for certain others, by
serving them through caring, a man lives the
meaning of his own life. In the sense in which
a man can ever be said to be at home in the
world, he is at home not through dominating,
or explaining, or appreciating, but through
caring and being cared for.

In many ways, Mary had ordered her life very well;
yet it semed to me—and to her as well, I think—that
there was no great comprehensiveness in her caring.
Many compromises can be made with life—there are
many solutions that are safe and involve little risk but
result in living life at half measure, and this is not really
living at all. Frank's compromise is far and away the
most common today, and yet every indication is that
Mary's compromise will be more popular in the future as
men and women become less needy of practical sustenance from one another.

It is much easier as a professional psychologist or a
concerned friend to help people discover ways of getting
what they want than it is to help them to decide what it
is they want in the first place. In the latter problem, the
would-be helper's biases almost always enter in and it is
always difficult to know what will be right for another.
And yet, as I reviewed all of Mary's relationships with
others—her friends, family, the children with whom she
worked—it became clear to me that, in never having had
the experience of relating closely in a primary relationship, she had missed out on sampling the kind of caring

human union that for most adults is basic. And she had given up on such relationships before trying them out in a meaningful way.

Although she had dated a number of men as a younger woman, all of her relationships had been rather superficial, involving repeated dating and sex but not real sharing, intimacy, and mutual support. She was capable of mutually supportive friendships with other women, but men were a bit of a different species for her. Boyfriends had disappeared from her life in the past, and she had felt rejected. She attributed these rejections to the fact that she was somewhat overweight. It had been two years ago, when she was twenty-seven, that she had more or less given up on men. Since that time, she had paid little attention to her weight or to making herself physically attractive. Because she had asked, I outlined for her what I saw and made some suggestions concerning how she might begin to know men as human beings, at first in settings where such relationships would not be confounded with dating, sex, and commitment problems. If I had been seeing Mary professionally, I would in time have arranged for programs to assist her in improving her appearance. But people like Mary, who have their compromises with life this well worked out, don't often ask for or accept much assistance.

To my knowledge, Mary didn't profit from our talk. To move forward she would have had to go through a kind of adolescence all over again, and that would have been extremely difficult. This is what most of her newly divorced friends would be doing, but their lives were uncertain and disrupted like that of the adolescent. Mary had things set for herself. Why rock the boat?

Mark's Prison

Mark literally had it made. At thirty-five, he quickly had become a very successful attorney in his community. He liked his work and was very good at it. But unlike most successful men, Mark did not take his work too seriously. He was bright enough to work a moderate amount and still be ahead of most others with whom he had to compete. He had another important advantage—striking good looks and charm, which are assets in any business. Mark had been a bachelor long enough to learn many of the practical aspects of taking care of himself. He enjoyed cooking, and although his repertoire was limited, it was very good and functional. As for the other mundane tasks of household management, he freely hired others to help him. He owned a beautiful home on the outskirts of the city and from time to time would give fantastic parties for his friends.

Those who had known Mark for only a few years assumed that things had always come easily to him, but this wasn't the case. Ten years before, when he was a law student, he had fallen in love with and married a slightly older, beautiful, and accomplished young journalist. For a time, this was an idyllic relationship for Mark. He had a woman whom he loved and respected and who cared for and stimulated him. To him she was a never-to-be-equaled superwoman. She was the ideal combination of mother and mistress and a respected professional as well. But as time went on, it became clear that he was not enough for her, and for reasons that he never really quite understood, she decided to leave him when she received an attractive offer to join the staff of a larger city newspaper. At twenty-five, just one year out of law school, Mark was devastated. He had never before been disappointed either in his love life or in his career, and he vowed that it would never happen again. He swore that in any future relationships or career situations he would have the upper hand, no matter how hard he had to work to get it. And indeed, by the age of thirty-five he had gotten it. He was the envy of many of his friends, both married and unmarried, in part because he was always in charge, always in control, always on top. Never was he involved with less than two women at a time, and often there were three or more. He was accomplished in all the skills involved in dating, sex, and maintaining relationships. If he had honestly taken the autonomous-adulthood inventory that I provided for you earlier, he could have entered more of those skills in the *Excellent* column than most singles I've known.

I asked Mark late one night how he managed his personal life. His response was strikingly honest. He told me again of his former marriage, the separation which had devastated him, and his vow. "I decided," he said, "that I was bright enough and strong enough to become really independent, and I did it. I discovered autonomous adulthood before you had named it."

"How," I asked, "are you so successful with women?"

"There's one simple answer to that one. I always need them less than they need me. I always see them less than they want to see me. I always have more women than I need, so the loss of one can never be a great loss. I set it up so that I always win and never lose."

In spite of his near-perfect score on my little in-

ventory, Mark is not the ideal model of the autonomous
adult that I would want to hold up for you, and that is
because he is preoccupied with winning, not with living. To me, his avoidance of meaningful and caring
relationships with others is just as much a compromise with life as any of the other compromising prisons
I have outlined. It is the most comfortable prison of all
but for this very reason the most secure and tightly
bolted. It works so well and hurts so little that he may
never be motivated to find his way out.

The case studies presented here represent a broad
range of types of autonomous-adulthood problems. The
most subtle deficits can be the most insidious because
they are associated with the most secure of single prisons. Are you in one? What's keeping you there?

5
How to Change

*The important thing is this: To be able at any
moment to sacrifice what we are for what we
could become.*
             —*Charles DuBois*

My one major concern in writing this book is that,
no matter how sound the advice I give in it, its impact
on you may last only a short time. Although you will
find suggestions in subsequent chapters that will assist
you in learning to overcome your autonomous-adulthood deficits, I know how hard it will be for you to
change your own behavior or to sustain such change
if it doesn't bring the desired results immediately. For
example, if you are an inexperienced man thinking
about learning to cook, you may easily be stopped before you start by such a practical consideration as obtaining the basic kitchen equipment and food staples.
If you are typical, you don't know what supplies you
need, you are unsure about where to purchase them,
and you may be reluctant to spend the money on such
an uncertain project anyway. Add to these obstacles,
particularly if you are recently separated, a certain self-
consciousness about performing this task in the first
place and about your ignorance in the second. Say you
overcome all this; you still don't know the first thing

about cooking! So then you go to buy a cookbook. But which of the hundred available should you buy? And which of the many recipes in the one you buy should you try to prepare? What should you do about the fact that all the recipes are for four to eight people when you are only one? And what the hell do sauté, simmer, poach, beat, fold, grate, and puree mean? Wouldn't it be better to just go out for dinner and forget the whole thing?

Or suppose you want to get involved in new activities and meet new people, where should you begin? The newspaper lists only a few of the potentials, and the more you need new activities, the less able you usually are to judge what would be good or where to find it. Participating in new groups is difficult for most, and trying it alone is particularly difficult. Getting out requires a *chain of actions:* finding what's available, choosing, planning for the time in advance—perhaps arranging for a baby-sitter—and, finally, going. It's easier to watch television and hope someone invites you somewhere. And like it or not, we all tend to fall back on what's easier.

It is this chain of actions that makes it so difficult to get a good home-cooked meal, a new, interesting activity, or a new friend. And, quite possibly, the first few times you struggle through the chain will not yield anything good. Falling on your face is part of being a beginner. Learning any new skill or developing any new repertoire is usually more trouble than it's worth *at first.* Things take more effort initially, the rewards are less satisfying than they will be at a later point, and failure is discouragingly common. These are just some of the reasons why acquiring autonomous-adulthood skills is tough and why most of us can use all the help we can get to change.

SELF-DISCIPLINE PRINCIPLES

Hence, in this section is presented a set of five self-discipline principles that can help you accomplish these difficult beginnings. There is no magic in these principles, and you have probably heard of some of them before. There is a lot to be said against them—they are a bit simple-minded and boring, and they require your taking your good intentions more seriously than you may want to—but *they work*. They have helped me do some things I've had trouble doing. A substantial amount of research shows that they work for people in general, and I have used them successfully with many clients in my practice. One of our earliest behavioral scientists, Benjamin Franklin, used some of them successfully on himself, and Franklin was a master of self-discipline and new learning.

Because I myself sometimes find these self-discipline procedures tedious and expect you may too, I'm not going to take any more space than is absolutely necessary to outline and discuss them. But once you assimilate them, you'll understand the rest of this book better, and you can employ the principles to actualize any of the ideas for change that you find here or anywhere else. Even though they are not the most exciting things I have to tell you, they may be among the most important. They can help you learn to cook or find the love of your life. They are worth considering.

Here is the set of five principles, with individual discussion of each one to follow:

I. Goal Setting
II. Graded Assignments
III. Self-Observation and Recording
IV. Self-Imposed Consequences
V. Environmental Planning

Before we go more fully into these principles, let's get one thing straight about autonomous adulthood. Adult autonomy does not mean doing everything well; it means doing the things you need or want to do well enough to suit *you.* For example, if you don't know how to cook as yet, it would probably be helpful for you to learn to put together a few basic dishes for times when you are ill or too tired to go out for dinner. Beyond that, it is your choice whether you decide to eat out most nights or whether you would prefer to learn how to make good home-cooked or even gourmet meals for yourself or others. The idea is for you to be able to meet all your own needs insofar as is humanly possible. Then you won't be a slave to searching or waiting for the one who will. And you won't be so likely to ruin your relationships with those you do find by heaping all those unmet needs on them. Adult autonomy simply means meeting your own needs in ways that make most sense to you.

Principle I. Goal Setting

The first step in getting anywhere is to decide where you want to go. If you have rated your priorities in tackling your inventory of skill deficits as suggested in the last chapter, you have taken the first important step in improving your ability to live well alone. But your autonomous-adulthood profile doesn't specify concrete goals. If, for example, you have a deficit in cooking, you now need to specify how good a cook you want to be. When I asked a client with this priority what he wanted to achieve, he said, "Well, I'd like to be able to cook simple meals for myself every night. They don't have to be fancy, but I'd like to be able to cook myself a good meal and enjoy it alone. I hate to eat out alone, but I see no reason why I shouldn't be able to sit down to a meal by myself at home and quietly enjoy it. And I wish I could cook really good meals for an occasional female guest or a foursome. Then, I'd know that I was really successful if I could prepare a larger dinner party. And I wish I knew how to get together a fancy spread for a night-time party. I'd like to learn cooking, but it's hard to begin."

Now, that's a fine set of goals, but as one big goal, it looks impossible. It will not only look much easier, but will *be* easier, if it is broken down to five subsidiary goals:

1. To cook simple meals for yourself.
2. To enjoy eating alone.
3. To cook entertaining and more complicated meals for small groups of friends.
4. To provide a large dinner party.
5. To provide adequately for a large party.

Even the most simply stated goals often must be broken down into smaller subsidiary ones. I remember a friend who said about his life goals, "For me, things are simple. All I want to do is meet the love of my life and everything will be fine." Whether or not everything would be entirely fine given that outcome, it is, by itself, a legitimate goal. But how to achieve it? Among the many possible subsidiary goals leading to this ultimate one are

1. To become involved in activities where likely other-sex persons may be found.

2. To initiate conversation with other-sex persons.

3. To ask for continued contact with desirable others.

4. To conquer fear of rejection and to handle rejection when it occurs.

5. To try out numerous methods for meeting others, including a blind date, an initiation to a stranger, ventures into novel situations, etc.

Now, if you want to begin working on your autonomy, take just two minutes with a pen and paper and write down as many goals for yourself as you can. Don't organize, don't set priorities, and don't eliminate anything. Use your autonomous-adulthood inventory results if they will help, but don't limit yourself to things suggested there. If you would like to lose weight, be healthier, or stop smoking, write these down too. The principles we're discussing can help you achieve any goal. The question is, What do you want in order to be a happier, healthier, more satisfied person? Where do you want to go?

Now, when this is done, take another two to five minutes to organize and eliminate. Draw a line through any goal that you're unwilling to spend at least a few

minutes a day on. Be honest, now, and eliminate some
things. Then, as before, rank what's left by importance
on the ABC priority system. If you have lots of As,
rank them A1, A2, A3, etc. Now, rank them—as before
—according to the ease with which they can be achieved.
As you do this—and it should take only a few minutes
—not only are you developing a list of goals for yourself
with the priorities all set, but a greater order to your
life may already begin to emerge. If you haven't done
it yet, let me urge you again to try. You'll get much
more out of this chapter and this book, and I think it
will help.

The next step is to pick one, or at the most two,
goals to begin working on. As with the skills selections,
the best goals to begin with would be the ones with
high ratings in both categories. Ease is especially important because if you follow all I have to suggest, you
will be learning a *system* of self-improvement. By starting with relatively easy goals, you'll give yourself the
best chance for success, and this early achievement will
motivate you to use the system on more difficult problems.

Now to break them down. When you have one or
two goals that you're willing to spend time on, ask yourself what subsidiary or short-term goals must be met
in order to achieve the major ones. Becoming healthier,
for example, may translate into improving your diet,
increasing your exercise, modifying your sleep, and so
forth. I have tried to delineate subgoals to be achieved
in each of the areas covered in this book, and there are
many helpful books on housekeeping, cooking, financial
management, automotive maintenance, and other prac-

tical skills to be found in any library. However you do it, your crucial first task is to find your subsidiary goals, the initial steps to your larger goals. Do as much of this as you can right now. However ignorant you are of the small steps, you certainly should be able to come up with one subsidiary goal. Purely for purposes of illustration, here is a brief listing of some major goals and the subsidiary goals which might accompany each one.

1. Better Budgeting
   a. To know where money goes.
   b. To construct a financial statement, including monthly income, fixed expenditures, savings, discretionary income, etc.
   c. To construct a budget including all items in *b.*
   d. To stay within the constructed budget.
   e. To use discretionary income more efficiently.
   f. To construct a statement of lifetime financial goals.
2. Tolerating/Enjoying Aloneness
   a. To be alone without feeling fear or depression.
   b. To be able to go out alone.
   c. To enjoy going out to dinner, traveling, and other out-of-home activities alone.
   d. To enjoy being alone, doing nothing.
   e. To enjoy solitary activities at home.
3. Goals for Housekeeping
   a. To do adequate home maintenance.
   b. To keep things in order on a day-to-day basis (i.e., to keep clothes in closets, dishes washed, etc.).
   c. To learn how to do all periodic housekeeping

tasks (i.e., wash clothes, dust, vacuum, wash floors, etc.).

d. To execute periodic tasks listed in c.

In every skill area such as housekeeping or cooking, you need to analyze whether your problem is in not knowing how to do the thing in question or whether it is in just not doing it. Do you need to learn how to do something or do you simply need to get yourself to do it? The principles outlined in this chapter will help you do either, but the subsidiary goals and initial steps will differ depending on whether your problem involves learning or doing.

It is usually best if you don't attempt to work on a large number of subsidiary goals all at once. Pick one or two for starters. Remember you are learning a system for changing your own behavior. Once the system is learned, you can apply it to any problem. But take care—since one major objective of the system is to make big things more manageable—to make molehills out of mountains—don't blow it by attacking so many subgoals that things become unmanageable again.

In counseling a newly separated man who lacks many autonomous-adulthood skills, I generally advise him to learn to cook simple meals for himself and, perhaps, to work on establishing better habits for keeping his home neat. Until he masters these first two, I advise him to get his house or apartment cleaned once a week if possible, go out to dinner as needed, purchase most of his items for entertaining, and otherwise delegate necessary chores. Even subsidiary goals often do not represent small enough steps, however, and what is needed is a breakdown into *graded assignments*.

Principle II. Graded Assignments

Now it's time to plan real action by specifying concrete things you can do to begin to achieve the subsidiary goals you have chosen. Take the first step in the chain to achievement by asking yourself this question: "What is the easiest thing I can do to get started?" And I mean *easiest*. I want to repeat the all-important fact that it is much better to be too easy on yourself at first than too hard. Starting out easy enhances the probability that you will do whatever it is in the first place and that you will be successful in the second. Starting out easy improves the odds that you will be caught up in the project and extend yourself beyond what you initially planned. The idea is to break down the initial resistance to engaging in an unfamiliar task and to establish new habits surrounding it. If possible, pick an assignment for yourself which will take only a few minutes a day. If you get more involved and spend more time than that, it's a bonus. If not, you've still begun to change and have completed your assignment. Here are the characteristics of a good assignment:

1. It must call for specific and concrete action.
2. It must specify a time period for completion.
3. It must not involve actions which exceed your capabilities (i.e., it must not involve skills you haven't yet learned or can't readily master).

If at all possible, your self-made assignments will be best if they build on one another successively. Consider the following sample assignments for the beginner who wants to learn to cook simple meals:

1. Cooking
   a. Buy one or more basic cookbooks in the next two days.
   b. Make a list of equipment you'll need (see basic cookbooks for suggestions).
   c. Make a list of staples you need (i.e., sugar, flour, salt, spice, etc.).
   d. Purchase needed staples and equipment.
   e. Develop at least three simple menus for meals within the next three days. (The standard fare in most American restaurants represents simple cooking. Just write out what you like.)
   f. Read about how to prepare each of the things included in the menus developed above by tomorrow night.
   g. Purchase the supplies needed for at least one menu by tomorrow evening.
   h. Prepare at least one menu in the next four days.
   i. Systematically increase by one menu a week the repertoire of meals cooked.
   j. Try your own variation of recipes you know and begin to develop a more individualized repertoire.
   k. Invite at least one friend this week to share a menu that you prepare.
   l. Prepare one menu for three or more guests in the coming week.
   m. Pick one more complex menu each week for one month.
   n. Add to the enjoyment of your meal by adding the accouterments of fine dining (i.e., a table-

cloth, folded napkin, attractive place setting,
music, good wine, etc.) at least twice a week.

When you begin your assignments in cooking, don't
hesitate to use shortcuts. On initial endeavors, you may
want to use frozen or already prepared entrées to which
you add a self-made salad and perhaps a baked potato.

In line with being easy on yourself at first for the
reasons we've gone over, remember you can stop when
you have achieved the goal you want to realize. When
you become autonomous in the sense that you are able
to meet your own needs, you have done enough. You
may or may not find that you want to become a gourmet cook after learning to prepare simple meals, or to
take a course in personal financial management after
you learn to make a budget. Go just as far as you want.

In using assignments like this with yourself, it is
important that you state them explicitly so that you will
know whether or not you are moving along toward your
goal. Write down each assignment so that you have a
written contract or agreement with yourself.

Examples of graded assignments in other practical
areas of autonomous-adulthood skill-building are listed
below. You should add your own time specifications to
any assignment you give yourself.

2. Budgeting
   a. Make a diary of all expenditures.
   b. Make a list of all monthly fixed bills such as
      rent, telephone, utilities, etc., and subtract the
      total of these bills from your total net monthly
      income.
   c. Make budget estimates or requirements for all

other expenditures such as food, clothing, entertainment, savings.
d. Make yearly goals for expenditures and savings.
e. Set a budget goal for a week or month.
f. Stay within the above constructed budget.
g. Revise budget on a weekly or monthly basis to be more in line with experience and new goals.

3. Housekeeping
   a. Purchase any recommended housekeeping guide.
   b. Make a list of supplies you'll need.
   c. Purchase needed supplies.
   d. Read about any housekeeping skill you need to develop.
   e. Straighten up house every day before going to bed at night or leaving in morning.
   f. Contract with yourself to do necessary housekeeping once every week, ten days, or two weeks as your needs require.
   g. Keep a list of needed household supplies.
   h. Make a schedule for less frequent cleaning chores such as window cleaning, stove cleaning, refrigerator washing, dusting bookshelves, cleaning closets.

4. Furnishing and Decorating Your Home
   a. Make a list of all items you need with approximate costs, ranked in order of priority.
   b. Visit a specified number of stores for furniture or art in a specified period.
   c. Decide on a style or decide to mix styles by a certain time.

    d. Ask friends where furniture of the kind you want can be purchased.

    e. Regularly examine used-furniture advertisements.

    f. Seek out opinions of friends regarding furnishings and art in your home.

    g. Purchase and read magazines on interior decorating for suggestions.

Beyond these sample projects, assignments that are relevant for you in any area of activity will become apparent as you read about the activity and begin to do something. The important thing is the concept of giving yourself assignments—making contracts with yourself that are specific with regard to what you need to do and the time it will take you to do it. It is also important that, wherever possible, the assignments start out simple and become increasingly more difficult, complicated, or extensive. And it will be best of all if the doing of the earlier tasks develops skills that can be used as components of later, more complicated tasks.

Principle III. Self-Observation and Recording

It is important for you to establish a systematic way of recording whether and how well you complete self-determined assignments. Even though this may seem to be an unnecessary step in self-improvement, both research and clinical experience show it is not. Some daily recording of the completion of your own assignments accomplishes many things. First, self-observation keeps you honest. It focuses you on keeping your commitments to yourself and concretely shows you when you have kept them and when you haven't. Second, self-observation provides a reminder to do what you have decided to do. If you carry a note pad and pencil around and record the number of initiations you make to others, or if you post a graph on your refrigerator door and record new recipes accomplished, you are more likely to be prompted to repeat the new activity. Third, written self-observation will give you the feedback you need to decide that the assignments are too difficult for you or to reward yourself for completing them. Fourth, self-observation recordings may help you appreciate gradual changes much more than you would otherwise. If, for example, you are trying to cut down on the calories you consume each day, your weight loss may be so slow it is discouraging unless you record both calories and weight loss and see the improvement reflected in the record. Fifth, self-observation data give you more to brag about: "I've learned six new recipes and run a mile a day since I started this program two weeks ago." Any extra reinforcement you can get from others for making beneficial changes in your life is good.

It is probably because of these advantages that the available psychological research tends to show that written self-observation by itself can often effect beneficial change in people's lives. I believe that such record keeping is essential to any self-improvement program. When I start observing something I want to change, I know I mean business, and I start changing. When I don't write it down, my good intentions get lost in the demands of day-to-day living.

More often than not, the kinds of assignments needed to build autonomous-adulthood skills lend themselves to the easiest form of self-observation recording. Such assignments can usually be stated so that you need record only whether they were completed or not. If you have one or two assignments per day or per week, you can use a calendar and simply note on it whether and when you accomplished them. A somewhat more effective method is to make a special recording calendar of your own which lists each self-assignment and provides blank spaces for your notes. Placed in an often-seen location (e.g., on the refrigerator door), this sheet can serve as a powerful reminder to do assignments and record them. Here is a sample:

Recording Calendar

Assignment	Mon.	Tues.	Wed.	Thurs.	Fri.	Sat.	Sun.
Initiate new contacts at least 4 days this week	+		+	+ + +	+		+
Prepare at least 2 evening meals for self		+				+	
Jog every day	+	+	+	+	−	+	+
House neat on random check (4 +s = weekly success)	−	−	+	+	+	+	+
Go to one group meeting this week			+				

Frequently, you will have assignments which you don't do every day. Even so, it is best to post them on your daily calendar. In the example above, preparing meals is to occur only twice in one week, and going to a group meeting only once, but each item fits well into the daily-recording format. The idea is to record what you do as simply as possible but without losing the advantages outlined earlier.

You will need a slightly more complex but more informative method of record keeping if you are working on something that has a relatively high daily rate. For instance, if you need to record the number of people you talk to each day for your social-skills program, or if you are counting calories, cigarette consumption, or other such things, you'd better carry a pad and pencil or a portable counter with you. Also, for high-occurrence data it is best to make a daily notation on a graph, preferably one that contains data reflecting the pattern that existed before you began the change program. Not only will this help you even more to appreciate gradual change, but it will also help you give yourself more reasonable assignments. If, for example, you wish to reduce gradually the amount of time you watch television or the amount you eat or smoke, a week of just observing yourself will tell you what an initial easy change would be. It will also give you a better understanding of the cues which trigger your TV watching, eating, or smoking. In addition, graphing this high-frequency data will help you see not only gradual change but change obscured by day-to-day fluctuation—such as weight loss.

Principle IV. Self-Imposed Consequences

Now, if you liked self-observation, you're going to love self-imposed consequences. But, if you hated self-observation, you will probably detest this principle of using reward and punishment to help you effect change: whenever you give yourself an assignment, you can sweeten it by agreeing to give yourself a reward when it is completed or you can punish yourself if you fail to perform the assignment. In some ways, this is the most artificial self-discipline technique I will suggest to you because it calls on you to be the rewarder and the rewarded, the punisher and the punished. Those who appear to have the best "natural" self-control seem most able to use this principle effectively on themselves, often without even being aware of doing so. If you agree that people do things either to feel good and virtuous or to avoid feeling guilty, you can see that most of us do use reward and punishment on ourselves, though not as effectively or self-consciously as we might. Thus, we are more at the mercy of our feelings of self-worth and guilt than is usually good for us. It would be better, I think, if we could eliminate these philosophically untenable emotions altogether and rely on more beneficial self-imposed consequences to control our behavior. In any case, following Principle IV for a while will help you to realize the rewarding and punishing effects of these emotions and also to gain greater control over the consequences you impose on yourself.

Once you have found an initial step toward your goal—an assignment—and a method for recording its completion—self-observation—you have the structure in which to place self-reward or self-punishment. When you make your initial agreement with yourself to do an assignment, you can specify the reward you will allow yourself if you do it and/or the punishment you'll get if you don't. You can promise yourself any freely available commodity or activity contingent on completing the assignment (e.g., you can go to that movie you've been wanting to see after you do the dishes). Or you can withhold anything which is available to you until you have done the assignment (e.g., you can't do your usual TV watching until you have done the dishes). Or you can require yourself to do something you don't want to do if you fail to do the assignment (e.g., you have to get up at 6 A.M. and do the dishes if you haven't done them before going to bed).

There are some basic guidelines for choosing consequences. It is usually best if you initially use rewards only, and those rewards are generally best that you might not otherwise allow yourself. Sweetening the deal is one way to get you to look more favorably upon changing. Of course, if you are the very self-indulgent sort, you might do better to find things to withhold from yourself until assignments are met. That's O.K., though less preferred generally than the reward method.

Next, try to choose something that really makes a difference to you. You are more likely to work hard at self-improvement if the payoff for doing so is high than if it is insignificant to you.

Finally, pick a reward—or punishment, as the case may be—that can be administered relatively soon after you have done each small assignment. People often fail in their use of self-imposed consequences because they make them too major and too distant from the behavior they want to control. Promising yourself a trip to the South Sea Islands for completing a difficult year-long project will usually not provide as much ongoing incentive for day-to-day activity as a meaningful *daily* reward for spending an hour a day on the project. If you wanted to use a trip such as this to help your motivation, it would be better to put aside a certain portion of the vacation's cost at a number of completion points throughout the year, or to purchase the items you'd need for the trip as you progressed on the work. And, of course, it would be best to supplement that with a good program of daily or weekly consequences. Remember, frequent rewards for small steps will usually work best.

Using self-imposed consequences in the way I'm suggesting here is, of course, somewhat artificial. Some people feel it's demeaning to treat themselves this way, and most have trouble employing this principle religiously. But it will work if you do it right. And, like all the other special methods recommended in this book, it can be dropped when it's no longer necessary. For a short time, I used a self-determined reward to force myself to begin jogging in the morning. Now I can't live without jogging, and allowing myself to jog could serve as a reward for doing something else that was difficult to begin. So what if it takes some artificial maneuvers to get you started down a path that's good for you? If you're the one who decides to use the self-discipline tool, you're still in charge and you've begun. You aren't going to be observing, recording, and rewarding yourself for life. These tools are just to get you started on a new and better path.

In fact, I think these principles can often be misused if they are applied for long periods of time to overcome persistent resistance. If you still have to force yourself to engage in some activity after a prolonged period of effort, it's very likely that that activity is just not for you. So, when you begin to use the tools outlined so far to begin something new, it is best to establish a preset time when you will reevaluate your need of them. If, at the end of that reasonable period, the new activities have not at least begun to feel good to you, simply for themselves, consider dropping them. Thus, if jogging had not begun to be pleasurable in itself for me, I would have stopped jogging and looked for other forms of exercise that might have suited me better. *Persistent* resistance to doing what you think would be good for you has great value when it tells you that you were probably wrong and motivates you to do something differently. To force yourself to begin something new is all right and often necessary, but there is something wrong with a life of self-imposed coercion.

Principle V. Environmental Planning

One final principle that may help you gain greater self-discipline is based on our knowledge of how environmental cues can trigger behavior. For example, the sight of a refrigerator can trigger eating, the sight of cigarettes can prompt you to smoke, and a messy desk can set off a chain of nonproductive fiddling. But environments can be changed so that they more readily elicit or inhibit what we want them to. One of my clients found, for example, that he could cut down his smoking by keeping his cigarettes in his secretary's office at work and in the basement at home. Another changed the triggering capacity of her refrigerator by putting pictures of fashion models on the door, along with a graph of her weight loss. Another found she could control her impulse spending by simply leaving her credit cards, checkbook, and extra cash at home each day. In each of these cases, the individual set up his or her environment so that unwanted behavior would not be so automatically set off. You can do the same. For instance, you may find that an inexpensive pocket calculator makes it easier to keep your budget up to date or that a well-organized kitchen makes cooking more pleasant and thereby more frequent.

Often, just environmental change of *any* kind will break up old unwanted patterns. If, for example, you find yourself in the rut of going home after work every day and consuming a flat TV dinner while viewing a series of flat TV programs, don't go home! Do something different—anything different. If you find yourself unable to get necessary work done where you work, either go somewhere else to do it if you possibly can or change your working space in some significant way. People's behavior patterns get stuck to particular environments. If you don't like the behavior patterns you have, you can help change them by changing the environment with which they are associated. If you know the specific environmental cues associated with your particular unwanted behavior patterns, you may be able to do a great deal just by modifying those specific cues. What are the environmental cues that elicit your unwanted behavior? What are the environmental cues that could facilitate desirable behavior? How can you change your environment to make it easier to do the things you want to do and harder to do the things you don't?

PUTTING IT TOGETHER

Now that we've analyzed each of the principles separately, let us see how they might fit together for a custom-tailored self-improvement program. Paul found that his highest-priority goal was to have a more active social life. As subsidiary goals, he identified the following:

1. To meet new people.
2. To develop the skills for making new friendships.
3. To see his established friends more often.
4. To entertain people more often.
5. To find out those things about him which people liked or didn't like.
6. To change his behavior to become more socially likable.

Paul set out assignments from suggestions given both in this book and in others. Primarily, they involved cultivating activities where he might meet people, moving out of his regular circles daily, approaching new people, inviting friends for lunch or cocktails at his home, and, later, finding out from close friends the things about himself that were attractive and those that were not. Each Sunday evening, he would sketch out for himself assignments for the coming week and a recording sheet on which to note their completion. In addition to this self-observation, he entered in his personal telephone directory the names of all the new people he met in his ever-increasing excursions into the world. After a few weeks, he had at least some simple assignment every day that would bring him into contact with old or new friends. Thus, he had something to observe every day for which he could impose consequences.

In choosing his self-imposed consequences, Paul decided to use television watching. He realized that he watched too much of it anyway and knew that it kept him away from people. He used TV watching as a daily reward for completing his sociability assignments: if he completed these, he allowed himself to watch all the TV he wanted; if not, he couldn't turn it on. Although, strictly speaking, Paul didn't apply environmental engineering specifically to the increase of his social activity, he did modify his environment by storing his portable TV in a closet. To reap his reward, he had to get out the TV and hook it up. This procedure also had the effect of decreasing his *automatic* TV watching.

It is important to remember that almost everyone who develops a self-change program has difficulty sticking with it. Most will at some time or another stop religiously giving themselves assignments or forget to self-record or fail to use the self-determined consequences or neglect to maintain the helpful environmental engineering. When this happens to you, don't despair. Your self-discipline program is not a total failure because you slip up on it for a day or a week or even longer. When this happens, try to find out if your program is unrealistic, redesign it if necessary, and try again. As you look at a program that has ceased to work for you, ask these questions: Are the assignments too difficult? Have you given yourself too many? Do they skip necessary prerequisite steps? Are they too vague and nonspecific? Is the self-recording too difficult? Does the written self-observation fail to reflect the central aspects of what you wanted to change? Are the recordings failing to jog you into working at your self-assigned daily and weekly tasks? Do the data fail to reflect your progress? Are the self-determined consequences too distant from the behavior you want to influence? Are the rewards or forfeits inconsequential—or have they become so? Are you using punishment exclusively and not adding positive things to your life through your self-control program? Are the rewards so important to you that withholding them is too difficult?

Above all, don't catastrophize if you fail to live up to your contract with yourself. Simply review the principles, redesign the program if necessary, and return to it. Such failure is almost inherent in the struggle to change. It is a problem only if you allow it to discourage the struggle altogether.

Just one reminder: the five principles make up a basic tool kit for self-control and change. You may not require the tools, they may not suit your style, or you may never get around to using them. But they work: it's up to you.

FIND A MODEL

The principles given thus far will help you to change *independently*. But anything you can do to make change easier is O.K., and finding a good teacher or model will do just that. In general, newly single people will profit greatly from having a close single friend who has mastered more of the autonomous-adulthood job description. Having a friend walk you through the first few attempts at the new job can ease the journey considerably, prevent some mistakes, and cushion the disappointments. Don't wait for a teacher to begin change, but keep your eyes open for one.

RESISTANCE TO CHANGE

Most of us are stubborn about changing our personal behavior, not only because we find such change extremely difficult to achieve, but also because we have become attached to our habitual behavior. No matter how dysfunctional it may be, it provides a reassuring continuity to our lives in the midst of all the change around us. Well-established patterns of personal behavior, positive or negative, reflect the ways in which we have learned to deal with the world. A change to something better is generally a change to something unknown—and the unknown is always fear-provoking. In addition, changing to something different means losing something inherent in what is left behind. There are always some benefits from even the most disordered and painful behavior patterns. To change, one must be willing to give those benefits up with the understanding that the benefits which changing will bring are likely to be far greater. But often, the old benefits must be given up first before the new benefits are realized. That makes change harder.

Another reason that people find change so difficult is that they hate to admit there is anything wrong with the way they are. It is almost as if people say to themselves, "If I have to change, that means that I have a serious problem for which I am to blame." This is an attitude that you must talk yourself out of. Everyone is less than he would like to be. No one is to blame for that. And, for that matter, no one is more virtuous for being able to undertake change. You simply get less out of life by continuing behavior patterns that bring problems, and you usually can expect more out of life by embracing changes you think will make things better. Everyone can profit from some change; no one is to blame.

Still another resistance to changing your life may go something like this: "I'm just this way. I can't change. I have no willpower." It may be that you're not yet ready for change or that you do not yet have the requisite self-control skills to effect change. When you are ready and have the skills, you can change. Willpower is a purely fictional label which we have chosen to give to this combination of adequate motivation and appropriate skills. The notion that you have a fixed amount of willpower which resides in your personality is incorrect and destructive; it leaves you powerless to change, and if you hold to it, you're sunk.

I have noticed one final resistance to change in those who have been coupled and who must now learn the skills for living singly. To formerly coupled people, such changes can symbolize a commitment to single life—an unwanted commitment because they want to become recoupled. For them, learning to enjoy being alone or to see to their own needs in new ways is viewed as antithetical to being a part of a couple. And yet, I think it is this kind of demand for rigid interdependence in relationships that contributes so much to destroying them; being an autonomous adult is good in our time whether you're single or coupled. The requirements of contemporary relationships have changed from a demand for predictable interdependence to a demand for independence, mutual sharing, and fluid change of function. I hope you won't avoid learning how to be an autonomous adult because you think this will be inconsistent in some way with your being part of a couple in the future. Being autonomous will only make you less needy of a relationship and better able to respond to what it will really demand of you.

Of course, people are often only dimly aware of these resistances to change. I have outlined them here so that you may become more aware of any which particularly apply to you. As we've seen in Chapter 2, ideas, thoughts, or internal sentences that get in your way can be worked on systematically too. If your resistance to change needs treatment, you can work on that resistance while at the same time moving stubbornly and systematically toward change itself.

EASIER SAID THAN DONE

Throughout this book, you are going to find ideas and prescriptions for change that are easy to endorse but difficult to actualize. If you have trouble being alone, for example, it will be easier to see the wisdom of the program I will suggest for remedying this than to actually carry it out. If you're involved in a serious relationship conflict, it will be easier to see the wisdom of the no-fault communication I will suggest for exploring it than to actually practice such communication at the height of your conflict. Some changes that must be made to acquire a really secure autonomous adulthood may take years of slow and persistent work. Seeing that a change needs to be made is only the first step, but it is the step that puts you on your way. Continual change toward a better life is the most you can expect. It's O.K. to be on your way. In fact, being on your way is what it's all about.

6
Living Alone and Coming Together

Man's loneliness is but his fear of life.
—Eugene O'Neill

It may be impossible to live without a culture.
—Kurt Vonnegut, Jr.

ALONE, LONESOME, LONELY

HAVE YOU EVER been desperately lonely? I mean anxiously, painfully, fearfully lonely? It is a bottomless, nameless fear, and a pervasive, overpowering boredom. You would give anything to escape it. It is dark outside. You wait for the phone to ring; you make yourself a drink, smoke a cigarette, search the television for something interesting enough to erase the discomfort. You go to the refrigerator, but nothing there can fill your hunger. You try to read, but nothing you pick up can command your attention. You can't concentrate. You run through the names of people you could call or the things you could do to get out of this spot. Perhaps you telephone someone and feel better for a time, but only for a time. You're ashamed of yourself for being so unable to cope with a little solitude—though it doesn't seem so little—it feels as if it will last forever. You wonder if the feeling can ever be erased. Why is this solitude so upsetting? In one way or another you get through that night. You hope not to have to face another like it for a long, long time, and perhaps you make plans to ensure that you won't.

If something like this hasn't happened to you at one time or another, you are probably just better than most of us at escaping the experience of loneliness quickly, before it hurts very much. It can be encountered at any time: when you are out alone for dinner and all the world seems to come in pairs; when you go home after a party with only the memory of the superficial din of too many people who have had too much to drink; after you have tried to talk to someone you really can't talk to and wonder why you bothered.

You are lonely but far from alone in this dilemma. Being alone is a fundamental and inevitable condition of man. And because so few of us are educated to be alone, loneliness is an almost universal human problem. No one can experience our problems, our pain, our life as we experience them. In the final analysis *all* of us are alone. And yet we are dependent on other people for many things (though not as dependent as we sometimes feel). The dilemma of being dependent but ultimately alone is not a comfortable one. I have no prescription for resolving it, but I can suggest ways in which you may reap benefits from the most negative reaction to it—loneliness. You can use the pain of loneliness to discover more about yourself and life, and you can learn how to make voluntary solitude more valuable and fun.

J. Krishnamurti says it well: "When the pain of loneliness comes upon you, confront it, look at it without any thought of running away. If you run away you will never understand it, and it will always be there waiting for you around the corner. . . ."

It is natural for us to reach out for the distraction of company or entertainment to turn off the pain of loneliness. But this remedy is merely palliative; the problem returns and must be remedied again and again. The frantic attempt to avoid loneliness can be most readily seen in newly separated individuals who compulsively spend every evening running from distraction to distraction. If you are in the initial throes of separation craziness, your running is understandable and perhaps even necessary.

But after a time, if you want to grow, you must stop running and avoiding and escaping. You must *embrace* loneliness, despite the pain, in order to get beyond it. This is the only way you can break its hold on you; you must sit with it, experience it, give in to it, search out its meaning. Initially, this bad-tasting medicine is better taken in small doses, but it must be taken. Before describing the dosage possibilities for you, let me tell you more about the treatment and its possible effects.

Eventually, when you are ready to experience unwanted solitude, you must block your escape hatches—put down the telephone, turn off the TV, ignore the refrigerator. Then, you must sit down or go for a walk alone and give into and explore your loneliness. I can't give you a detailed road map for how to do this or any promises about what the journey will bring, but I can offer some guidelines. If your loneliness is anything more than a mild preference for company or a benign boredom, you are probably avoiding something unpleasant. If your loneliness is uncomfortable enough to warrant the name, you will try to escape it and the escaping indicates you are trying to get away from something. What is it? What are the thoughts you don't want to think? What are you really afraid of? What is so bad about your own company?

Using these few questions as guidelines, let your thoughts travel where they will and see what you can learn. Don't expect to discover anything profound right away, and *please* don't struggle with or limit yourself to the questions; just relax and *be* lonely for a while, and see what happens!

Once again, I have no way of knowing what you will find. From a good deal of experience with others, I could name some possibilities. But I am confident that, if you stick with this venture, what you learn will be far more personally meaningful than anything in my catalogue of possibilities.

One of the more common experiences is that loneliness is not so bad when you accept and embrace it. Part of its sting comes from the feeling that it is beyond your control. When you decide to get into it, to make it your own, you are, from that moment, in charge of it, and hence of *yourself*. You have taken that first small dose of the medicine, and even if it tastes horrible, you may discover a certain pleasure and sense of mastery in the fact that you are at least able to tolerate it. And then, perhaps from the next dose of solitude—or the next, or the one a year from now—you can learn things about yourself that you never suspected were there.

Some of the fundamental insights about what is

right and wrong in your life that can emerge from taking a good hard look at yourself may be exactly what you have been avoiding, and yet you may feel unexpectedly rewarded by both the pleasant and the unpleasant things you discover. If used properly, these insights may pave the way for either important life changes or new self-acceptance. Some insights about your own loneliness, for example, may come to you during your time alone. From my experience with others, I can foreshadow the following possibilities. In coming to grips with the issue of loneliness itself, try to see which ones apply to you.

1. Other people are really important to you, but you haven't taken adequate time for them.

2. Other people, while important to you, aren't everything for you, and some unwanted time alone is the price you have to pay for devoting yourself to other things.

3. You have been (a) too proud, (b) too lazy, or (c) too fearful to put yourself into situations where you can meet others.

4. Your relationships with others are superficial and leave your need for intimacy unfulfilled.

5. Because of painful relationships in the past, you have been avoiding people who could be important to you now.

6. You are allowing your lack of a partner to restrict your contact with important friends who are paired.

7. You are doing some things that drive people from you, such as (a) complaining too much, (b) de-

preciating yourself excessively, (c) being too aggressive, or (d) withholding yourself.

8. You are particular about friends and prefer being alone to being with people who do not meet your needs.

9. You have very few meaningful activities (creative operants) to engage in when alone.

10. You have for a long time lived with others and, as a result, being alone is strange and fear-provoking.

11. You have just gone through some transition in your life and need time to accumulate new friends.

12. You don't know how to have fun by yourself—you never had to learn; no one ever taught you.

13. Your limited interests make you boring to others and to yourself.

These insights are just a few of the more common ones to be found from self-examination on the issue of loneliness. The possible insights relevant to you are, of course, limitless.

As you get into your own thoughts about loneliness, you may find that you are simply catastrophizing about the experience or about something else. Perhaps you will now hear in your solitude the persevering and irrational cassette that your distractions have been drowning out. Your catastrophizing cassette may be about anything. If it is about loneliness itself, it may sound like this: "I can't stand to be alone. I am worthless without a partner. My life is devoid of purpose without someone to love. I will always be alone. Loneliness is my punishment for the wrongs I have committed. I shouldn't have to be alone; I've been cheated. . . ."

If you have read Chapter 2, you already know how

to treat this kind of nonsense. If in your loneliness panic you are simply catastrophizing about an unfamiliar, unpleasant condition, it is important that you begin to talk yourself out of it and get along with the business of living. A little time alone can't hurt you, a little reluctant solitude will not kill you. People have survived for years by themselves; certainly you can make it through one night or one week or even a few months if you absolutely have to. You may prefer to be with others; you may have few satisfying things to do on your own; you may need to learn how to have fun by yourself; you may need to plan your time better so that it is more filled with other people, but being alone can overcome you only if you let it.

You may have to reindoctrinate yourself in experiencing loneliness by the same methods employed in the issues of anger, guilt, and worthlessness. The reindoctrination process will undoubtedly take some time, much of which will have to be spent alone. But doing it can free you from a desperate need for other people; it can free you to pursue new, creative, and enjoyable activities on your own without the crutch of a companion; and, most important, it can free you from fear. To be free of fear is to be really alive.

No matter how free you become, however, there will still be times when you happen to be alone and would prefer to be with others. I call this feeling *lonesomeness*, a mild displeasure involving no panic, no self-pity, no catastrophizing. Simple lonesomeness is normal and not a signal that anything is wrong. It is merely a signal to do something different. The cure is to seek out other people or to involve yourself in solitary activities that give you pleasure. If you experience occasional periods of wanting to be with others when you're not, you're lonesome—go and be with others.

The state of *aloneness* is enjoyable absorption or contented relaxation in solitude. It is discovering the joy of your own company, the unhindered delight of doing exactly what you want to do when you want to do it. It is, like love, one of life's peak experiences. If you have never been there or have been there only rarely, you have much to look forward to. If you're lucky, you may have the experience of going from the panic of loneliness to the joy of aloneness in one episode of solitude.

One of my clients went through such a metamorphosis. Judy had suffered frequent attacks of loneliness for many months before she came to me for help. She had grown up in a small Midwestern town, the youngest of three girls in a close-knit family. She had always been bright, getting good grades in school without a great deal of effort. During her first two years at a college in Chicago, she lived with two roommates in a dormitory. Then she moved into an off-campus apartment, which she shared with close friends, and dated many men before settling on Joe in her junior year. Shortly after graduation she and Joe were married. They remained in Chicago, where he went to work while she attended law school. In the fourth year of their marriage, Judy got her first job as a fledgling lawyer, and things really seemed to be going well for the couple. With some help from their parents, they soon had enough money to purchase a town house on the north side of the city. To all their friends, it seemed as if they had it made.

But things were not quite as rosy from their own

points of view: they were bored with each other. And Judy had begun to question herself. As she explained it, she wasn't sure who she was; she had developed in a safe cocoon of family, friends, and a familiar college, reinforced by a safe, respectable, but emotionally cool love relationship and marriage. It wasn't a bad marriage, she said, but it was a dull one.

"Finally, after that first year out of law school, when I stopped worrying about making it, I knew I wasn't happy. I envied the people who had gone away to college or professional school or to travel in Europe or to do anything out of the ordinary to challenge themselves. Then an opportunity for a job with a Los Angeles firm came up for me. It was a really good firm, and the job would allow me to learn much more about my specialty. So I talked this over with Joe, and taking it seemed the only thing to do."

Despite their separation, neither Judy nor Joe had wanted a divorce, which was still an open question. During the first few months in Los Angeles, Judy was terribly lonely, but she realized that this was part of the bargain. She wasn't seriously concerned about it until after about nine months, when her loneliness and ever-deepening depression seemed worse than ever. There were reasons for her being alone a good deal. By far the youngest and most inexperienced member of the firm, not only did she have a great deal to learn, but the older, more established people overloaded her with work. And for the first time, she did not have a man in her life or the friends she was used to. Because she was still ambivalent about Joe, she had done very little dating, and there were no other young women at her office to whom she could easily relate. Her depression was becoming increasingly self-perpetuating; her feelings of dejection and helplessness sapped her efficiency, caused her to work more hours to make up the work, and contributed to her inertia in making contact with others.

After discussing the reasons for her depression, I persuaded Judy to begin exploring groups where she could meet other people. Then, in the third session, I suggested that she consider embracing her loneliness when it next struck. When she walked in for her fourth appointment, she looked radiant. She said, "Well, I think I've got it," and told me the following story.

"Two nights ago, I was really blue. I came home from work and was too tired to do anything but watch a series of nothing programs on TV. I was lonely and miserable and beaten, and I started crying again for no reason. About eight o'clock I called a new friend in LA. She wasn't home. Then I called Joe and he wasn't home. So, I felt even worse. It was as though I was really afraid of something, but I didn't know what it was. I was so lonely, it seemed there really wasn't anybody or anything that could help. I felt so totally separate and cut off. I thought of calling my family or friends in Chicago, but I didn't want them to know I was feeling so bad. And I knew there really wasn't anything they could do anyway. They probably wouldn't even understand, and besides, my phone bill has been ridiculous—it's over a hundred dollars a month. Then I remembered what we had talked about . . . I decided to drive to the ocean and walk along the beach and see what happened. I was going to embrace loneliness if it killed me.

"As soon as I got in the car, I felt a lot better. At least I was trying something that could be constructive.

Once I got down by the water, the surf seemed to have a calming effect, and all the panic that I'd felt before was gone. As I walked along the beach, I thought about how nice it would be to be there with someone I loved. But I wasn't, and I was going to make the most of what I had. I thought about being with my friends in Chicago and wished that I were there. But, again, I didn't feel sorry for myself about it. I had chosen to come to Los Angeles, and it was a brave decision. I realized that it had some costs—costs that were heavier than I had ever anticipated, but that I was still able to pay if I had to. At that moment I felt particularly strong, and I was proud of myself. I didn't especially like where I was, but I was happy that I had the courage to be there. I guess the loneliness panic that I had experienced before then became what you call lonesomeness. I would have preferred that things were different right then, but I realized I could live with the fact that they weren't.

"Then, I started to think about how I could make it better. The first thing I came up with was that I should start seeing some men, and really put myself into it. I mean, I wanted this separation from Joe. I wasn't happy with him, although I like him a lot. I figured I might as well begin to try this single trip as completely as possible. Then, I could really tell whether I wanted it or Joe. And I decided that I had to cut back some at work. Those old men are working me blind, and I refuse to continue to work that hard. The worst thing that can happen is I'll lose this job, but there are plenty of other jobs I can get here or in Chicago. There's no reason for me to ruin my mental health for that damn firm. The third thing I decided to do was to really try to get involved in some of those groups. To be honest, I've only gone to one, and I did that because you wanted me to. I see that I've got to give myself more. Then, I felt a lot better, because it seemed to me that these changes would make my life a little more livable than it's been.

"I walked along and looked at the white waves rolling in from nowhere, and I looked up at the stars and I sort of marveled at it all. I sat down in the sand and thought, 'Isn't life really interesting!' And this is where it gets hard to explain . . . it was sort of a mystical experience. I saw the universe as an infinite number of separate things all related to one another. I saw myself as a part of this but separate and absolutely unique. This separateness which was so frightening to me a couple of hours before was a part of the whole scheme of things, part of the un-understandable beauty of it all, a part that I would have to accept no matter how I felt about it.

"I got home late that night and slept until very late the next morning. I went out for a fancy lunch and, instead of feeling sorry for myself for having to eat alone, I really enjoyed it. Then, I went to work, and the first thing I did was make a date with a guy I sort of like whom I have been holding at arm's length. Then, and only then, did I get to work. And I think I accomplished more that afternoon than I typically do in a day. I don't know if I'm cured," said Judy, "but I sure have had a good time in the last two days."

Judy wasn't cured. She had recurring episodes of loneliness as well as frequent bouts of lonesomeness. But her peak experience at the beach was a breakthrough and the beginning of a better life. She learned that loneliness could be worked through, and she made some basic changes that served to round out her life and make her less of a loner. She experienced the transformation from loneliness through lonesomeness to aloneness.

If loneliness is a problem for you, or if lonesomeness occurs very often, you probably haven't learned well enough how to have fun by yourself. You're not unusual. We Americans are gregarious people, often insecure in solitude, and more than a little unsure of what to do with ourselves when alone. Most of us have learned that the really good times in life always involve others. Not many of us are capable of enjoying a good meal alone, whether at home or in a restaurant, a vacation in solitude is an unusual experience, and many recreational activities are viewed as the exclusive domain of couples or groups. Loners, so we are taught, are strange and unhappy people.

To counteract and overcome this early cultural training, you must develop a repertoire of activities you can engage in when alone. Particularly if you have found that your loneliness is a result of simple boredom, the development of such a repertoire is a high-priority area for achieving autonomous adulthood.

Since the enjoyment of so many pursuits has been associated with other people, you may feel they will only be depressing if engaged in alone. And, indeed, some of them might prove to be just that, but the only way you can find out which ones can give you pleasure as solitary activities is to try them, one by one if necessary. I suggest that you view these experiments as self-made assignments in acquiring autonomous adulthood.

One final word about loneliness, lonesomeness, and aloneness. To one degree or another, loneliness may always recur for you. It is a reflection of a very human response to an inevitable dilemma. Don't view it as failure when it looms upon you after you think you have gone beyond it. Just remember what you have learned and use it again and again.

LONELINESS TOLERANCE TRAINING

In this section, you will find some guidelines for programming and getting control of the time you spend alone. If you were to consult me professionally about this problem, I would begin by prescribing a specified amount of time alone. I would ask you to pick a time—usually an evening of your choice—when you can be by yourself. For that particular period, I'd ask you to turn off all those appliances you use as crutches—the radio, the television, the stereo—and I'd ask you to take your phone off the hook. You could do whatever you wanted except for those things I've just ruled out: go for a walk or a drive, plan a trip, do yard work, make music, cook something, write a letter, sew, shadowbox, read, or just think—do anything. The important thing is for you to remain alone and rule out all forms of passive entertainment. There is no need to explore your own thinking in depth during these times—you don't have to meditate. All you need do is be alone.

The best length of time for this activity varies from person to person and depends on your initial tolerance for being alone. It is far better that you start out with a short time period that is too easy for you—perhaps no more than an hour or two—than one that is too long and difficult. Don't push it at first. It is also helpful to arrange in advance for some social contact at the end of this aloneness period. Thus, for example, you might decide to engage in this exercise between eight and ten o'clock some evening before visiting friends.

You can gradually increase your time alone from session to session. The eventual goal of this training in aloneness is for you to experience several entire evenings alone without accompanying feelings of distress. It is during these times that you *may* find yourself working from loneliness through to lonesomeness and into aloneness. In any case, the exercise will help you discover those activities that make you feel good in times of solitude, and you will learn if there is a need to add to your repertoire of solitary activities. Above all, try to find out how *you* can enjoy your time alone. You may never have had to learn this before, or you may have learned it so long ago that you need to learn it again.

One great advantage of increasing your aloneness tolerance is that you are in charge of your own time alone. In each activity, you are not reluctantly alone; you are alone by your own choice. There is no pressure and there is no obligation to seek out others—that is exactly what you have decided *not* to do. You are experimenting with yourself alone, and you are to be congratulated for trying to stretch yourself.

With due allowance for individual variation, almost anyone who follows these procedures should be able to increase his or her tolerance of aloneness to some degree in a matter of weeks. But don't be surprised if your aloneness tolerance continues to improve slowly over months and even years as you become more accustomed to aloneness and less frightened by it. If, for example, you have always lived with others and now are alone for the first time, it may take you quite a while to be totally comfortable alone. Don't worry about it; just work on it.

Most of the people I've counseled who have trouble being alone give themselves a lot more trouble by being hard on themselves for what they perceive to be a very serious shortcoming. It is only that they feel the discomfort of being alone more acutely than others; the feeling is familiar to everyone. You've been taught to be unhappy and lonely when you're not with other people. Don't punish yourself for having learned it so well. If you are more dependent or fearful of solitude than others, this is just your way of making life more of a problem than it really is. If you want to learn to become better company for yourself, you can.

COMING TOGETHER

When people couple, they typically cut back on two of life's most sustaining activities—creative operants and close friendships. When people uncouple and become single again, these are the two primary activities in which they must reinvest. And it is primarily the quality of these investments which determines whether single life is experienced as lonely and boring or found to be meaningful and fulfilling. Single life has perhaps the greatest potential for important social relationships because the single person experiences greater need of them and fewer restrictions on using them. In most cases, the single person is free to develop a friendship system including both men and women, both couples and singles, and people of all ages without having to answer to anyone. Single life, for you, may be the most lonely alternative or it may be the most social. It all depends on how you use your freedom.

It is a fact that the nuclear family as we know it in this country—a small and mobile unit, cut off from the larger family and community—is a rare social grouping. Many social scientists, including myself, believe that it is essentially an unhealthy form of social organization, because it requires people to satisfy too many of their most basic life needs within an inordinately limited sphere. One of the many pressures the nuclear family suffers today is that the marriage is set up for failure by being called upon to provide more than it possibly can.

Each of us has many dimensions to our personality —a unique set of interests, abilities, and sensitivities. To develop each dimension, to exercise each faculty, we need contact with others who can share or contribute to the full range of our potential. Although it is nearly impossible for any one other adult to play such a varied role, couples often isolate themselves from other people who could stimulate their continued growth. They allow those dimensions of their personalities in which the mate is unable to participate to atrophy and die. And then, sometimes years later, they find their life dull and confining and resent the losses which their pairing seems to have brought about. The more unenlightened blame their partners for their losses. This sequence is not necessary, of course, but it is a difficult trap to avoid in a society which programs it so nicely. One of the many advantages of single life is that relationships with others who share your needs, interests, and abilities are limited only by your capacity to find and maintain them.

Single people who tend to view their singleness as a temporary condition to be endured on the way to an important heterosexual relationship often view their friends as stopgaps until a lover-mate promotes them to a more valued status. For most, the lover-mate does come along sooner or later, and the friends may then be phased out or retained only for infrequent superficial sociability. This is when extreme pressure is created for the couple to meet all of each other's needs. It is a formula for failure often leading to the conclusion that something very serious is wrong in the relationship. The individuals may separate and reenter a broader social system, but if this move is again viewed as temporary until the real Mr. or Ms. Right comes along, the stage is set for a replay of the same human tragedy, with the concomitant loss of meaningful friendships and the wealth of experiences to be had through broad-based human sharing.

A working social-support system is necessary for a fulfilling life for almost everyone, no matter what his life circumstances may be. To be distressed at not having it is normal—and, in this society, not having it is the norm. A good deal of the stress in this culture, both personal and societal, comes from the pervasive lack of a meaningful community in our lives. Single people, especially newly single people, may feel this void most

acutely because they are deprived of that overtaxed sub-
stitute—the mate. The desperate loneliness that single
people so often feel is largely caused by this more or
less universal need for meaningful community. But because couples *seem* to be less lonely and because coupling is the culturally prescribed remedy, single people
often pursue a mate with a vengeance. At the same
time, record numbers find marriage a confining trap
and leave it for a single life. For many, it is a repeating
cycle—an uncomfortable choice between loneliness and
confinement.

Perhaps inevitably, counterpressures are building to
open up the family and liberate all its members from
the rigid and confining ties of a closed system. But as
yet, we have not developed new social forms to accommodate these new pressures and still meet the continuing human need for intimacy, security, and belong-
ing. Until such forms are developed and integrated into
the social fabric, you are on your own. Acquiring the
freedom which comes with the peaceful acceptance of
our inevitable aloneness is the first part of the two-
part answer to this fundamental dilemma: the other
part involves participation in the broad-based human
sharing available to you through friends. Acquiring and
maintaining a functioning friendship system is essential
to reaching a healthy autonomous adulthood.

It is, of course, impossible to prescribe the appropriate social-support system for any individual. People's
styles differ, and one person's comprehensive social network might prove overwhelming to another for whom
a narrower or quieter one is ample. In my experience,
people generally know whether or not their current
friendship network is adequate to their needs. If you ask

yourself the right questions about your own network, you should be able to readily determine how well you are doing in this department. In addition to the questions you come up with for yourself, ask these:

1. Do you have at least one person nearby whom you can call on in times of personal distress?
2. Do you have several people whom you can visit with little advance warning or apology?
3. Do you have several people with whom you can share recreational activities?
4. Do you have people who will lend you money if you need it, or those who will care for you in other practical ways if the need arises?

If the social-support system represents an area of deficit for you, it should be one of your highest-priority targets. Understanding how the following unspoken maxims of a rigid, inward-looking social system unnecessarily limit your friendships will help you surmount those restrictions to gain a fuller life.

Maxim I. Lovers Are Better Than Friends

Although few people would strongly or openly endorse this maxim, most live by it. They do so when they cancel an engagement with a friend because a lover or even a casual date comes on the scene. They do so when they allow their friendships to atrophy when a new love comes into their lives. They do so when they place greater emphasis on pleasing lovers than on pleasing friends. They do so by assuming that others would almost always rather be in the company of a lover than a friend. They do so by seeing something perplexing in friendships between men and women.

This damaging maxim is so pervasive that you will have to work at dispelling it in yourself and others. Repeatedly, you will find that couples assume you are uncomfortable with them unless you bring a partner along. You will find that friends place you in a secondary position in relation to their dates or lovers. And your own other-sex partners will frequently put their friends in a back seat in relation to you and be deeply hurt if you fail to follow suit.

If you are truly convinced that these two forms of human sharing are equally important and that a broad system of social contact and caring is important for psychological well-being, if you really see that all human friendship, love, and caring are basically the same, then you will have to reeducate yourself and those around you. Watch yourself practice Maxim I and decide if you want to hold on to it.

Maxim II. Friendships Should Just Happen

For reasons that are not completely clear, many people are reluctant to pursue friendships actively, especially new ones, in spite of the fact that they suspect this is exactly what they need to do. I know many men, for example, who go to great lengths to locate and pursue potential female partners but who rarely consider going out of their way to develop friendships—in part because they have never really understood how important friendships could be to them and, in part, because they see such pursuits as unmasculine and a sign of weakness. My unsystematic observation is that cultivating friendships is a more formidable obstacle for men, who are taught they should be strong, independent, and competitive, than for women, who are less saddled with these particular burdens.

Most people in this society are still in pursuit of the nuclear-family life-style, and it is not easy for any individual, single or coupled, to bring greater freedom and broader meaning to his or her life through others, much as he or she may want to do so. As I've already argued, the achievement of this freedom and meaning requires an active social-support group able to serve many of the functions that an extended family and closely knit community could provide under a healthier form of social organization. Building such a group is not an easy task because it does not fit well into our dominant social structure, in which all relationships are secondary to coupling. It takes some work in this inhospitable environment to build the kind of social-support system you need. But many others who feel a need similar to yours will welcome the broadening of their social-support system that a relationship with you can represent, and still others who may be less aware of their own needs for broader social support will realize its advantages once it is offered to them.

There are three basic guidelines for finding new friends: first, pursue your own interests; second, keep your eyes open for promising acquaintances; and third, be persistent in your efforts to establish relationships.

You must pursue friendships persistently until the momentum of a well-functioning social-support system takes over. For many reasons, people's good intentions regarding social contact typically far outnumber their constructive actions. Many potentially rewarding relationships have been lost to mutual inertia on the part of two well-meaning, would-be friends. But, once you

are able to get something started which proves rewarding, the friendship is likely to continue, and your initiation will probably be reciprocated. As with all other
changes you may be making in your life, you can tackle
this challenge one step at a time. Simply peruse your
own social milieu and pick one person you'd like to
spend more time with. If your social milieu does not
yield others in sufficient numbers, broaden it until it
does by pursuing your own interests in groups. Then,
invite those you find to share some activity with you—
perhaps as simple as a luncheon date or a drink after
work. Not every contact of this kind will lead to something worthwhile, but if you keep on making them,
some of them undoubtedly will. When you find another's company rewarding, don't hesitate to continue
initiating further contact, and don't wait for your invitation to be reciprocated. This kind of social nicety
isn't necessary—don't hold back because of this out-
dated convention.

Don't restrict your friendship contacts to any one
type—singles, marrieds, same-sex, or other-sex, but if
you are newly single, do consider the special advantages
of initiating and cultivating the friendship of other
same-sex singles. Same-sex single friends have the most
in common generally, and their need for friendship is
more apt to be reciprocal. Newly single people can learn
a great deal from an old hand at the singles game. As
a result of my own observations, I usually advise people
who are newly single or those who, for other reasons,
need to develop a new social-support system, to pursue
actively the friendship of at least one same-sex single
person. These people, like yourself, do not have a
built-in, ready-made companion to rely on or answer to.

Hence, they are more in need of your companionship and more readily available to you. They can share your growth and pain without being threatened or necessarily judgmental. They can profit from your experience as you can from theirs. You have a good deal in common initially simply as a function of your mutual attempt to master living as a single person. So, while not restricting yourself to same-sex single friends, try not to be without one.

Maxim III. *Single People Should Confine Friendships to Other Singles*

Although most of us do not consciously support this proposition, many single and coupled people act according to its dictate. Singles are often hesitant in their relationships with couples because of their fear of intruding. If they visit with both of their married friends, they fear they are intruding on the time the couple would rather spend together. If they see their married friends individually, they fear they are taking their friend away from his or her spouse. For their part, married people often feel that their single friends are involved in a lively, swinging singles scene and fear this makes their own company stodgy by comparison. As a consequence of these popular misconceptions, many singles see their coupled friends infrequently and then usually with a partner in tow. This confinement represents a great loss to all involved. If you are or could be the friend of both members of a couple, I urge you to see them together and let them know of your acceptance of a threesome. This social grouping may well be one of the most valuable forms of human sharing. Most couples do their socializing with other couples, but more often than not, only one, or at the most two, really close relationships exist among the four people. Frequently there are none, since so much couple sharing is only superficial sociability.

If you can achieve a friendship with both members of a couple so that you are comfortable with each one individually and both together, you will be contributing immeasurably to their lives as well as your own. My own friendships with coupled people who like each other are among the most rewarding ones for me. With three people, there are three possible dyads, and if each one is positive, it can be extremely satisfying. (With four people, on the other hand, there are fully six dyads operating, not to mention all the possible coalitions. This social grouping is bound to be more complicated—a complexity that frequently interferes with the development of intimacy.) With three people who trust one another, there is unique potential for people to relate in new and important ways. A husband or wife can observe how his or her mate relates to the friend, and the single person can be allowed a close view of the couple's relationship. A trusted single friend, just by his or her presence, can serve to break up destructive patterns which a couple may develop in the absence of social checks. And the single person can learn much about how other people handle their intimate relationships. There is also greater potential for fluidity in a threesome in that one person may pull back and be alone without leaving the others without a companion. In threesomes, a more equal or democratic relationship can prevail between the sexes—a nonsexual and nonsexist camaraderie among all three. Having a pair of your friends to yourself can free you for really interacting with them as people rather than worrying about integrating a fourth into your circle. There isn't anything wrong with a fourth, of course, but it is important that each member of the threesome realize that the fourth isn't necessary.

Sometimes, of course, your friendships will be confined to one member of a couple. This, too, can be most constructive for everyone concerned, and there is no need for you as a single person to feel guilty about taking someone away from his or her spouse or family. Ordinarily, this is probably one of the best things you can do for your friend and his or her spouse. The isolation of married people from singles confines the couple to the marital-family unit while it fuels the single's isolation. There is every reason for strengthening the friendship ties which complement each participant.

Maxim IV. *Close Friends Must Be of the Same Sex*

We pay a very high price when we define the relationships between men and women as extraordinarily different from other kinds of human sharing. Not only do we mistakenly look for salvation in one such romantic relationship, but this distorted view effectively cuts out half of the available people from our friendship circle, forcing us to miss the unique advantages which a close but nonromantic relationship with an other-sex person can offer. Such relationships are particularly important now, in part because they are so uncommon. Typically, we develop rather predictable ways of interacting with the people we get close to—with other-sex lovers and same-sex friends. Often, we develop stereotyped ways of manipulating them or keeping them at a distance. An other-sex friendship, however, is sufficiently different from these other two forms of intimacy to make us aware of our stereotype patterns and to challenge us to find more straightforward and spontaneous ways of relating. Other-sex friends can be uniquely valuable in helping us to be more ourselves, thus encouraging us to be more genuine with others, and can teach us as nothing else can that relationships between men and women do not need to be so very different from other kinds of friendship. They can help us dispel the unrealistic romantic notions that so often poison the long-term relationships of lovers.

Other-sex friends are also especially valuable for helping to build autonomous adulthood, in that they can teach us the skills that are more often the specialties of their sex, in a situation free of power struggles or one-upmanship games. This, I think, is one of many advantages of the communal-living movement, which has developed primarily among the counterculture young. Although many communal-living situations are managed in a traditional way, they potentially provide a unique opportunity for efficient on-the-job training for autonomous adulthood. In addition, and perhaps more importantly, this social form gives people a chance to develop close relationships across the usual boundaries of marital status, sex, and age. Communal living may very well not be the social form that eventually replaces the popular alternatives of conventional married life or solitary single existence, but it is one form that offers the potential advantages of meaningful community life.

Maxim V. *Best Friends Are the Only Worthwhile Friends*

People do not confine their search for the one and only to lovers; in looking for friends as in looking for mates, we frequently make the mistake of seeking out only those who will fulfill all or most of our needs. As a consequence, we may spend a good deal of time without important others in our lives, and when we find them, we become possessive for fear of losing any part of such a limited social system.

There is more than one kind of friend just as there is more than one kind of love. Being single can provide you with the freedom to get the most out of each type. Some friends are ideal for shared recreation, others for long philosophical talks, others for mutual learning and teaching, and the most welcome—those to whom you can turn in times of trouble. Best friends are frequently those who serve you, as you do them, in many ways; but such friends are not always readily available, and even when they are, they cannot speak to all of your needs. If you can open yourself to friendships of every kind, you will probably find there are new sides of you of which you were only dimly aware. Growth often requires encountering the unfamiliar. Use your single freedom to find what's out there and what's inside you.

Maxim VI. *Friends Are Always There*

Your friends, like everyone else, have limitations. While best friends are, by definition, usually there when you need them, other people can do only so much for you. And because of their own limitations, problems, and failings, other people inevitably let you down from time to time. Those who are unforgiving of their friends typically do not have many. And those who hope that others can solve their problems in living are frequently disappointed. In the final analysis, we are all alone. This is an existential fact of life, important to remember when considering the central place of others in our lives.

WHAT NEXT?

The most obvious thing to do if your friendship system needs bolstering is the most important: you simply need to increase the amount of contact you have with others who are or could be your friends. To do this systematically, simply make a list of *all* your friends and potential friends. Then record, preferably by date, the *initiations* you make to them. Count everything (telephone calls, luncheon invitations, dropping by their home or office, invitations for dinner). If you like, record their initiations to you as well. With this self-recording as a basis, proceed as outlined in the last chapter to give yourself assignments to increase the number of your contacts. (Include rewards for meeting the assignments.) If your pool of actual and potential friends is too limited, make a list of activities in which you can become involved that will lead to other people. Then assign yourself participation in these activities. It may also be necessary to assign yourself the task of making initiations to others you find in these and other places. Keep using the guidelines in Chapter 5 to get yourself going on making new friends and cultivating old ones.

Now, I could tell you more explicitly how to find other people, how to go about building acquaintances into friendships, how to choose friends, and what to offer them. Whatever help I might give on this, however, is given in the next chapter, because people typically require it much more for new dating contacts than they do for friendships. When it comes to friends, most people know exactly what to do; the problem is getting them to do it. If you need to do something about your friendship system, I think you know what to do; do it.

PART III
HOW'S YOUR LOVE LIFE?

7

How to Find People:
Where to Look; What to Do

It's the first step that costs.

—*French Proverb*

FINDING PEOPLE

"I'VE TRIED, but I just can't seem to meet any decent men. This is a crummy place to be single." Marie, a personal friend, was twenty-eight years old, attractive, and single. She had lived with a man for two years but then she had ended the relationship on her own initiative about nine months before. She had done her very best in the previous six months to meet suitable men, both for companionship and with the hope that she might find another more satisfying primary relationship. But her luck had been poor, and she was getting rather discouraged. I asked her about the various methods she had used in looking.

"First off, I want you to know that even though I've looked for men in all the usual places, I don't like to do that sort of thing at all. It's degrading; it makes me feel cheap. I think those kinds of things are better when they happen spontaneously. I don't like playing this stupid singles game—it's not my style. Every good man I've ever had, I met *legitimately*, either in a class at college or at work. We got to really know each other

205

first and then a relationship blossomed naturally. That's the way I like it best, but that's not happening now."

"You don't meet any men where you work now?" I asked.

"As a grade-school teacher? You must be kidding! There are only four men in the whole damn school, and all four are married and dull."

"Well," I asked, "what about other contacts?"

"Oh, I've had a couple of blind dates with guys that my friends set up for me. One was a disaster, and the other was just dull. On the first one I was scared stiff. I built it up to be a really big thing and got upset about not having the right things to wear and not looking good enough. When this guy showed up he was just as nervous. We went to a movie and then for a drink afterwards. We had nothing to talk about. When we got home, on the basis of this marvelous relationship, he got physical. I turned him off immediately and sent him home and never heard from him again. I suppose that's just as well. We had nothing to say to each other anyway. The second one was pretty much the same. At least with that one I didn't build it up to be a big thing, and I wasn't disappointed. It was no big thing, believe me."

"What else have you tried?"

"Well," she said, "I took an art class both to learn and to see who I could meet, and I went to one meeting of a ski club."

"And?"

"And nothing! There were two guys in the art class and neither one interested me at all."

"And the ski club?"

"Nothing. The meeting was a complete waste of time. I didn't meet anybody interesting and I left early."

"Well, what about parties?" I asked.

"That's another losing territory. All the parties I'm invited to are with my fellow teachers and their husbands. The parties are fine, I suppose, as far as parties go, but they sure are no place to meet men."

"How about bars or nightclubs?"

"The singles-bar scene? Oh, no! I have been that route before. That whole superficial, noisy, meat-market scene depresses the hell out of me. If I'm so hard up that I have to go looking for men in bars, what does that say about me? And the men you meet in bars, *ywaaakkk!*"

"What about meeting somebody in the supermarket, the bookstore, anywhere? What about getting picked up, or picking up somebody?"

"That also strikes me as a little cheap," she said, "but if the right man approached me in the right way, it might be O.K. But, of course, that hasn't happened. One slick customer approached me in an art store once and said, 'My, you're pretty.' All I could think of to say was, 'Yes, I know,' and I walked off in the other direction. Anybody with a stupid opening like that certainly wouldn't be worth my while."

"Well, I guess we have exhausted about all the usual alternatives," I said. "Have you considered computer dating or using the newspaper ads?"

"Only for a millisecond," she said. "Both of those things are too humiliating and too risky. I mean, you wouldn't know who you were ending up with; you could get some nut. I'm not that desperate yet."

Now, Marie may be a little less adventurous than most, but unfortunately, not much! Her laments are very typical, and each complaint has an element of truth in it. Our culture does not provide many really easy ways for single adults to meet each other. With a few exceptions, most methods are tainted in some way so that the single person feels that he or she is somehow cheapened or made out to be desperate or a loser for actively seeking companionship through these means.

Marie's problem was twofold. First, she simply was not doing enough to cover all of the available territory. Meeting men was something she thought she shouldn't have to work on. Her second difficulty was in viewing so many of the truly legitimate and useful ways of meeting men as cheap, superficial, and beneath her dignity. Single men and women want to meet, and that is good. What is not good—what is in fact tragic—is that they do not meet in anywhere near the numbers they could. It is not because they are unaware of where to find each other, or how to begin interacting with each other; it is largely because of the nonsense single people tell themselves about the process of meeting other single people—the fearful notions they have about taking even the smallest risks and the fears they conjure up about being hassled (typically a woman's concern) or rejected (typically a man's concern).

I can give you many good suggestions for places to meet suitable people, and I can practically guarantee that you will be successful in meeting them if you persist in the search and follow the suggestions. But I also know that few if any of the ideas I have to offer about where to meet the other sex will be new to you. And most importantly, I know that if you have a problem in this area, it is most likely a problem in lack of persistence, not one involving a lack of knowledge. I know that if you live in a relatively quiet area (i.e., a small town or city), you would tell me there is nowhere to go, the place is socially dead, and so forth. And I know that if you live in a large city, you would tell me that people are distant, superficial, difficult to meet, and so, very often not the type you want to get involved with. What's more, I know you're right . . . these generalizations do have some basis in fact. It is often difficult to meet the kind of people you want to know better, and that is just why *you have to work at it*. Telling yourself that you live in a poor place to meet others, that you want such meetings to occur spontaneously, and that you have tried some things that didn't work only further fuels your own worst enemy—inertia.

The one essential thing you must get through your head if you want to meet others is that you will need to work at it—not desperately, but persistently. Of course, if you are very unselective and easily pleased, if you will settle for the first Tom or Jane to come along, you may not have to work all that hard at it. However, the fussier you are about your other-sex companions, the more you will have to work at finding them. This work will have to involve some false starts, some disappointments, and perhaps some hassles, inconveniences, and rejections.

Assertively meeting other people may require you to do some things that do not come naturally to you. But unless you are very different from most human beings, the other-sex friends you make, the quality of your affectional and sexual ties—your love life—form an extremely important part of your existence. If you are physically healthy, your satisfaction in living is usually a function of at least two things: the gratification found in your work and the quality of your interpersonal relationships. How hard have you worked at the preparation for and maintenance of the occupation which demands so many hours of your day? By that yardstick, how hard are you willing to work at finding those people who can help fill your other hours with mutual understanding and affection?

It is odd, but nevertheless true, that many people have the absurd notion that they should be able simply to stumble over the most fantastically suitable man or woman. If you are another unfortunate victim of this unrealistic, irrational, and self-destructive notion, take time to begin dismissing it. The origins of such notions are not difficult to trace. The beautifully spontaneous meeting is an element in almost any love story we may read or see portrayed. For most of us, the first amative attachments we had were in school, where we were surrounded by many other single adolescents who were also most interested in dating—and hence, in us. Even so, we often forget how difficult those early adolescent beginnings really were.

If you wish to find other people now for good companionship, sex, love, marriage, or whatever else, you must work at it. What's more, you must approve of working at it. Look upon it as an important *second job*. Far from meaning that anything is wrong with you, taking on that job vigorously and happily means that you are a realistic, adventuresome, and alive human being who will, in all probability, get what you are looking for far sooner than you think.

I have learned some things that may help you undertake this second job and really enjoy it. Let me begin by telling you about trout fishing in Oregon. There is a beautiful small trout stream in western Oregon to which I migrate in the fall of each year. I drive up through small logging towns to a campsite just deserted by the summer tourists. The camp is isolated, the leaves are changing to their autumn colors, and it is a wonderfully tranquil place to be.

I make this journey to fish for the large ocean-going rainbow trout called the steelhead. There is one important thing to remember about fishing for steelhead: the average angler doesn't catch one very often. The Fish and Game Commission tells me that it takes about eight to ten hours of fishing, on the average, to land a steelhead. And because I fish from the bank with a fly rod and am only an average fisherman, my catch record is somewhat more sparse than that. When I do hook a steelhead, though, it is really something. For my money, this is the most exciting game fish in the world, beating any other ocean-going fish no matter what its size.

Another thing to remember is that steelhead hang out in certain "slots" in the river. Slots may change from year to year, but once I know where steelhead are most likely to be, I am more likely to catch one. And yet, it is always possible to catch one at any place in the river, especially when they are on the move. I never know when I'll get a strike. It could be on my first cast, it could be at the end of a long three-day trip, or it could even be next year.

Finally, and most important, there is only one thing that will prevent my enjoyment of fishing for steelhead. I can ruin the whole adventure if I get too serious about catching one. If I become too goal-oriented and forget to enjoy all the other wonderful aspects of the trip—the drive, the scenery, the companionship or the solitude, and the challenge of this experience—only then do I spoil things. Only if I take myself and my activity too seriously can I destroy what is otherwise so beautiful.

I tell you this personal story because it is analogous in so many ways to what I want to tell you about taking on this job of finding other-sex companionship. First, although both jobs take a lot of work, they are not only worth the work but are enjoyable in the doing if you look at them in the right way. Appreciating the beauty of the process and the challenge of the task is the key to approaching both endeavors.

Just as the steelhead are more likely to be found in one spot than another, the people who will interest you are more likely to be found in certain places than in others. If you become a good fisherperson, you will want to know about as many of these places as possible, and you will work persistently, albeit happily, to cover as much territory as you can. And you will always remember that you can make the most exciting strike of your life at almost any point; some places are better than others, but all are possible. Furthermore, you will realize that you are playing a probability game: the more hours you spend, the more exposure you have, the more likely you are to see the fish rising. You will learn that you must be persistent in trying again and again; you must cover all that territory both thoroughly and repeatedly. And most importantly, you will learn that there is joy along the way as well as in the outcome of your efforts. Sometimes the fish won't be biting, but an experienced angler rarely takes this personally and spoils the sport.

If you can view your endeavors to meet other people as an exciting part of life in which you may learn something as you go, if you can get into the process of doing it and put your dream of the outcome in the back of your mind, you will become a happy and successful angler.

Now let's consider a sort of fishing ground which you might try sometime—a big-city singles bar. Though it is shunned by many singles, it can be a good place to meet other people. If you visit one, however, you will probably find that many of the people there are not having a very good time. Some, especially the women, do not do "this sort of thing" regularly and are more than a little bit ashamed at just being there. They look standoffish, as though they are telling themselves that they shouldn't have to go through this, that they should be able to meet a man in a more respectable atmosphere where they could relax. Others, more often the men, bear a kind of desperately serious expression. They are out to "score," which may mean anything from finding a good one-night stand to finding a suitable marriage partner, and they seem obsessed with the outcome, whatever it is. They are preoccupied with the necessity of coming up with some brilliant opening line, concerned about finding *the* girl before the next guy scores with her, and afraid of looking stupid or of being rejected. If you emulate these people by taking yourself and what's going on here too seriously, you won't have a very good time either. And, I might add, you will be less likely to achieve whatever it is you want.

Let's take the most practical and constructive way of looking at this setup. If you don't set your expectations too high, there are many advantages in going to a singles bar, especially if you are just beginning to meet others. One advantage for a new angler is that this is a pond in which there are a lot of fish, and most of the fish are biting. Almost everyone has come for the same reason—to meet someone else, and it's appropriate and expected for both men and women to initiate conversations. Brilliant opening lines are in no way required or expected, and something as plain as "Would you like to dance?" is quite sufficient as an opener. All men, and especially those who are somewhat shy and afraid of rejection, will more than appreciate a welcoming glance or smile from a young woman and often welcome even more a direct initiation. The women are generally there to be approached for a conversation or a dance, and many are discriminatively looking for more. Although everyone may be a little self-conscious about the process, it is designed explicitly for people to meet one another.

If nothing else, the singles-bar setting is an eminently good setting in which to practice *initial* interaction with the other sex. It is the ideal slot for rapidly learning how to get something going, keep something going if you want it to, and stop it if you don't. If you are a woman, you will probably need to say no oftener than you would really like to, but here you can get good practice in a relatively protected setting for saying no confidently, assertively, and respectfully.

Unfortunately, the singles bar also tends to offer a good practice ground in developing a thick skin. It is among the most impersonal, competitive, and superficial settings for meeting others. Singles in many places tend to be careless of one another's feelings, but such indifference is especially notable in a singles bar. Knowing that many of the people encountered will be unsuitable for any kind of relationship and also fearing rejection, many singles adopt an exaggerated, "cool" facade to get them through their venture. If you visit this fishing ground, you will in all probability experience some very cool customers and some rejections of one sort or another. But all methods of finding others have disadvantages. It should help you to know what the disadvantages are and to know that they are a part of that method rather than a personal shortcoming.

The basic secret for catching a fish in this fish pond is to throw in your line; that is, *talk* to those you think you might want to get to know. Talk when you can, and make arrangements, with appropriate caution, to get better acquainted with those you like. If the time comes when you cease to enjoy this, if you get embarrassed or even desperate—like some of those around you—try to talk yourself out of it, and if you can't, leave.

But remember, this is also a place in which there is a lot more going on than your own little drama. Like the trout stream, the smoky, crowded, and somewhat crazy singles bar has beauty in it too. It has advantages and possibilities to enjoy and learn from—you merely have to look at it in the right way to see them. And if you can see them at a singles bar, so much the better for you in settings where the beauty is more apparent and the shortcomings less obvious.

There are ways of looking at all new exploratory adventures that will soften the sharp edges and help you to view them more joyfully. Perhaps the most helpful attitude in this particular quest is one in which you recognize that your explorations in meeting members of the other sex wherever they are represent a healthy, adventuresome curiosity about life, other people, the things they do, and the ways in which they come together. You can learn something from every experience you allow yourself to have, and—with very few exceptions—from everyone you meet. They each have their own fascinating story to tell if you will but listen. It may not be a story that will absorb you for a long time or provide the basis for a continuing relationship, but it represents a unique view of the world which you may sample. Don't set for yourself the goal of meeting a new partner in every new heterosexual contact you have, or you will be frequently disappointed, frustrated, and discouraged, and will miss many good experiences. Consider what you are doing as a reaching out for life, looking at what it has to offer and taking as much as you can. Keep the larger and more difficult goals in mind, but in the back of your mind. Realize that you have nothing to lose by simply being friendly as you go along involving yourself with life and with learning new ways of relating to it.

TWO BASIC SECRETS
OF MEETING OTHER PEOPLE

With this background, I am now going to give you two basic and most important secrets for meeting other people. But, like so many basic secrets of life, they are deceptively simple—and besides, you already know them. Because of this, you may be tempted simply to dismiss them. Please don't. Think about each secret seriously; evaluate how well you execute each one in your own life. In order to meet compatible other-sex persons, you need:

First, to develop a fulfilling social network, involving people and activities that are interesting for you and bring you enjoyment.

Second, to go out into the world often and be prepared to approach others and be approached by them.

In addition to the overriding necessity that we have established for a social-support system or network for the well-functioning single adult, there is a lot more to be said on the advantages of such a system in regard to your search for other-sex companionship. First of all, bear in mind that keeping up with activities and people who interest and entertain you will inevitably lead to others, and it will be only a matter of time before you are thrown into contact with people of the other sex. If finding others is a problem for you, it is important that you realize that *it is only a matter of time*. There is no need to panic. There is only a need to get moving and cultivate a determined and active patience. When you are busily and productively engaged in interesting activities and rewarding friendships, there is less longing for sexual and love relationships, so that you are free to seek them out calmly and philosophically rather than pursuing them with desperation.

Those who appear to be in desperate need of others are usually not very attractive or effective. Desperate seekers seem to have very little to offer because they are so consumed with their own need. They are ineffective because they feel their life's worth is riding on each encounter. Few of us want to be the object of another's all-consuming need for love and fulfillment; none of us can ever fulfill such an unrealistic demand. So, if you want others coming to you, display some independence, cultivate your other interests, and have much more to offer than your own need. If you have to, play this role a bit, but know that this more self-sufficient *you* will come naturally if you have a good deal going on in your own life—if you have a broad matrix of social contacts and absorbing interests.

Many of my single friends and clients have told me the same thing. When they feel the most need of meeting other people to begin sexual or love relationships, the world seems an empty and lonely place. But when their lives are the fullest and they have the least yearning for such relationships, eligible people seem to drop out of the trees. This is so, of course, because alone time flies when you are absorbed, busy people meet other people, and independent people are relaxed, secure, and attractive. And, remember, you will become more independent by behaving more independently. Your own activity and social-support system can enable you to be independent and can provide you with ever-expanding opportunities to meet eligible others. How good is it?

The social and activity networks in which you or any of us move, however, may not always yield just the people for whom we are looking. The most universal lament of all unhappily single people is, "Where is everybody?" The deceptively simple answer is, everywhere. More specifically, other people can be found in or at the following: parks, museums, restaurants, bars, coffee shops, bookstores, record stores, art stores, furniture stores, grocery stores, clothing stores, other stores, outdoor markets, lectures, movies, sports events, concerts, plays, fairs, club meetings, banks, laundromats, elevators, offices, tennis courts, bicycle paths, parties, work, beaches, lakes, resorts, hotels, conventions, buses, trains, airplanes—the list is endless. I'm not trying to be cute or facile in listing these places and events for you. I am only trying to point out what you might be overlooking. People are all around you wherever you go. You can, with just a little added effort, get to know them. When you initiate a conversation with a stranger in any of these places and arrange for some future contact, you are picking someone up. There is *nothing* wrong with this and much right with it. I recommend it, and most of the remainder of this chapter will instruct you on how to do it well. Some places will obviously be better for meeting people than others. Typically, settings where people go for relaxation and entertainment are the most fertile. It is to these places that many people really go in order to pick up or be picked up by others. A park on a Saturday afternoon or the pool of a resort hotel are, of course, more natural "slots" for singles to meet one another than are movies or bank lobbies. But wherever you encounter other people represents a viable possibility. In Los Angeles, for example, it is not uncommon for singles to pick one another up on the freeway. Too gutsy for you? Keep reading. There are easier things to do to work your way up to such courageous reaching out.

HOW TO PICK UP PEOPLE

Now let's get down to business and analyze what you need to do in order to increase the number and quality of your contacts with other-sex persons. The first thing to do is to assess your own best slots for meeting others who will have the most in common with you. Your object, of course, is not to meet as many peo-

ple as possible but to meet attractive and suitable people, and your best and most fulfilling relationships will
be with those with whom you have a good deal in
common. Hence, analyzing your own interests is critical
to your determining the best places to look. Again, your
creative operants are of great importance. If your interests are very limited, you will not have as many suitable places to go to meet others and, indeed, you will
not be as well equipped to attract those you do meet.
In Chapter 4, I introduced you to Karen, a woman so
deficient in creative operants that the bars in her community were her only slots. Her interest in drinking did
not attract many people, nor did it provide her with a
wealth of stimulating material for discussion. The treatment program for Karen was primarily directed at increasing the number of her interests, in part so that she
would have more appropriate places where she could
meet others of both sexes. If you find yourself in the
same situation as Karen, your first step should be to
sample various activities which might be of interest to
you.

If your interests are many, your task at this stage
will be a relatively easy one. If you tend to favor outdoor
activities, you would do well to consider involvement
in special interest groups with this focus such as the
Sierra Club, ski clubs, rock-climbing or diving clubs.
Many organizations, colleges, and city programs offer
organized outdoor trips and instruction in outdoor
sports.

If your interests run to politics, you should consider
exploring various political groups in your community
such as the political parties, the American Civil Liber-

ties Union, the Americans for Democratic Action, and so on. Involvement in a political campaign is an excellent way to meet many others.

If your interests run to music, you can look for other people in clubs featuring the particular kind of music you enjoy, at concerts, in classes, or in record stores.

Of course, we live in a society in which many interests are more or less sex-typed. Thus, women are not liable to meet too many men in courses in cooking or sewing, and men are not liable to meet a large number of women in motorcycling or rock-climbing clubs. On the other hand, if you are one who might develop an interest in a typically other-sex activity, you are in a uniquely fortunate position.

It will help if you analyze your interests and the slots they represent in a systematic way. If increasing the number of your contacts is a serious objective, I strongly recommend that you get a piece of paper and make a list of all your interests, vocational and avocational. Then, alongside each interest, write down all the possible places that people sharing your interests would frequent. Leave nothing out. Remember that you can meet people anywhere, and people lead to more people.

To expand your list of possible places to meet others, it might be helpful to check the Sunday edition of your local newspaper, where activities for the coming week and month are often listed. If your list is still a rather meager one, this means that you have too few creative operants and need to do further work in this area.

The next step in analyzing your list of possible

places to meet others is to set priorities in the following way. Rate each activity, indicating the level of interest it has for you by giving it an A priority for high interest, a B for moderate interest, and a C for relatively low interest. Next, grade each activity in terms of density—the likelihood that it will lead to your meeting other-sex companions. In general, those activities which are not sex-typed against you and which provide opportunity for relatively heavy exposure to other-sex companions would be best. I have prepared a list of this kind for myself and share it with you here as a possibly helpful example. Those activities which average highest in both interest and density are obviously the ones which I should pursue when looking for other-sex companions.

Your Author's Slots

	Interest	Density
Parties	A	A
Professional conventions	A	B
Nightclubs featuring jazz music	A	B
Nightclubs featuring soul music	A	B
Nightclubs featuring rock music	B	B
Nightclubs featuring folk music	A	B
Singles bars	B	A
University campuses	B	A
Medical school campuses/hospitals	B	A
Professional lectures	B	B
Bookstores	A	B

	Interest	Density
Singles organizations	C	A
University libraries	B	B–C
Lectures in allied professions	B	B
Trips	A	A–B
Skiing or ski clubs	A	A–B
Tennis courts/ tennis lessons	B	B
Museums	C	B
Outdoor clubs (Sierra, etc.)	B	A
Political organizations	C	B
Rock-climbing or climbing clubs	B	D
The beach	B	A
Group bicycle trips	A	B
Group backpacking trips	A	B
Group boating trips (river running)	A	C
Sailing lessons	B	C
Skiing lessons	A	B–C
Cooking classes	C	B
Street corners	D	A

Note: the last item on my list, "Street corners," is thrown in simply to remind you once again that you can meet the most desirable person of your life at a place of very low interest. Singles organizations, singles bars, and airports attract a lot of people, and if you are skilled at using such settings, you may be able to do very well indeed. In a high-density area like an airport, you need skill in approaching and talking with others and the ability to quickly evaluate the potential for some kind of relationship. Such areas are more commonly thought of as pickup settings and yield the most for people with well-developed pickup skills.

Someone good at picking up others is simply good at initiating conversation, adept at continuing it, and capable of asking for or signaling a desire for further contact. Such skills are obviously going to be very useful to you no matter where you meet other people, for whatever purpose. What I have to say about these skills should be relevant to you no matter how timid you are about the straightforward pickup.

All the initiation-pickup techniques to be discussed here can be used by women as well as men. Some of the boldest techniques I will mention are ones my women friends, colleagues, or clients have had the guts to use. Nevertheless, it is true that men still bear the primary burden and joy of this initiation process. Some of these pickup techniques will be used primarily by men, while other, more subtle methods are, at this stage of our development, more generally suitable for women. Before providing a list of possible techniques, let's have another list—one reviewing the attitudes that will do most to facilitate the techniques for you.

1. Your life is not on the line. Your worth, success, or self-esteem do not depend on the response of the other person. If your approach is positive, friendly, considerate, and respectful, the response you get will generally be the same. The answer to your proposal of future contact may be a negative one, but the way in which it is delivered should generally be kind. If it is not, that means that the other person has a problem; you don't.

2. Your initiations do not have to be clever, smooth,

and professional. Indeed, initiations which are too smooth, slick, and competent are often suspect and less effective than more human, faltering, but sincere endeavors.

3. Making initiations to other people is adventuresome, courageous, and healthy. If you want to make contact with others and have the aplomb to do it, congratulate yourself for having the guts to embrace life.

4. Your looks are not of paramount importance. Unfortunately, most of us have normal insecurities about the way we look. As people accumulate experience in living, they usually find that there are many others who find their particular physical appearance attractive. Even those characteristics that you may find displeasing in yourself are sometimes very pleasing to others. Most people will never be as critical of you in this regard as you are of yourself. Try to forget these insecurities and move ahead in your adventure of meeting other people.

5. Being rejected does not make you worthless. There are many reasons why any given person might not be interested in either your initiation or in future contact with you. Many of these reasons have little or nothing to do with you, and you should manage as well as possible not to take them seriously. To gain anything worthwhile, you must take some risks. Being rejected is a risk that you will be taking in this endeavor, but rejection is not the end of the world. In dealing with it, you may learn some important things about yourself and about life.

6. It is the process of meeting other people, not the outcome, on which you should focus. Pay attention to what you are doing and try to enjoy it. Attempt to for-

get about success or failure and the ultimate objectives of your endeavors.

7. View your efforts in picking up as *practice*. At first, you may wish to practice merely by *thinking* about what you would say in order to initiate a conversation in a specific situation. Just go around for a day or a week and practice coming up with initiation lines. Then, simply practice initiating a conversation with some same-sex person, and then with other-sex individuals in various settings. Don't wait for the love of your life to come along in order to begin this practice. Practice on anyone and everyone you see. You don't have to follow up every initiation with a proposal for future contact. Just practice, practice, practice.

8. Experiment, enjoy, have fun, smile, be friendly. You are engaging life; live and be glad you can do it.

MORE PICKUP LESSONS

Janice found herself eying and being eyed by a very attractive man as she drove along the freeway. Her car and his bobbed back and forth as each person tested the other. This brave hunk of man finally got up enough courage to smile at Janice, there was eye contact, and she was getting excited. But the man flipped on his turn signal, moved into the far right lane and drove out of her life forever—or so he thought. Janice was disappointed, but in a surprising burst of courageous energy said to herself, "Damn it, this man looks too good to get away." Before she quite knew what she was doing, she had followed her target off the freeway and into a

supermarket parking lot. Now came the real test, because she had to wait for him to come out of the supermarket. When he did, she closed the sale; she got out
of her car, walked over to him, and said, "Hi, my name
is Janice and you just looked too good to get away!"

The man's jaw dropped; then he said, "Who, me?"
with obvious delight. They had a short conversation and
exchanged telephone numbers, and he called a few days
later.

This kind of bold, direct, and courageous approach
can often provide the highest payoff, and there is no
reason why it needs to be restricted to the male of the
species. Unfortunately, women who are able to do this
are rare, but those of my acquaintance who have done
it are usually gratified by the positive response they receive. Even if the approached person is unavailable because, for example, he is married, the response is usually
an affirmative one that shows he is flattered and pleased.

Carol was a recently separated mother of three
young children. She would no more attempt to emulate Janice's tactics than leap from a fortieth-story window. She did, however, want to meet men and needed
help in developing some initiation skills of her own.
She asked the members of our separation-adjustment
group to help. In the building where she worked, there
was a man with whom she exchanged greetings from
time to time, but she did not know his name and, although he seemed willing to be friendly, he had never
done anything about it. The group tried to encourage
Carol to approach him in the company lunchroom or
elsewhere to engage him in conversation, but she felt
this was just too difficult. In the group setting, she
practiced some possible initiations we suggested, and

didn't do at all badly. But she just couldn't see herself repeating these approaches outside the group. I then recommended what I think is the most universal, low-risk technique for such situations: that she merely look at her intended friend a little longer than usual—communicate her interest simply through eye contact. She agreed either to initiate a conversation with him or to try the eye-contact method at least once before the next session. And when the session came, she reported proudly the following story. She had seen Mr. X in the lunchroom and looked at him for just a fraction of a second longer than would be polite.

"Right after lunch," she said, "he came by my office and nervously asked me if I had seen some movie. Before I had a chance to answer, he said, 'Would you like to go?' and I agreed. I guess I picked up a man, huh?"

While women are put at a disadvantage by training which incorrectly suggests that more assertive behavior is inappropriate for them, it is to their advantage that very subtle indications of interest may stimulate an initiation from a man who would otherwise be too shy or too preoccupied to say the first word.

Both Janice and Carol were effective in getting what they wanted. Their approaches differed widely, but both represented useful, effective pickup techniques, and illustrate the extremes in assertiveness. Both extremes can work and may be called for in different situations. Obviously, the broader and more flexible repertoire of initiation techniques you can develop, the more situations you can use to advantage.

The most commonly used initiation strategy is, of course, somewhere between the two extremes. It is simply to talk to another person about an easy topic. The three basic topics to use in such initiations are the *environment*, the *other person*, and *yourself*. And there are two ways to initiate these topics: either offer a comment or ask a question.

The most natural and innocuous of such initiations involves comments about the environment. A woman once picked me up by complaining about the elevator service in the building in which we both worked. I lost no time in continuing and expanding the conversation. I liked what little I knew about her by the time we reached the fourth floor, and when she exited from the elevator, I did too, even though I had several floors more to go to my own office. At that point, I asked if there would be any chance of my getting to know her better, and when she let me know there would be, we quickly exchanged telephone numbers and got together later that same day. Here, for your own adventure seeking, are other opening lines:

"It's a beautiful day, isn't it?"

"That's a good book you are looking at; I enjoyed it."

"Great show, don't you think?"

"That's a beautiful Cézanne."

"What do you think of this place?"

Yes, these openers are banal. But they do get the talking started, and there's usually still time for you to warm up and become more personal. Remember, it's more important to start talking than it is to say something wonderful, and it will be a hell of a lot easier when you stop worrying about being wonderful.

The next technique, closely related and also fairly innocuous, is to remark on something about the other person. A compliment is almost always useful if delivered respectfully and cheerfully. In general, initial compliments are better if made about something that can be talked about. Telling a woman that she has a pretty face may be flattering, but unless she's had a nose job she wants to talk about, it leaves little room for discussion. Commenting on a curious piece of jewelry or an unusual tie makes for a better beginning because its owner is almost sure to have something to say about it. (Putting your compliment in question form can be very valuable here: "Where did you ever find it?") And don't restrict your compliments to the simple things you can see. One of my clients easily picked up a man by complimenting him on his cologne. And a college professor was delighted when a young woman approached him after one of his lectures to tell him she really liked the way he moved when he talked. She said, "You know, you are very relaxed with your body; you move like a construction worker." As you might have guessed, my friend lost little time in asking this extremely perceptive woman out for the evening. In a similar vein, a musician friend of mine notices when women respond well to his music. He will compliment a woman by noting her appreciation and asking if she is a musician herself.

So, whenever you see someone you want to talk to, see if there isn't something about them which you can remark on. Here are a few passable openers:

"I like your sox" (an icebreaker).

"You look sad" (to be used judiciously).

"You look familiar" (trite but reliable).

"You're the handsomest man I've seen all week" (bold but effective).

"You're the happiest person I've seen all day; can you share it?" (who could say no?).

In regard to our third technique—saying something about yourself in order to communicate with another—I remember one time when I was in a bar in Los Angeles and saw a particularly attractive woman standing in a corner alone. This bar was always so jammed with men and so competitive that it was unusual to see a woman this appealing remain alone for more than thirty seconds. Being human, I began telling myself some stupid, self-defeating sentences which ran something like, "She's probably with someone and is waiting for him to return. If I talk to her, it would just be an intrusion. Someone will get to her first. There are many better-looking men in this place. She's really attractive. Why would she be interested in me?" (I have just as much right to be neurotic as the next person.)

But I had studied this problem in myself and others long enough to recognize my self-defeating sentences. So I turned them around into an opener. I walked up to her and said: "Are you waiting for somebody special to talk to, or will I do?"

"No," she said ambiguously, but her attitude made it clear that I would do just fine.

That was the beginning of a fine relationship, and even though the line just popped out, I've always been rather proud of that initiation. It is noteworthy for the way in which what I said was built on my hesitance. I was feeling insecure, but, at least that time, I flipped the insecurity around and came up with an opening remark which shared that feeling and protected me at the same time from the rejection I feared. It might have been better, of course, had I not felt so insecure in the first place and had no need to protect myself from rejection. But I did, and I learned that even negative feelings can be used and shared.

Many of the openers that share something about yourself also provide you with a question that guarantees a response. Thus, when traveling, you might tell someone that you are visiting his or her city and don't know the good places to go for entertainment. Naturally, you then ask for some advice on such places. If the conversation seems at all promising, and especially if the other person seems to share your interests, you might then wish to ask for company on your tour—and get it!

Even if you don't use self-disclosing remarks for openers, bringing in this kind of talk sooner or later will help other people talk with you. Volunteering *free information* about yourself—your occupation, your current situation, your feelings—invites the other person to respond to you and your interests.

One of my friends always uses the self-disclosure technique whenever he needs to make a direct and fast approach to someone. He simply explains, "I know this is rather abrupt, but I figure it's now or never. You seem to be a very attractive person, and I was hoping I might get to know you better. Do you think that might happen?" This is another example of dealing with a rejection by anticipating it; you make it difficult for the other person to accuse you of being abrupt if you have already recognized that aspect of the situation and dealt with it.

The technique of disclosing something about yourself covers everything from the most mundane remarks to the most direct of approaches. Here are a few examples:

"I'd like to get to know you better."

"I'm new around here and need to know some things about the area. Could you help me?"

"I thought that was a boring lecture. What did you think?"

"Will I be glad when this day is over!"

"I hardly ever do this, but I'd like to ask you out for a drink."

"I'm looking for someone new to talk to, and I'm taking a chance on you."

Note that two of the foregoing approaches end with a question. So did several of the earlier sample openers. If you wish to talk with someone and are stuck for an initial remark, see if there's a question you can ask. Is there, for instance, any information you need? Ask for it. Unfortunately, there is one serious problem with question asking: interaction can very easily end after you've got the answer. (What do you do now that you know where the post office is?) If the other person does not take you up on your desire to start a conversation, you may still have to produce a quick comment on one of the other topics in order to sustain the contact. But at least a question gets *you* talking, and that's important. Here are some common questions:

"Do you know of a bank nearby?"

"Do you have something for a headache?"

"What did you think of that concert?"

"Do you know any good nightspots?"

"How are you today?"

The main idea, you see, is simply to start talking. It doesn't matter so much what you are talking about. If you can be clever and creative, so much the better. If you can't, don't worry about it. Most opening remarks made by most people most of the time are rather trivial and superfluous. That's not the point; meeting other people and talking to them is. So, whenever you see someone you would probably like to pick up, just begin talking in a friendly and interested way. If you can't think of anything to say, quickly run over the three topics—and take the plunge, with almost any comment or question.

There are still those times, of course, when it is truly impossible to begin such a conversation. In these cases, writing notes can be extremely effective. I have one friend, for instance, who freely admits that he uses his business cards for this purpose more than he ever does for business. If he spots a woman to whom he is attracted, he writes her a little note on the back of his card: "I think you are a very attractive person. If you're available, I would like to take you out for lunch or a drink sometime. Please check one: 1. Yes. My phone number is ————. 2. No, thank you."

Although my friend certainly does not get to know all those to whom he writes such a note, he has had no unkind rejections using this method, and all those whom he has approached have seemed flattered and even impressed by his boldness. A graduate student friend of mine uses the same method to pick up women in the library, where talking is restricted and a vocal approach might disturb others. Again, his batting average is nowhere near perfect, but he has never been turned down rudely, and his tactful ingenuity has frequently paid off. Another man of my acquaintance executed the ultimate in the quick pickup. He saw a young woman in a restaurant whom he found extraordinarily attractive, but, alas, she was with another man. Scared but determined, my friend approached the couple's table and said to the woman, "I don't want to interrupt your lunch but if you want to discuss that TV part I mentioned, please call me," and he presented his business card (he was connected with the television industry). She thanked him and called. Nothing ventured, nothing gained.

This class of approach is, of course, very direct, but there are circumstances in which more subtle initiations are not possible. In most pickup situations, time is limited and there are other restrictions. If you don't strike when the opportunity arises, it's gone forever. The pickup situation is by its very nature not the safest of circumstances, but it can provide a very exciting test of both your skill and your rational thinking about rejection. And it just could lead to a secure and meaningful long-term relationship.

Let's briefly review what you must do to find and get to know others.

1. Decide that it is good and right and healthy to work actively on meeting other people; decide to do it.

2. Begin practicing immediately; begin today to think of openers in various situations. As soon as possible, initiate conversations with same-sex strangers, then with other-sex persons whom you do not wish to pick up. *Practice.*

3. In some way or other, move out of your regular daily schedule each day.

4. Analyze your interests and your resulting slots for meeting other people.

5. Systematically, make a plan to cover some of the slots today, this week, next week, and so on.

6. If you can, assign yourself graded, sequential tasks and reward yourself for accomplishments. For instance, think of at least one initiation line today; make at least one initiation to a same-sex stranger in the next two days; go to one of your newfound slots during the week; talk to one other-sex stranger in the next two days; and plan to ask for further contact when and only when you want it. Don't rush this one! Just get some exposure and practice, and the rest will come.

The problem of what to say *after* you have made your initial contact remains to some degree; but frequently, because of the way one topic leads to another, this will be no problem. I have taken up many pages on the initiation problem because my experience suggests that this is where people run into the most difficulty; once we're over that hurdle, "what to say after we say hello" is relatively easy—we've had more practice at that.

The basic dynamic of initial interaction is very understandable. Assuming that both people have some initial desire for interaction, they will typically engage in conversation directed at finding a common ground for continued talk. A good conversationalist is one who can find things of interest in the particular knowledge or experience of the other. Thus, as a psychologist, I enjoy talking to cab drivers and bartenders about the people they deal with, to physicians about the psychosomatic problems they are called upon to handle, to salesmen about the psychology of their selling approach, to teachers about the way they capture the interest of their children. The basic secret in finding such common grounds of interest is to offer and listen for free information—

that is, to indicate as quickly and efficiently as possible what your interests in life are and to pick up on the interests of the person to whom you are speaking.

Suppose, for example, a man approaches you and says, "I'm new in town and I was wondering what people do for fun around here." Now, this one sentence has a wealth of material for continued interaction. The free information that the initiator is new in town can be used for a discussion of where he came from, how he likes it here, where he lives or is staying, and what occasioned his move or visit. In addition, it provides an opportunity for you to give a good deal of free information about yourself simply by answering his question—not only with what "people" do for fun but what you do.

It is possible, of course, that in any given interaction you will not find a common ground for interesting discussion. Although this is less likely as you increase the number of your interests and your ability as a conversationalist, it will still occur. This is not to be viewed as a failure for you or the other person, but simply as a fact of life. It is part of the probability game that you are playing in actively engaging with life and other people.

It's usually best, of course, for both you and the other person to engage in this kind of initial interaction —sounding each other out—before you make any sort of date. In any case, your first encounter with a stranger can be relatively brief and noncommittal. Someone who at first appears quite attractive to you may prove to be disappointing, and there is usually no point in dragging out contact with the other person once this has happened. So, for a next meeting, if any, while you still barely know the new person, consider having coffee, a drink, or lunch together, or meet for some other relatively casual, short-term activity. If things click, you can prolong the time or make another date.

If you follow the advice I have given you in this chapter, I can practically guarantee that you will meet suitable people in short order, and that the material in the next chapter will be relevant to you before you know it. So—start practicing and keep reading.

8

Getting Together

Life is a journey, not a destination.
—*Argus Publications*

SCOT AND I were out for a leisurely lunch, catching up on events in each other's lives and enjoying a good, honest talk. Six months before, Scot had been the reluctant partner in a separation from his wife of fifteen years. He was a professor in the business school of a nearby university, and he had never been what you'd call a flashy person. Since his separation, however, there had been some changes in his physical appearance and style of life. His horn-rimmed glasses had given way to contact lenses, his new slacks were tightly tailored and flared, and he had traded in his old sedan for a new sports car. He now lived in the Marina Del Rey, which is the ultimate American singles city. I was both personally and professionally curious to know how his transition to single life was coming along. I asked how it was going.

"Well," he said, "it's up and down, but I think I'm doing O.K. in most things. But you know what's the worst part of it? Dating—even the word gives me the creeps, but what else do you call it? It makes me feel ridiculous. I mean, I'm a grown, hardworking professional man. Most of the time I feel confident and sure of myself. But on those first dates, I feel worse now than I did as a kid. I feel like I ought to be dressed up in my saddle shoes and my seersucker suit carrying a pink-and-white corsage. I get unexplainably nervous; I don't know what to talk about; I fumble; I'm just not myself. I don't get it; it's like I was sixteen again, and for the first time in as long as I can remember, I don't know what the hell to do. I've changed my style and my dress to keep up with these pretty kids and to feel more confident, but it doesn't help much. This dating business is a younger man's game."

Scot had a pretty bad case of dating discomfort, but the general topics about which he was complaining are common to almost all those who reenter single social life after a period of settled coupling. I remember talking with Amy, a twenty-four-year-old woman who, after ending a two-year affair, was also concerned about reentering this form of socializing.

"You see," she said, "I know how to do the dating thing, but, damn it, I just don't want to. I mean, here come the losers, the grabbers, and the little boys. I don't want to put up with them in order to find another human being I can care about. It's as simple as this: I just don't want to be bothered. But at the same time I know that I *have* to before I can get it on with someone else. I'm no prude; I love sex, but I don't want to have to worry about it every time I go out with a man. But, you know, it's always there. I just don't want to have to worry about all that—I just don't want to have to hassle with it."

I give you these brief profiles of two attractive, intelligent, and fairly together people to make two important points. First, all single adults are at least a little apprehensive and reluctant about initial dating. They are so because they are not sure of what they are getting themselves into and they are not completely sure of what they are supposed to do. The rules for such socializing are in great flux, and no one really knows what to expect or what is expected of them. This is a situation loaded for apprehension. Second, Scot, Amy, and most other single adults react this way because they overemphasize the difference between adult dating and other forms of human companionship. If Scot and Amy could think about this category of socializing as simply another form of human sharing—a chance to share companionship, recreation, and understanding with another human being—if they could merely let things happen, confident in themselves (as I am for them) that they would know what to do in almost any situation, they would relax, do better, and have more fun. In all probability, they would most impress those they see by not trying to impress them; by being at ease with themselves, they would naturally set their companions at ease. Since there are now almost no rules for such adult companionship, Scot and Amy are free to make their own, and as long as they are decent to their companions, there should be no problem.

Although I will try to provide some guidelines in this chapter on the various issues that arise in initial dating, my most important piece of advice is, "Not to worry." When Scot goes out, he will be concerned about where he will take his date, what he should talk about, how to get her home if he doesn't like her or, if he does, how and whether to get her to be affectionate, how gentlemanly he should be in these days of women's liberation, what he should tell about his former marriage or other current relationships, what is expected of him in terms of affection, sexual initiation, and so on and on. Amy, because she is both younger and more experienced, has fewer worries. Primarily, she will be concerned about retaining some control in the relationship and not being overpowered in all decisions. And she will be concerned most about how to say no to anything from rejecting a suggestion about where to go for dinner to rejecting sexual advances when she's not interested. Women who are older and less experienced usually have most of the concerns which Scot expressed as well, but almost every woman, regardless of her experience, has primary concerns about saying no.

It would be better, of course, if both Scot and Amy could simply enjoy whatever adult companionship has to offer and see how they feel as relationships develop. I realize that this advice—not to worry—may be a little hard to follow. But the more familiar you are with the issues and the more you feel that you will know what to do when any of them arises, the less you will worry about them. Hence, the rest of this chapter is going to be more specific about—and probably more helpful to— those who are beginning the dating process again. Although the more initiated single person may find some of it rather elementary, many problems in dating are covered here, and each reader can check off what he or she already knows. By processing this knowledge in a more systematic way, even the experienced may be helped, if only to deal better with their less experienced partners.

There has been very little research on single-adult life-styles, but there are some studies on the personal adjustment of the divorced showing that better adjustment is related to more and better dating after separation. Our own research suggests that dating is particularly important during the first year; it appears to be of great value in the reconstruction of self-esteem and a new life with other people. And yet, the newly single often avoid it because they are afraid and uncertain about what to do; after all those years of being centered on one person, they don't know how to act "on the outside."

In dealing with dating, sex, and love relationships between men and women, I shall be going on the assumption that men are more often the initiators and that it is more crucial for them to solve the problems of initiation and dealing with rejection than for women. Concurrently, women are assumed to be more often the recipients of initiations, confronted with the problem of responding to them. It is a fact that being able to say no in various contexts is generally of more concern to women. Although I shall discuss how both men and women can learn to play reciprocal roles, in most cases I am assuming the more traditional ones, especially in the initial dating context. By a very narrow definition, this approach may be called sexist. By my definition, it is merely realistic. To write about things as if they were different because I might think it would be better if they were would be a disservice.

ASKING FOR DATES AND SAYING NO

Jack: "Hello, Molly, this is Jack Parker calling. How are you?"

Molly: "Uh, I'm fine. Hello."

Jack: "It's a nice day today, isn't it? What are you doing?"

Molly: "Uh, yes, it is a nice day. But I'm not sure who you are. Did we meet somewhere?"

Jack: "Oh, I'm sorry. I met you at Todd and Evelyn's party last Friday night."

Molly: "I'm still not sure that I remember who you are. I met so many people at that party."

Jack: "Well, I'm an insurance salesman, and we talked about movies—remember, we talked about Fellini and Humphrey Bogart—things like that."

Molly: "Oh, yes. I remember now. I'm sorry I didn't remember your name."

Jack: "I remember you were having some trouble with your car. Has that been worked out yet?"

Molly: "Uh, yes, it has, thank you."

Jack: "How have you been since I saw you last?"

Molly: "Oh, fine."

Jack: "Say, I was wondering what you are doing Saturday night."

Molly: "Well, uh, I'm busy Saturday night."

Jack: "O.K., what are you doing Sunday? I was thinking of taking a drive to the coast."

Molly: "Well, uh, my sister is coming over on Sunday and we plan to do some baking."

Jack: "Oh, I see. Could I take you out for dinner next Thursday night?"

Molly: "No, that's bad too."

Jack: "Well, how about sometime next weekend, then?"

Molly: "Next weekend I'm, uh, going skiing with some friends."

Jack: "Oh. Well, I'll call again."

Molly: "O.K. Good-bye."

Jack: "Good-bye."

This, dear reader, is how not to do it. This sequence is filled with examples of bad human relations on both sides. Let's analyze the problem first from Jack's side. For starters, he should have identified himself as completely and quickly as possible and moved ahead only after being sure he was recognized. Obviously, this would have saved embarrassment on both sides, and even if it were not needed, it would have given Molly a little time to figure out what was happening. In addition, although it may have been useful for Jack to make a little conversation about other things before asking for a date, it was not necessary, and, since he really had nothing else to say, it was awkward. It would have been better for him to get right to the point. It was also awkward of him to ask what Molly was doing at a particular time. It was none of his business and wasn't what he really wanted to know anyway. The essential thing to understand in the process of making arrangements is that *the initiator is not usually asking for companionship for only one narrowly specified occasion.* Almost always, the initiator is stating a wish (i.e., I'd like to go out with you sometime) and is asking for a positive or negative response (i.e., would you like that or wouldn't you?). So, if you are the initiator and are interested in more than a certain engagement at a certain time, ask in one way or another what you really mean—whether the object of your interest would like to join you sometime. Once you get a response to this general question, the settlement on time, place, and activity will be rather simple.

Molly didn't help much. Poor Jack was drowning and pulling her down with him, but she didn't have the good sense to save them both simply by defining what the question really was and giving her answer. It is fairly apparent that she didn't want to go out with Jack, but she never really said that. While it can be argued that Jack and Molly were conversing in polite code about spending time together, I submit that this form of communication is neither effective nor thoughtful. To telegraph coded messages about any sensitive matter is a bad practice because it is hard to know another's code and always difficult to decode. Misunderstanding and distress are almost inevitable with such maneuvers. It is almost always better to identify the issue with another immediately and communicate about it clearly.

Nonproductive coded messages are common in initiation situations in which the invitee wants to say no but is uncomfortable about it. Many of us have unfortunately never learned that it is kinder and more respectful of others and ourselves to say no when we want to. Or, having understood that, we still fail to form the word when the critical moment arises. As a result, we begin a pitifully destructive game of saying yes or maybe in one way while saying no in others—a confusing code. We take the course which is easiest in the short run but by far the hardest in the long run, and we often end up hating ourselves for it and dreading a postponed confrontation with the one who has to keep asking to find out what's happening. Men are often worse about this than women because saying no is a newer, less practiced thing for them.

Molly could have simply acknowledged that Jack was suggesting that they go out sometime and could have given her real answer to that question. She could have given either of two very acceptable answers to Jack's opening invitation, depending on her interest in seeing him. Type 1: "I would very much like to go out with you sometime, Jack, but Saturday night is just a bad time." If she wanted to, she could tell Jack why Saturday night was unavailable, but she would not be obligated to. Type 2: "It's flattering that you would like to go out with me, Jack, but I can't right now because. . . ." The plausible excuses are many. Molly could indicate that since she had just broken up with her husband or boyfriend she wasn't yet ready to begin dating again. She could, if it were at all true, indicate that she was dating one person rather steadily and wasn't interested in broader dating. Alternatively, she might say that her social-dating life was already overly full and that she was not yet ready to go out with anyone else.

Molly could also have said that she did not want to go out with Jack, period; she did not owe him any explanation. I think it is kinder, however, to offer some ego-sparing explanation if there is one which is generally true. Although opinions differ on this point, I believe in the courtesy of caring for other people's feelings when we can. You are not obliged to do so; you may reject an invitation with no explanation, but what is the harm in going a little out of your way to protect another's feelings? Singles dating life can be rough. Why should single people not try to take care of one another as much as possible?

The central rule that we have developed over the course of counseling many singles who have difficulty saying no on this and many other issues is to advise them to respond in the following way: "I can't (or don't want to) handle that because. . . ." In most cases, of course, the word "can't" is not quite accurate because most of us are able to handle many things with which we would rather not deal. It is merely a figure of speech which softens what might be taken as a rejection.

But, if Jack pressed Molly about her reasons for saying no or argued with her about them, she would do better to actively assert her right to her own decisions and her own reasons and completely avoid further discussion of the matter. While caring for the feelings of others is important, it is equally important to avoid engaging in argument or justification with those who do not respect your own rights and feelings. You never have to justify your decisions. Your feelings are what they are; state them, stick to them, but avoid debating them. Allow your compassion for others to protect their feelings as long as that does not hurt you. But do not allow your compassion to interfere with what you do or what you want.

FIRST TIME TOGETHER—RELAX

Let's suppose you're going out for the first time with someone you don't know very well: you probably have some questions about where to go, what to do, and how to act. In this section, I am going to try to anticipate as many of those questions as I can and give you some answers that make sense in terms of my experience. No matter how much you have developed socially as a single person, you probably still feel more or less uptight about meeting someone new. Even the most enjoyable of initial encounters can involve a series of complex, often subtle communications as two people define themselves in relation to each other. Some forethought concerning what to do, how to act, and what to say can save you possible grief and misunderstandings and make you just a little more sure of yourself. While I shall go into some detail on each question, there is one cardinal rule that applies to every one: *Do whatever will make you and your companion most comfortable.* Anyplace you go, anything you do or say is good if it increases your mutual ease in becoming better acquainted and enjoying each other.

Where to Go

There seem to be three important considerations in deciding where to go, your first time together. Pick a place where both of you will be comfortable; pick an activity that allows at least some time for you to be alone together in a place where you can talk, and get acquainted; and avoid unduly expensive or lengthy engagements that would tend to overemphasize the importance of this initial encounter.

The first rule is fairly obvious. If you are uncomfortable, you will be less able to be yourself, to make your companion comfortable, to respond to the subtle cues he or she will be giving you, or to give out cues yourself. If your companion is uncomfortable, he or she will suffer all of this and, of course, associate this discomfort with you. In choosing a place to go, it is more important to be comfortable than impressive. Ordinarily, intimidating restaurants, formal get-togethers with business associates, or recreations which one partner doesn't understand will violate this criterion. A quiet get-acquainted drink, a simple dinner, a trip to a concert featuring the kind of music you both enjoy, followed by time together, are far better choices.

If you are the invitee and your companion suggests a place to go where you would be uncomfortable or even bored, don't hesitate to tell him or her. Make it clear, of course, that you are rejecting the place and not the person, and offer some reasonable alternatives if you can. As in other things, go out of your way to protect the other's feelings, but not so far as to participate in something you cannot enjoy. Here's an example of how you might convey this:

"You know, Joe, I'm very eager to go out with you, but I'm not sure I'd be comfortable driving with your four children to the coast to see your former mother-in-law when we really haven't had a chance to get acquainted yet. Could we start off by doing something that would be a little easier for me, like going on a picnic or something?"

Regarding the second rule, keep in mind that the central purpose of most first appointments is to get acquainted. This is not likely to happen in activities which exclusively involve time with other people or passive entertainment. Doing something with another couple (double-dating, it used to be called) may be reassuring and take the rough edges off the acquaintanceship process, but it definitely slows up your getting to know the other person. Similarly, you aren't going to share much personal information in a discotheque, where you have to shout above the music even to order your drinks. So, get in some alone time together—the more the better.

Finally, extraordinarily expensive or lengthy engagements are generally poor choices, since such encounters involve a considerable investment by both parties. Believe me, it's easier to reconcile yourself to the fact that you don't particularly want to continue seeing someone after spending an hour over a drink than it is after an entire weekend of skiing for which you've volunteered to pay. And it is easier to say no to someone who has treated you to a cup of tea than it is to a person who has forked over a hundred dollars for an evening in the city. A luncheon, an invitation to your home for dinner, a game of tennis, or a short sail followed by some talk time are better alternatives. Take it easy—and perhaps that's as good a way as any to sum up the three rules. Remember, if you and your companion do find you want to stay together longer or to meet again, you can.

What to Talk About

First of all, I hope you'll try not to worry too much about what to talk about your first time of getting together. Nothing can make you more tongue-tied than worrying about what you're going to say. If you are overly concerned about this, you may be making the mistake I discussed earlier of viewing dating as something terribly different from other kinds of adult companionship. In general, you will simply want to talk about the same kinds of things you talk about with other new acquaintances.

But to really get to know others, you've got to get personal. You have all sorts of things to find out about them—their history, where they've been, what they've done, and how they feel about it. You'll want to find out what he or she does for a living, for fun, for friends; his or her life-style, standards, and values. And you'll especially want to get a line on where he or she is in regard to personal relationships with the other sex. You want this information, I hope, not to come to some instant judgment of the suitability of this person as a primary partner but simply to get to know him or her as a person. Of course, you will use this information to determine how the two of you will fit together in some relationship just as you would with any other new friend. And, of course, the other person will usually be working to get the same sort of line on you. So, between you, there's plenty to talk about. In fact, there's potentially more to talk about at this point in your relationship than there ever will be again.

There are basically two kinds of intimate sharing, and you may find it useful to know the distinction between them. *Confiding* is sharing personal information about yourself, your own history, your feelings about yourself, and your feelings toward others in your current life—with the exception of the person you are with. *Openness* is turning your attention *to* this person and sharing your feelings about him or her, discussing your hopes or fears about his or her feelings toward you, and exploring the quality of your relationship. This open communication is the more difficult for most of us, but it is also the more critical type of sharing for the building of real intimacy. You can begin open communication early by sharing any honest, positive impressions you have of the other person. And you can easily share your own feelings of uncertainty about how you are coming across to your companion in the early stages of your time together. In other words, openness can begin early in relatively nonthreatening areas, setting the stage for later openness in more difficult but more essential ones.

In general, though, the building of intimacy is furthered most during the initial stages by confiding. Again, early confiding may be restricted to relatively neutral topics and later spread to more intimate confidences. If you are sensitive to yourself and your partner, you can usually determine the level of openness and confiding with which you are both comfortable. Your own self-disclosure is often the easiest way to signal that personal intimacy is O.K. with you, and it usually prompts your companion to greater sharing. You may be concerned, of course, that such intimacy on a first encounter may be premature. No such thing. It is best, at least at some level, that your relationship with one who might become important to you begin with open, honest, and significant communication. Generally, the longer you wait to begin the building of intimacy the more self-conscious you will be about it. Sex often begins early; why not a little intimacy?

Your Relationship Status and History

When any two people begin a relationship, each begins to learn where the other is in regard to relationships. Although the timing of this exchange of information will vary from couple to couple, at least some of it will be expected fairly soon. It is generally agreed, for example, that it's only fair for people to reveal their marital status very early in the sequence. And to really know someone, you need at least a brief outline of their *relationship history* and at least a sketchy notion of their current *relationship status*. In this day, the acquaintanceship process is typically much faster and less formal than it was even a few years ago. It is quite appropriate —and indeed often expected—for such an exchange of information on the first meeting.

In discussing the need for telling family and friends about your separation in Chapter 1, I introduced you to the short-story/long-story notion for communicating the necessary separation story to others. The same idea applies here. Sooner or later, and more often sooner, you will want to indicate where you've been and where you're at in relation to relationships. Early in the acquaintanceship chain, you can ordinarily give that information in short form, or incidentally in the dialogue about other things. The purpose of this sharing is obviously not to stimulate jealousy or to seek therapy for whatever relationship problems you may have, but to allow the other person to know you, to know as much of your past as is relevant at any given stage of your acquaintance. Being deliberately vague or mysterious about current or past relationships is one of the ways people play dating games and keep their partners off balance. Honesty, in measured and carefully delivered doses, is far better than mysterious silence in such matters.

Also, it is one of the best ways to elicit the same sharing of information by your partner; self-disclosure prompts self-disclosure. As you offer something of your personal history and see how it is received and to what extent it is reciprocated, you can judge accordingly how much more to offer. In this way you can start this process slowly and pace your mutual sharing so that both of you are comfortable with it. If you are uncomfortable at the prospect of early self-disclosure, just go somewhat more slowly. The process will be the same; it will merely take longer. But don't wait too long—try to get into it as soon as you can.

In your mutual sharing, you are basically getting to know one another on the one issue which will most directly affect you each in relation to the other—how each of you thinks about and handles relationships generally. Now, that's important; such discussions build intimacy or signal incompatibility. On a more specific aspect of this issue of relationships, the comfort of both parties is not always the only consideration. For example, it may be uncomfortable for your new friend to tell you that he or she has a spouse and two children in the suburbs, but it is absolutely necessary for you to know this in order to make your own decisions about the relationship. And you, of course, owe the same honesty to others.

A friend of mine, during his throes of separation from the woman he'd been with for some time, began seeing another. Wanting to reassure his newfound friend of his interest in her, he chose to speak negatively to her about his partner of two years. He was critical, blaming, and complaining. His new companion, who later became his wife, told him how turned off she was by this performance.

"When you talk like that," she said, "it makes me wonder how you talk about me when I'm not around or how you would talk about me if things didn't work out between us. The way you treat her is likely to be the way you would treat me. And I don't always like what I see." My friend learned quickly and shut up. He also saw that being kind to his former partner was more reassuring to his new partner than his making unkind remarks had been. He felt he had learned a profound lesson.

Many of us move from one relationship to another without a neat closure of one before beginning the next. In these competing or overlapping relationships, the way we treat all the people involved is a measure of our humanity and caring, and to the degree that the people we become involved with are also human and caring, they will so measure us. Singles can take care of each other even when they don't get along or are in competition.

So, in the beginning exchanges of your relationship history and present status, try to keep in mind the lesson learned by my friend—and overall, remember the necessity for honest self-disclosure, no matter how gradual.

FIRST IMPRESSIONS

When you begin to see someone you find attractive, it is only natural to want to impress him or her. You may do this by accentuating the things about yourself you think will be attractive to this particular person, or by playing up those tastes and interests you both share to make you appear more compatible. You may pretend to like certain pastimes, to hold certain views or ideals of which you think the other approves. You may conceal faults, enhance virtues, and generally present an image of yourself that is, although positive, fundamentally inaccurate. And you may very well get away with it. That's when the trouble begins: either the other will either reject you because he or she is not attracted to the kind of person you have presented yourself to be, or he or she will be attracted to you for the false image you have created. You lose either way. In the second alternative, you are stuck with the image you have created—stuck with an uncomfortable and impossible role in what otherwise might have developed into the most intimate of human relationships.

In their book, *Pairing*, George Bach and Ronald Deutsch cite evidence that people usually stick tenaciously to first impressions. In one way or another, they demand consistency with an initial impression and are disturbed by discrepancies. Besides your being stuck with that false first impression, the more you build it, the more difficulty you are building for the time when you want to relax and be yourself. You must then go to considerable effort to modify that first impression, often causing the other to feel confused and misled. Or you are forced to continue the pretense—ensuring that the inevitable confrontation with reality will be even more disruptive.

In any case, it's impossible to know what qualities others are looking for in a companion, and your idea of your perfect self may be less attractive and less human than the self you actually are. Perhaps the most important virtue of intimate relationships exists in the permission they give for each of us to be completely ourselves. You can rob yourself of such a relationship by trying to charm a potential intimate with an image you guess he or she would prefer. It is too easy to guess wrong. And, if someone you are attracted to really does prefer a person fundamentally different from the real you, you will be far better off without him or her.

ETIQUETTE

Where a woman is accompanied by a man, it is always assumed that the man is the host and he is expected to do the ordering (except at lunch, when she may give her own order). After the woman has had a few minutes to look over the menu presented to her by a waiter, he says, "What do you think you'd like to have?" She chooses, preferably the table d'hôte—the meal in which everything is included in the price of the entrée—and says what she will have, beginning with the first course if there is no extra charge for it. . . . Where a woman accompanied by a man is asked directly by the waiter what she will have, she looks at the proffered card and then tells her host what she wishes to eat except at lunch, when she may order directly. . . . Too, she may, at either lunch or dinner, ask the waiter a direct question if she wishes, such as,

"Are the snails prepared with much garlic?"
Then, if the answer is satisfactory, she turns to
her host at dinner and says, "Good, then I'll
have snails." [Amy Vanderbilt, *New Complete
Book of Etiquette*, 1963, p. 582.]

If things ever were this simple (or complicated),
they are no more. Changes in our society, particularly
those reflected in and furthered by the women's movement, have challenged all rules of etiquette governing
male-female relationships. Although these changes may
be slightly disquieting to some, the new mores allow
men and women to begin to work out relationships
which suit them—to do it openly in the beginning of
their time together and without the concern that they
are doing something unusual or in violation of some
standard. So the lack of rules need not be seen as a
tragic loss of values or custom, but may be viewed as
an opportunity to live and relate to others unbound
by somebody else's rules. While the simple issues of
etiquette concerning who orders dinner, who opens
doors, who lights cigarettes, and who pays for what may
seem minor, the way in which these issues are decided
can reflect how other, more important issues are decided
between the people involved. Without overemphasizing
their importance, you should be aware that they are
issues which, in one way or another, are to be settled,
and that the solutions and the way they are arrived at
can have implications for the rules by which your relationship will be governed.

Many of these etiquette issues are, of course, resolved implicitly. This is fine if both people do in fact

agree on the rules os established. Thus, if a man consistently helps his female companion on and off with her coat, through doors, and through public places, and the woman appreciates and graciously complies with and waits for these courtesies, these traditional rules have been implicitly agreed upon. In this case, there is no need to negotiate anything. If a man fails to do any of these things and his companion endorses this and clearly takes the initiative in these matters, there is similarly no need for discussion.

But wherever there is some concern about offending the other person through failure to follow traditional rules, or where there is conflict in people's preferences, there is need for discussion. The man is at a disadvantage in redefining the etiquette rules because it is generally he who is stuck with the more active, courtesy-giving role. A sensitive man may understandably be concerned about displeasing his companion by appearing discourteous when he merely wishes to be free of a rigid prescription for his behavior. For example, if a woman is obviously waiting for a man to display his gentlemanliness in some traditional way, this would be a poor time for him simply to go about his business without discussing the desired redefinition of etiquette on the spot. When it is more important to the man that he please his companion but he is unsure of how to do so, he may simply follow the traditional rule.

In general, the same alternatives are available to women, although they may be employed somewhat differently. A woman may simply take the initiative in putting on her own coat, opening her own door, or lighting her own cigarette. In these times of changing mores, this kind of behavior should be readily understood. Nevertheless, many women have told me that men of their acquaintance have been slightly offended by these bits of self-sufficiency, and if you are concerned about offending, one of the other alternatives might be more comfortable for you. You can verbally redefine the rule, or when the conventions are relatively meaningless to you or when a redefinition may come later, you can wait for the man's lead and follow it. Again, any of these alternatives is most acceptable.

The fundamental purpose of etiquette is, of course, to express consideration for others; hence the one basic rule is to be thoughtful and kind. The specific ways in which these qualities are shown are of no real importance, if they serve this purpose. In this spirit, contemporary couples trade off traditional courtesies to each other, irrespective of the conventional sex-role assignment of the courtesy. They retain the spirit of taking care of each other without the rigidity of the rules.

Who Pays?

The issue of who pays for what, when, and how is somewhat more difficult for most couples to settle, in part because it is more likely to affect and be affected by other factors in their relationships. In the past, there were many reasons why the male's traditional obligation to pay for everything made more sense. Foremost, of course, was the fact that ordinarily it was the man who initiated the occasion and, as host, was responsible for the expense. Relationship patterns are somewhat different today, and even a first time together can evolve so that both parties participate in deciding what to do and how or whether the expense should be shared. If not initially, such sharing often takes effect as the couple spend more time together. It cannot be assumed that men have more available funds for such entertaining, and many women now concerned with achieving equality and independence often see paying their own way as symbolic of that new status. They do not want the obligation of being treated; they do not want to feel bought and paid for. For their part, many men resent a rigid obligation to pay another's way and do not want to be required to purchase someone else's companionship. Many contemporary men and women feel that a more equitable sharing of joint expenses is not only more fair but more respectful of individual rights.

In general, I share that view and, as the question often arises in my work with singles, I shall offer some guidelines for considering it. One guideline is to think of shared recreational activities on the guest-host dimension. Thus, if any person invites another for a specific event, he or she may be assuming the role of host, and the expectation that he or she will take care of the expenses of the guest is warranted. Such an assumption becomes less justified as the time, place, and activity are more negotiated and evolve from both participants. For example, if a man invites a woman out to dinner, especially for the first time, she may reasonably expect that he will pay for it. If, however, she suggests that they go to a particular place for a drink after dinner, it would be just as reasonable these days for him to expect her to pay for some or all of this. But since such things are extraordinarily variable, *she* had better carry enough money to help out with the dinner bill, just in case—and *he* had better not accept her suggestion for after-dinner drinks unless he can buy them if he has to!

Sometime during the early stages of a new relationship, the couple should discuss the question of who pays. Perhaps it is least awkward for the woman to initiate the discussion, either directly or indirectly. If done directly, she would simply offer to pay for or contribute to the cost of some shared event. This would give the man an opportunity to state his preferred position on the general question and for the couple to reach some understanding about it. If done indirectly, either party could bring up the topic as part of a general discussion of contemporary relations between men and women. (Indeed, this is one of the best and most innocuous ways of feeling out the other person on any number of issues regarding dating, sex, and relationships.) If both people can discuss the money question openly, they can determine whether their expectations are congruent or whether there is conflict that requires negotiation. If the woman fails to bring up the question and the man becomes impatient, he has every right to bring it up.

If a couple decide to divide the expenses of their shared activities, such a division need not necessarily be rigidly 50–50. One person may simply have more money than the other and genuinely wish to assume the expenses of certain activities which the other could not afford. At one time or another, one person may be willing and able to put more than the other into the cost of their doing something that they could not otherwise do together. If they have developed a generally amicable guideline on their dating tastes and expenses, they will not need to discuss each occasion as a new problem—or go to the trouble of an exact dollar-for-dollar accounting. But if either member of the couple feels insistent on a strict 50–50 arrangement, they must negotiate in a more detailed way about what they will and will not do; also, they will have to gauge their activities to the budget of the less affluent—or more thrifty—member.

Once again, the outcome of this negotiation is less important than the process of arriving at it. A process in which both parties respect the feelings and budget limitations of the other should yield an outcome that strengthens and deepens the relationship—the more so because this is not an easy issue to resolve in a relationship; but it can't be avoided. When you don't decide this one deliberately, you decide it undeliberately, and the way you tackle it is likely to reflect the way you will, as a couple, decide other difficult issues. If you want an open, trustful, adult relationship in other matters, pay attention to this one. Though money isn't everything, money is a fact of life that all of us must cope with, and its handling in a relationship can symbolize a great deal.

In all relationship issues, it is fruitless to try to find the one correct way of doing things. There isn't any such thing. Rather, it is necessary to find ways of doing things that show respect for the rights and feelings and even the hang-ups of those involved. Though the questions of etiquette and who pays may seem trivial at first, the traditional rules on these matters give persistent and often subtle support for saddling men with all the privileges and burdens of social dominance and saddling women with all the privileges and burdens of social submission. These issues are important because their solutions symbolize the way your relationship is structured. Negotiating about etiquette and who pays provides an opportunity for accommodating to, and loving others.

DATING GAMES

When Ken walked into the group one Monday night, he looked like a beaten man. It was obvious to everyone that something hurtful had happened to this usually cheerful and self-possessed young businessman. When asked what it was, Ken shrugged and told us this rather involved story:

"I've got a woman on my hands who's driving me absolutely nuts. I've known her three weeks, and she's caused me more grief than my ex-wife did in six years." Urged on by the group, he continued, "Lenore and I met only three weekends ago. Our meeting was really romantic. She had run out of gas and was standing helplessly by her car when I drove up. She's a beautiful woman, and I was terribly attracted to her from the start. I drove her to a gas station . . . we laughed a lot and seemed to hit it off immediately. We've been together a lot since then.

"The first two weeks were great, except that Lenore was pretty uptight about sleeping with me, but after a week or so we'd broken down that barrier. We planned to spend this past weekend together, from Friday to Monday morning. Well, we were going to meet Friday at

my place for cocktails and dinner right after work—
anyway, *I* thought it was right after work. We both get
off at four thirty, and I expected her to be at my place
by five. But I was left cooling my heels in my apartment
until nine twenty, when Lenore comes waltzing in,
bubbling all over and carrying a large bag of groceries.
She says, 'Darling, I've got the most wonderful things
for our dinner.' I could have belted her! She carries on
about all the great things she's brought for dinner and
how glad she is to see me, while I try to stay cool and
see if she's going to have the courtesy to apologize for
being four and a half hours late.

Finally, I asked her where the hell she'd been, and
why she didn't call me. She said something like, 'Well,
we didn't specify a time, and I thought you were more
casual about time than you apparently are. I always like
to eat dinner late on weekends, and I went out after
work with some marvelous friends in the office. Then I
had to go home and change, and then I had to go out
and buy groceries for our dinner.'

"In the process of telling her how angry I'd been
the last four and a half hours, I confessed that I called
her at home and at work, where I had talked to one of
her fellow workers whom I know. Now, that was a problem because she told me that she didn't want anyone
at work—or her close friends, for that matter—to know
about us because they gossip so much. That never made
much sense to me, but I went along with it, but after
three and a half hours' waiting, I went ahead and
called. Anyway, when I told her about that, she really
flew off the handle. She accused me of totally misunderstanding her, of going back on my word, of being
ungrateful for the effort she went to for dinner, and of

being uptight and spying on her. And then she just stormed out. So it's me and the television set in there going crazy until about midnight, when the phone rings. She apologizes for being late and for getting so upset and running out. She told me she loved me. I accepted that apology, and I guess I apologized a little bit too, and then I asked her over. She said she'd gone to a nearby bar for a couple of drinks and was tired now and wanted to go home and go to bed. She was only five minutes away, and I couldn't really understand her, but I accepted it. She promised to come over 'first thing in the morning' and fix me a marvelous breakfast, and promised we could spend the day together. I almost asked exactly what time 'first thing in the morning' was, but I was trying to be cool, so I didn't.

"Well, I was up at seven thirty and by eight I was ready to have my marvelous breakfast. When she wasn't there by nine thirty, I started wondering the same sort of things I'd wondered about last night: Who were these marvelous friends at the office that she's been with after work? Where did she really go after she left my place? And if she loved me so much and was so apologetic and was only five minutes away, why couldn't she come over? Why was she so concerned about her roommate and other friends not knowing about me? And who else is she seeing? You see, I had tried to find out from her what other relationships she had, but somehow I was never answered, and somehow I never have learned about that.

"Now, at eleven thirty, she finally does come by, and she really can cook a great breakfast. But then, just as I'm about to plan the rest of our day, she says she has to drive out to her boss's house by the lake to deliver some papers. I offer to drive her and plan something out there, but she says no, her boss and some of his colleagues will be there, and it would be better if I didn't. Again, I wondered whether she's seeing her boss or someone else at the office, but I keep the wondering to myself. But at least by now I've learned to pin Lenore down on time. She promises to be back by five to fix the dinner we didn't have last night and go to a party which some of my friends were having. Well, she comes back at six (not late enough for me to say anything but late enough to bother me), and we have a really nice time and a fine dinner.

"We both were a tiny bit looped on drinks and the dinner wine, and we started to get friendly, you know, and I was just incredibly excited and wanted to make love—that woman can turn me on more than anybody I've ever known. But she didn't want to. She said it would just mess her up before the party and that we could always make love later. Well, then we go to the party, and Lenore attracts men like honey attracts flies. And she loves it. She spent about an hour out on the deck with Dick, an old friend of mine, *and* in the middle of the party she courteously excused herself and went into the bedroom to make a long telephone call. Well, I want to tell you, by the end of that party I was pissed. When we left and got into the car, I let her have it. I told her all the things she'd done wrong and all the things that I'd been wondering about since Friday. Did I get any answers? Hell, no! She just cried and asked me to take her home, which I did gladly. When I pulled away from her at the curb, I laid rubber just like I'd done in high school. God, this whole thing is just like high school, isn't it?

"Well, I had a hard time getting to sleep Saturday. I was mad at Lenore, mad at Dick, and maddest of all at myself. I finally got to sleep around three or four in the morning, and was up again at seven. When I woke up I began to have doubts about what I had done. I put myself in Lenore's position and saw that perhaps on Friday she just wanted to have some time with her friends at work and then change her clothes and pick up some things before spending the weekend with me. Even though I had planned to take us out to dinner, it was awfully nice of her to pick up all those things and to want to cook for us after working all day. And I could see how she might have misunderstood about the time. I sleep better in my own bed too, and if she were really tired, maybe it was understandable that she went home that night. And then on Saturday, well, I could see why it could be important to her to keep her private life separate from her office life—she might not want me to come and meet all of her bosses. And, of course, it's not her fault if men are attracted to her, and she and Dick really do have a lot of things in common.

"So, anyway, I finally began to feel guilty for my childishness and jealousy, and I called her up and asked if we could get together and talk. So I went over to her house about noon, and we had a really nice talk, apologized to each other, and hugged and kissed, and she told me again how much she loved me and I told her the same thing. And then, about three, she said I had to leave. Of course, I asked why, and she said that someone had called and asked her out for the afternoon to sail and go for dinner. I tried to find out when that happened, and I'm not completely sure about when it did, but one thing she said to me was that she didn't know how our talk was going to go, and if it went badly she just knew she'd have to be with somebody. So, I assume that she accepted the date after we had agreed to our talk. Well, I told her that and told her I didn't understand, and she just kept repeating the same excuse. Then she said that it was really me she loved, and she promised to call me after her date was over, and, if it wasn't too late, she'd come over and spend the night. Well, now I knew I shouldn't go along with that, but, you see, I didn't want her to sleep with anybody else, and I was kind of blown away by the whole thing at that point and just said O.K. and left.

"Well, I spent another lonely evening by the TV, thinking lots of uncomfortable thoughts. She finally called at midnight and said she had just gotten home and was really tired and that she couldn't come. She said, 'I still love you.' And this time, I was just beaten. I didn't say anything because I couldn't think of anything to say. I thought about calling her back to see if she really was at home, but that would have been humiliating. I confess, too, I even thought about driving by her place to see if her car was parked outside. I'm proud to say I didn't do that either. I didn't get much sleep last night, though. I just don't know what to do with Lenore. What do you think I should do?"

What we have here is a hard-core case of dating games. Clearly, Lenore takes the initiative and seizes the advantage in this game, and whether she knows it or not, she is an expert player. She delivers a smashing serve, and her follow-up shots are equally masterful. But Ken doesn't walk off the court either. He plays the game by responding in the best way he knows how but, as you have seen, loses every point. If things continue this way, he will probably opt out of the game sooner or later after many sleepless nights.

The sheer beauty of this ugly game is in its subtlety. For every move, Lenore has an acceptable rationale for her behavior. Each separate instance, taken by itself, seems innocent enough. But the pattern is obvious to the most sympathetic observer. Many of the popular types of dating-game behavior are represented in Lenore's maneuvers, and of course Ken also plays the game, albeit poorly, in his anger and jealousy and his attempts to play it cool, restraining his spontaneous reactions to the things which trouble him. I do not mean to imply that Ken would necessarily always be better off to level with Lenore in all matters; I am only indicating Ken's part of the game.

This scenario represents a game because the recurring transactions, though somewhat plausible on the surface, are determined by concealed or ulterior motivations. We know Ken's motivations because he has told us, but we can only guess at Lenore's. Furthermore, there is a repetitive win-loss quality to the interaction itself, as both players attempt to gratify their hidden needs. As Ken recounted his weekend, he fell into the most natural trap of the dating game's losing player: he tried to discover the *true* motivation for Lenore's behavior. The group contributed to this endeavor by listing all the things that Ken had thought of and then some. Perhaps Lenore was just a very spontaneous and thoughtless person, and there was nothing more here to find. Perhaps she was ambivalent about spending an entire weekend with Ken and was not comfortable with the level of commitment she felt that represented. Perhaps she wanted very much to get close to him but feared his rejection of her, and wanted to test him by putting him through this emotional wringer. Perhaps she had met someone else she liked better, but either was unwilling to tell Ken or didn't want to let him go as yet. Perhaps, suggested one woman in a flash of self-insight, she was afraid of her vulnerability to Ken and wanted to show repeatedly that she was not as vulnerable to him as he could be made vulnerable to her. Somebody pointed out that Lenore must care for him to some degree or she wouldn't go to all this trouble to play such an elaborate game. Finally, somebody else pointed out that Ken would never be able to guess Lenore's motivations. In fact, he said, Lenore herself might very well be unaware of them. Now, that was helpful. Ken would never know for sure what Lenore's motivations were, and though he could ask her, her track record suggested that she would very likely be unable or unwilling to tell him.

Ken spent a good deal of time in the group focusing on his jealousy, his bewilderment, and his anger at himself. The inwardly directed anger was a result of his blaming himself for being unable to see the game quickly and change it. Like so many losers of such games, he was downing himself because someone chose him for her game and treated him badly, because he played along, unwittingly and defensively, and because he lost. This, of course, is Ken's most serious mistake.

Allowing your self-esteem to be determined by the behavior of another is a deadly trap. It divests you of control and makes you more vulnerable than you ever need to be. When other people treat you poorly, this says infinitely more about them than it does about you.

Because we live in interdependent relationships with one another, we are all vulnerable to those who, for whatever reason, choose to break commitments or otherwise prey on that natural vulnerability. But in fact, no one can ever make a fool of you; they can merely breach common trust and disappoint you in the process. When you think that you are diminished by the behavior of another, you're wrong. The group was especially helpful to Ken in reinforcing this view. Ken was not depreciated by Lenore's expertly executed game. His reactions, while less than perfect, were most understandable, and now that he saw the game for what it was, he could decide what to do about it. Indeed, participating in the game and losing it showed him what the game was all about and illustrated at least one way of *not* winning it.

Most people who are single for any length of time and active in the single-dating scene will be the object of some dating-game maneuvers. When this happens to you, it is critical that, no matter what you do about it, you think about it properly. Remember, you can never decipher with certainty the motivations of those who initiate the game, so don't waste your time trying. Furthermore, you are not depreciated by the unfortunate behavior of another person; such actions are primarily his or her problem. And, finally, being "taken" in such a game teaches you something about how *not* to play it.

Ken told his story just as he had arrived at a choice point. He could opt out of the relationship and the game altogether. He could accept Lenore as she was and make no attempt whatever to change her. Or he could decide to stay in the relationship and attempt to change his and her behavior in order to stop the game. We explored each alternative together. He wasn't ready to throw in the towel as yet, he said, but he would if there were many more weekends like the one he'd just been through. In realizing this, Ken recognized that he had ultimate control. He saw that he could stop the game instantly and at any time by simply refusing to play it. That seemed to help.

In discussing Ken's second alternative, his accepting Lenore as she was, we pointed out that he could decide the games were Lenore's problem and that, although they provided a minor nuisance for him, he didn't have to do anything to put an end to them. Like a pacifist, he could merely refuse to fight and accept this little part of humanity just as he found it. Ken thought this solution had a nice ring to it, but he had to confess that this honestly wasn't him. He very much wanted Lenore to stop playing the game and felt he had to stop seeing her if she didn't; he just couldn't honestly accept it. Parenthetically, it is my educated guess that a show of pacifist behavior from Ken resulting from this total acceptance of Lenore would have been a more effective way than any other to put a stop to her game. But Ken correctly rejected this approach because it wasn't right for him, so we had to move on to the final alternative.

The last course of action, trying to stop the game, meant playing to win. Winning meant the end of the game; playing meant consciously doing whatever would end it. As long as Ken continued to interact with Lenore and she continued to play the game, he would be playing too. Since he could not accept her totally, he would hope to be able to change her behavior. Whether he liked it or not, he was placing himself in a position where he had to manipulate her in his attempt to change her behavior. Whether he became outraged at what she did, ignored it, discussed it at length, refused to interact with her unless she behaved the way he wanted her to—whatever he did that involved him in this struggle would be part of the game.

In looking for a winning strategy, Ken could see that what he'd been doing was not the game plan of choice. He had lost and felt bad, not only about Lenore but about himself. Whatever he had to do to win this game, it was clear that he must stop doing what he'd been doing. We knew that this game like all others takes at least two to play, and we suspected that Ken's reactions were a significant factor in sustaining the game for Lenore. His anger, jealousy, and frustration had undoubtedly been a part of her confirmation or payoff, whether she was out to prove her lack of vulnerability or Ken's greater vulnerability, her independence or his dependence, or whatever. To stop the game, Ken had to react differently in some significant respect. Following this line of reasoning, the first thing he might try, the group thought, was simply to stop showing anger, jealousy, suspicion, disappointment, and hurt pride. But how, when he felt all of these things so strongly?

All the group members agreed that Ken would do well to have a calm, understanding, nonaccusatory talk with Lenore. He had to let her know that her actions made him feel bad—to admit his vulnerability rather than denying it, only to reveal it later in a fit of temper.

He was advised to be open with her about how her behavior affected him and their relationship. The consensus was that he might find it worthwhile to ask her to confide in him as to the nature of her other relationships. In order to facilitate this, he not only would have to assure her of his acceptance of whatever he learned but also would have to mean it. Although this was difficult for him, he knew that anything was better than his agonizing uncertainty. It was time he knew the real score.

Finally, I summarized what Ken's game plan could be: First, he would calmly tell Lenore that, while he didn't like some of the things she did, he realized he still was unable to stop her from doing them, and that he still liked her; that he further realized he was vulnerable to her and that she could hurt him, but that since there was absolutely nothing he could do to change her behavior, he was going to stop trying. Next, after telling her these things, he would try not to react with negative emotion to any of her game maneuvers and would avoid her as much as possible during those times when he could not maintain his more philosophical attitude, always reminding himself of his option to quit playing whenever he chose. Rather than hope to deal with her pleasantly and in an accepting way when she was maddeningly late, I recommended that he simply leave and go about his business. The shock of not finding him waiting for her might be good for her, especially if he could be calm and nonpunitive about it when she later caught up with him. Ken especially liked this suggestion. The strategy, of course, was to cut off the reward or payoff for Lenore and to put Ken back in control of himself as much as possible.

Our reasoning was that, when Ken admitted his vulnerability to Lenore, he would do a good deal to eliminate her need to prove it. When he reacted calmly to her, he would remove the angry attention we guessed helped to maintain her behavior. And when he refused to wait for her for unreasonable periods of time, he would cease to reinforce her discourteous disruption of his time and attention. Perhaps most important in all this was that the strategy would give Ken a viable, consistent stand to take in relation to Lenore. He need no longer be so unsure of himself, to be buffeted about by his own vulnerability and Lenore's unpredictable actions. He would gain control of himself.

To pull this off, Ken would have to see that his blaming Lenore was illogical, destructive of his ability to deal with her, and generally a waste of time and energy. He objected that he didn't want her to "walk all over him," but the group pointed out that she was walking all over him only if he saw it that way and that he was vulnerable to her mistreatment only as long as he chose to be. Realistically, nothing that she might do to him could do him any real harm; she could only hurt his pride and inconvenience him a little. It was further pointed out that, while he could do almost nothing to *ensure* a change in her behavior, the maneuvers that helped protect his own feelings could also bring about some change in her. True, he would still be playing a game, since he could hardly turn off all interest in effecting such a change in Lenore. He was not being completely straightforward about his objectives.

Does a person have the right to be this manipulative? Of course he does! He has the right to want what he wants and to employ ethical means to get it. Far from being unethical, failing to act childish when one feels childish represents growth toward maturity and control. Unthinking or rigid honesty is not always a virtue. If Ken wanted to go to the trouble to deliberately control his reactions in order to discourage Lenore from her games-playing, that was his right. Here's the motto I suggested to Ken: *Don't play games unless you have to; but if you have to, play to win* (i.e., to stop the game).

Several other good suggestions were forwarded by the group. John, a group member, offered two important strategies: that Ken actively prove he could respond well to unpleasant information, and that he reward Lenore for her honesty, punctuality, thoughtfulness, or whatever else he wanted to encourage. John told of a recent personal incident: a woman in whom he was most interested called to break a date with him. At first, she didn't tell him the reason, and he accepted without a word her apparent unwillingness to talk about it. But when she finally did confess to him that an old boyfriend was unexpectedly coming to town and that she felt obligated to see him, our model group member said he understood completely and praised her for her honesty and openness in telling him. She then called him at seven thirty the morning after the broken date to reassure him that the reunion was fine but uneventful and that she couldn't wait to see John again. "So," he advised Ken, "whenever Lenore does something right, tell her; let her know you can be trusted with things you don't want to hear, and she'll tell you more."

Ken looked like a different person after that session,

and the group was invigorated by the good hard work they had done for Ken and themselves. What was the outcome? Ken did very well from then on, with a little periodic bolstering from the group. Lenore continued to play her games, but with reduced intensity, and at this writing was slowly opening up to Ken. Nevertheless, where their relationship will go is less important than the distance Ken and the group covered in their struggle to cope with the dating game.

Men, of course, initiate their share of dating games. The maneuvers illustrated in this case—breaking commitments, chronic lateness, vagueness about other relationships—are as common to men as women. A more direct maneuver engaged in by men is *breaking precedent*. When men establish such precedents as regular calling and regular dating, they can convey a telling message by breaking one of them and then denying, when confronted, that any message was meant at all. This, of course, is usually nonsense, and it is well to identify this game calmly if it is played on you. Other game plays engaged in by both men and women: failing to call when promised; stimulating jealousy by excessive talking of other relationships; inconsistency in expressing feelings ("I love you" but I call you once every three weeks); stating future intent but failing to make good on it (promise me you'll fly away with me so I can neglect to invite you); failing to show up for an appointment (the topper).

In each of these cases, I usually recommend that the object of the game identify it calmly and in a nonaccusatory manner. Although good players in the dating game can always find an acceptable rationale and deny the gamy quality of their behavior, they cannot deny the feelings their behavior produces in you. If the other cares for you, he or she will ordinarily care about and be responsive to those feelings—justified or not. Rather than arguing about what your partner *should* do or how you *should* feel, you can begin to talk about how both of you can behave to make each other feel better. If, as the object of the game, you can show your willingness to work at that level—to listen and to work things out—you may be able to stop the games. But don't count on it!

Good game players are hard to change. Before undertaking the task, be sure it's worth the effort. And remember, there's nothing wrong with playing to win.

BEGINNING AGAIN

Dating is good for you. Especially if you are one of the newly single, all the evidence indicates that dating can be one of the very most important things you can do to feel good about single living. True, at first it can make you feel a little silly, a little awkward, a little out of place. Problems often arise as two people begin to know each other and try to adapt to each other's needs without denying their own. In some ways it is harder now because there is no set of rules to prescribe your own or others' behavior. But for this very reason, you may now begin immediately to relate to a person rather than a role. And you can begin to build a relationship that suits your mutual needs. The lack of a predetermined script for early relating allows you to practice real communication from the beginning. Though there are

aspects of the process that are going to be a little uncomfortable, it is a process from which you can learn
and grow. Don't let the minor irritations that come with
beginning again hold you back. Do it!

A GUIDING PRINCIPLE

Many of the matters discussed in this chapter are
a bit superficial, I know. But these simple matters represent the first building blocks on which any relationship
will rest. How these early problems are met can foreshadow the way an entire relationship will develop.

There are some consistent philosophical threads
running through the advice I have offered on each problem—threads which have been and will be interwoven
throughout this book. Let me specify and highlight one
of the most central. It is the principle of simply accepting other people for what they are rather than for what
you want them to be. This principle rests on the sane
adult's capacity to separate what he wants from an objective view of reality—what he can get. You don't
have to like the behavior of another person to accept
him or her—you must merely have the wisdom not to
hate that person for his or her failure to live up to your
expectations or needs. When you truly get this principle,
you see that the worth of others is not dependent on
their ability to meet your needs, and your worth is not
dependent on your ability to meet theirs. It is silly to
blame others for being unable to give you what you
need, silly for others to blame you, and silliest of all for
you to blame yourself.

When you fully understand this, your communications with others will improve dramatically. When people learn that they can tell you what they really think and feel without unduly hurting or threatening or disappointing you, they will. And, when they do, they will treasure you for this rare and liberating quality. And you will treasure many of them, for you will be able to take what they have to give without the haunting feeling that it is never enough.

9

Sensuality and Intimacy

Life without music would be a mistake.
—Friedrich Nietzsche

Imagination is more important than knowledge.
—Albert Einstein

THIS IS THE sex chapter. It is not about where and how to rub, although books which tell you that can be extremely useful. It is not primarily a chapter of sex statistics, although these have been incorporated where they can serve a useful purpose. And it is not a theoretical or moral treatise on sex. Rather, in the spirit of the rest of the book, this chapter is addressed to those sexual issues with which single people are most often concerned. First, and especially for the newly single, we will examine the current state of sex mores in America. Although what other people are doing may not give you any notions whatever about what you should be doing, your being up on current developments will at least let you know what to expect of others in general, and will be certain to help you in dealing with them. And of course, it's always interesting to know what other people are doing sexually.

Managing the beginnings of sex in any relationship often presents difficulties for single men and women, and so this will be the focus of a good deal of this chapter. As you already know, I have addressed almost all of this book to men and women equally. Doing so has been easier than I had imagined, because sex roles really are becoming ever more similar, and there is no question that an egalitarian, nonrestrictive relationship between the sexes is the wave we are riding. Yet, in the area of initial sexual interaction, more traditional role expectations and behavior usually persist. Men have more problems associated with initiating sexual contact and dealing with rejection, while women have more difficulty with the passive and sometimes defensive position or responding to initiations and saying no. And yet, as women increasingly take on the more active role in dating and sex, they inevitably face the task of initiating and the possibility of rejection. In some ways, such problems are more difficult because women are relatively unprepared for this role, and they often share the unrealistic stereotype which suggests that men are always ready for sex with any reasonably attractive woman. Given that perspective, a rejection may be viewed as devastating. Men are perceived as ever-ready sexually because they have been given the social role of initiation. For their part, as men take on the role of the one who must stop rather than start sexual encounters, they may be confused or frightened by it, and this reaction may interfere with sexual interest and performance. They may interpret attempts to place them in this position as a threat to their idea of masculinity. They may be reluctant to say no even when they want to very much because of their acceptance of the stereotype of the ever-ready male and their fear of what failure to live up to it will mean to them as well as to their partners.

So, in spite of the fact that conventional sex-role behavior is still maintained by most people most of the time in initiating early sexual encounters, everyone would now do well to have at least a sympathetic understanding of both roles and to develop the potential ability to play them. This chapter, therefore, will examine the psychology of both the assertive and the passive sexual roles. To the extent that men feel bound by convention to be assertive and women passive, we as men and women do have different concerns about initial sexual encounters, though there is nothing innate about all of this. And no matter which role you play, you will be infinitely better at it if you can more fully appreciate the concerns of the one who plays the other part. As relationships develop, of course, most people tend to break down these fixed roles and are able to move fluidly from one to the other. Indeed, this can begin much earlier than it usually does, and I hope that what is written here will help you achieve that if you want to.

The most important focus of this chapter has to do with the ways in which single people can think and communicate about sex—about its meaning, about its place in relationships, about making it better. Experience has taught me that, in the sexual realm, a constructive attitude about sex and a willingness to communicate and learn about it are by far the most important ingredients for a good sex life. There is no one right way to rub; sexual techniques that are pleasing to one person will be displeasing to another. Even more important, a sexual technique that is very pleasing to a partner at one time may be less pleasing at another and will become downright boring if it becomes rigidly repetitious. Good sex involves the ability to relax and enjoy the journey, to communicate sensitively about it, and to experiment and learn continually. Catching on to this attitude is by far more important than knowing all the moves.

WHAT'S HAPPENING NOW?

In Morton Hunt's recent book, *Sexual Behavior in the Seventies,* he reports the results of a large national survey of American sexual behavior, similar to that conducted by Alfred Kinsey in the late 1940s. A comparison of the results of these two studies tells us whether there has or has not been a sexual revolution in the direction of greater permissiveness. There has.

Among men and women under twenty-five, for example, 81 percent of the women and 95 percent of the men now engage in sexual intercourse before marriage. According to his data this younger group is more prone than older age groups to restrict their sexual intercourse to important relationships; but the younger sexually active singles of both sexes reported an average of two sex partners during the year prior to the survey. Even more liberal sexual attitudes and behaviors were reflected in the responses of singles between twenty-five and thirty-four. Sexually active single men in this age group reported that they had had an average of four sexual partners in the previous year. In the same age group, sexually active women had an average of three sex partners in the previous year. All these figures and others cited by Hunt are strikingly higher than those obtained by Kinsey a generation earlier. Among the young, sexual permissiveness seems to be restrained by the requirement for affection somewhat more than among the divorced and older single people. Considering the entire sample of both married and single people, Hunt found that 60 percent of the men and 30 percent of the women viewed sex as acceptable for unmarried men, even when there was no strong affection between partners, but only 44 percent of the men and 20 percent of the women found non-love-based sex to be acceptable for single women. There is, of course, a much more permissive attitude on this point among older single people than among older married people.

The change in sexual mores from a generation ago was also strikingly reflected in the proportion of people who said they had participated in oral sex. Approximately 70 percent of both men and women had adopted the active role in oral-genital relations (i.e., cunnilingus for men, fellatio for women). More extreme "swinging singles" behavior was found to be less prevalent, however. Among younger single people, for example, only 15 percent of the men and 4 percent of the women had tried partner swapping, but a large proportion of these men and all the women involved had done so only once. Nearly 17 percent of the young men and 5 percent of the young women had experienced sex with more than one partner at a time, although a third of these men and most of the women involved had had only one such experience.

So, while it is clear that there has been a dramatic loosening up of sexual mores in the last generation, the dominant standard among people, both married and single, seems to be characterized by the label "permissiveness with affection." On the other hand, there appears to be a large minority of individuals, especially older single people, whose views and behaviors are more accepting of sexual contact between individuals who do not necessarily have strong affectional ties. In general, sexual interaction is more varied and experimental than it was in the past, but group sex and partner swapping are restricted to a relatively small minority among both married and single people. In summarizing his findings, Hunt writes,

> Though many Americans now use as forms of role-playing coital variations that were shunned by previous generations, while they take a somewhat more unfettered enjoyment in their own sensations, by and large they have added to their repertoire only acts that are biologically and psychologically free from pathology. They remain highly discriminating in the choice of their sex partners and they continue to regard their sexual acts as having deep emotional significance rather than as merely providing uncomplicated sensual gratification.

Some readers may find this factual information somewhat frightening or intimidating because they may mistakenly view it as a demand for a level of sexual permissiveness with which they would be uncomfortable. The behavior of others cannot serve as a model in determining your own. Most single people who have been around at all realize the incredible variability in people's personal preferences concerning sexual interaction, and those who are enlightened respect one another's preferences. The norms reported in Hunt's survey tell you only what to expect on the average; they don't prescribe behavior for you or anyone else. People obviously should have sex with each other only when they both want to, using sexual techniques with which both are comfortable.

On the other hand, these data illustrate some hard facts that must be faced in developing one's own position regarding sexual interaction while single. Chastity is unusual for single people, especially for older singles. Those who hold to it are denying themselves and their relationship partners a form of meaningful and intimate sharing which most other adults enjoy. Such a unilateral denial of this important aspect of intimacy will often strain a relationship and make other alternatives more attractive, especially to the frustrated partner. Nevertheless, there is nothing wrong with this more conservative position on sex as long as one is aware of and able to cope with its disadvantages.

THE GENTLE AND CREATIVE ART OF MUTUAL SEDUCTION

Two true stories: A man and a woman have gone out alone for dinner on their first encounter. They are just beginning the crab cocktail when he turns to her:

He: Well, how about it?

She: How about what?

He: Well, you know, how about going to bed with me?

She: Gulp!

Another man and woman are beginning their first date. As they leave her door, she turns to him:

She: Let's get one thing straight. Just because I'm going out with you tonight doesn't mean I'm going to sleep with you.

These two stories graphically illustrate the two most common problems that people face in trying to cope with the initial phases of a sexual relationship: men, as the typical initiators, often fail to understand the simple dynamics of mutual seduction or are unwilling to take the risks involved in it; and women, more commonly in the passive role, are often so uncomfortable with their inability to say no appropriately that they either avoid situations in which they must say it or blurt it out inappropriately. When the roles are changed, the problem can be the same or even worse. So, let's look carefully at seduction and the various ways of saying no.

Seduction has suffered a bad press. *Webster's New World Dictionary* defines *seduce:* "to tempt to wrongdoing; lead astray . . . to induce to give up one's chastity," implying that there is something intrinsically wrong with the process of initiating intimacy between two people. Why? Certainly one of the two partners will be more interested in an intimate sexual relationship at any given time, or one will be the culturally sanctioned initiator. Someone has to make the first move, and surely most of us would rather have our interest gradually, gently, courteously, sensually aroused than be asked bluntly, "Well, how about it?"

There is a sensitive, respectful form of mutual seduction which involves nothing more than creative mutual communication between two people. It often begins before either person is fully aware of it and follows a path of such little resistance that no one is ever really jarred or surprised or seriously disappointed. Effective seduction is merely good communication with a sensual and playful flair, rather than a predatory process in which the seducer tricks and manipulates an innocent, unwitting other. When two people build intimacy together, one may be more of an initiator than the other, or they may trade off this role. It may be built quickly or slowly, but always *step by step*, involving increasingly more personal and open conversation and affection. Respecting this gentle, gradual process allows the intimacy to develop smoothly, at its own natural rate.

Seduction is talking—talking which develops mutual understanding. Almost everyone feels more comfortable with the closeness of sex after other feelings of closeness have been achieved through intimate talk in the forms of confiding and of openness. As two people share what is important to them through intimate talk, they can gradually allow their feelings about one another to find expression in affection and in sex.

If you are more the initiator in the mutual process, carefully watch the reaction of your partner. If the other person does not reciprocate the intimacy of your talk to the same degree, step back—don't rush it. Talk about the difference in your intimacy timetables if you can do so in a gentle and nondemanding way, but don't go blithely ahead without reciprocation. Others will ordinarily be more attracted to you if your conversation flows easily, if you make them feel comfortable, if you give evidence of liking and respecting them, and if you know them well. These attributes are, of course, supposed to be more pronounced in women than in men, but I suspect that much of this difference, as well as others I'll present, reflects the specialized roles we play in regard to the initiation of sex.

In the course of intimate talk, it is often useful for the initiator of intimacy to signal certain attitudes. Of the four attitudes I am about to formulate, the most important to establish, especially for a man, is that *sex is optional*. For example, if his amorous interest is in a woman who may be accustomed to fending off sexually aggressive and demanding men, it is important that he dissociate himself from that role. When anyone is pre-occupied with maintaining a self-protective stance, he or she is not liable to get very turned on. Good sex requires a relaxed, receptive attitude on the part of both people involved. Unfortunately, many single women who are accustomed to being rushed sexually have adopted a negative, on-guard attitude about it. When a man comes along who is easy and comfortable with whatever happens sexually, who is consistently caring and affectionate without being pushy, there is nothing to defend against. This frees the woman from her preoccu-pation with how she should respond to her partner, allowing her to get in touch with her own affectionate and sexual feelings. In our present cultural context, I believe that one of the most singularly seductive things a man can do is to allow his partner's sexual interest and ardor to find their own free expression—to let her feelings dictate what will happen.

The second attitude which enhances the growth of intimacy is that *affection does not have to lead to sex.* Again, because of the typical role division in seduction, it is often more important for women than for men to be assured of this enlightened position. The rationale is the same. A woman on guard about male expectations will often hold back from all but the most sexually unstimulating affection until she has made up her mind to have intercourse. Now, that's problematic, because it is often affection which allows each partner to discover his or her own level of sexual interest. True, affection forms the base of mutual seduction, but if a woman knows that she can freely show affection without necessarily progressing to sex, that she has a choice, she will be that much more likely to let go and participate in mutual seduction—if not this time, maybe next time.

And if you aren't prepared for that "not this time" —if you give freeing signals without really meaning them —you will appear very untrustworthy. And you will risk jeopardizing your entire relationship. Try to grasp what a relatively minor thing sexual frustration is. If you don't see the real wisdom of these freedom-saving attitudes, consider what David Seaburg tells us in his book, *The Art of Selfishness:*

"High in the art of living comes the wisdom of never letting anyone do anything for you until he is so anxious to do it that you know he is doing it with real joy."

Both men and women will sometimes be reluctant to initiate or participate in mutual seduction and love-making because they fear that the other will think badly of them. So, the third attitude to signal is this: *sex is good*—people who have sex when they want it are good, healthy, and moral human beings.

Another important concern that inhibits both men

and women from seduction and sex involves the meaning it will have either for themselves or for their partners. For this reason, it is often wise to signal what sex would mean to you in your relationship with any other person. Your intended partner may be reluctant to engage in sex with you because he or she thinks it means either too little or too much to you. Most people you encounter will like it better if your sex with them means more than mere sensual gratification, but they may well be relieved if you can let them know that your initial sexual contact does not carry with it the implication of a monogamous and serious commitment. Sometimes, of course, both members of a couple will endorse one of the extremes—either commitment or total casualness—and that's fine. But ordinarily neither extreme will be felt initially, and a mutual signaling of the meaning of your intimacy can make for far greater comfort and avoid many problems.

The fourth and last attitude to signal sounds rather simple-minded, but is no less important than the others. We are all a bit insecure in new relationships and need reassurance that we are liked and appreciated. And the one who is making all or most of the bids for contact or intimacy especially needs to hear this. It is rejection that men in the active role fear most, and in affectional and sexual contacts they fear rejection for inadequate sexual performance. For their part, women, typically placed in the passive role, fear that they are getting affectional and sexual attention only for sexual sport or because it is expected. To counteract such insecurities and concerns, signal this: *"I like you; you're doing fine."* Positive feedback about any likable quality of the other person can do much to further intimacy and trust in a budding relationship—or a well-established one, for that matter. To deal with the other's insecurities about sexual performance, you can signal that whatever happens in sex is O.K. as long as the two-person process is O.K. A relatively ideal sexual adjustment between two people takes time, and high expectations for near-ideal initial sex can ruin it. The achievement ethic is antithetical to good sex.

There is a consistent thread running through these attitudes that can be expressed in many ways, all conveying to the other such assurances as "I'm not dangerous to you; I will respect your rights, your space, your limits; I won't judge you by how well you fulfill my expectations; I won't dislike you if you don't give me what I want; I care enough about you to take care not to hurt you; you are safe with me."

You may rightly ask how you could ever signal such personal things early in a relationship. That's a difficult question to answer, but not impossible—and the answer deserves careful attention because comprehending it is basic to a real understanding of the sensitivity required of good seduction.

First, let's explore the subtle and sensitive art of indirect communication. It is an art as difficult to describe as to master, but one worth the effort required. It has the dual advantage of allowing you to express things earlier than you otherwise could and to set the stage for a more direct expression of the same things at a later time. Let's look at one subtle example of how indirect communication can be used to signal one or more of our four helpful attitudes.

Suppose you have been discussing your relationship history with your date and—as is natural—you have brought the discussion around to sex. You might say something like this: "You know, it's interesting that in all my important relationships it has never really mattered to me how soon I had sex or how good it was. Sometimes it came very early for me and other times it came late. Sometimes it was great at first and other times it took a while to really develop. How sex began has always been more or less incidental to how well the relationship worked out generally."

Now, this simple statement indicates many things. It says that sex is optional; that sex is not of overriding importance to you; that you are not pushy about it; that you can care deeply about another person in spite of the fact that he or she may not be the Mark Spitz or Billy Jean King of indoor screwing; that you don't judge people either positively or negatively on the basis of their performance or the timing of initial sex, and so forth. This is an indirect communication because you have delivered it in another context. Ostensibly you are not talking about your current relationship but about past ones. Nevertheless, most people will make the connection and assume consistency in your past behavior with what you will demonstrate to them in the present.

Even the things you say more or less directly can be stated in such a way that they constitute a gentle communication. Suppose, for instance, that you and your companion are both feeling amorous, but you have real doubts about any long-term relationship developing between you. In other words, you want to make love but you don't want to sign an engagement contract in the process. You may even have great hopes for this relationship but still be wary of any hint of commitment. In that case, you could say something like this: "I would really like to get close to you, but I would feel much more comfortable if we could do that without its meaning any promises for the future. I like you, I'm attracted to you, I want to get closer to you, but I'm afraid of doing anything you might interpret as a commitment, because I'm not ready for that." Clearly, this is a direct communication, but the words chosen convey consideration and concern for the other person's feelings and expectations, rather than a premature assumption that his or her expectations may be inappropriate, unrealistic, or unfounded.

My suggestions for indirect or modified direct communication may help you find your own opportunities and your own style for communicating these helpful attitudes. There is, of course, no rigid need to communicate all of them to everyone you see in dating-sex contacts. They are just guidelines for the times you might wish to put another person at greater ease with you. Of course, you will communicate differently with different people as you find different contact points for developing all aspects of a relationship. With some, your verbal seduction may involve humor; with others, it may develop through general intellectualizing about relationships; with still others, an open and direct one-to-one exchange may best suit your mutual styles. Hooking up with different people in different ways is part of the adventure.

Now, some of you may feel that, in writing this, I am coaching people in the delivery of seductive lines. You are correct—that's exactly what I am doing. But, to me, an effective "line" is simply a courteous, sensitive, kindly, and effective way of saying something you sincerely believe.

Compared to the complex subtleties of verbal seduction, the physical form is simple child's play. This is fortunate, since the physical part is so singularly important. Furthermore, the four helpful attitudes can easily be expressed in physical seduction. Again, the basic secret is the gradualness and sensitivity of your approach. You can begin it very early by the most innocuous and friendly touching. Anything that you can do to soften the rigid barrier of physical privacy to which most of us hold will begin the process. A touch on the arm or shoulder, a light caress of a woman's hair, the taking of a man's hand, or the brief contact of your bodies as you sit together may begin to ease through that barrier of private space. When you make these moves to touch, or when touching occurs accidentally, notice how your partner responds. Does he or she appear to like it, move closer, reciprocate, and extend the physical contact? Or does he or she seem uncomfortable, move away, or pretend that nothing has happened? If you get the warm, positive reaction, feel free to go up a step in the hierarchy of physical intimacy. If you get the cool, disinterested reaction, back off until you know the person a little better. Then try again and note the reaction as before. If you keep getting an uncomfortable or nonreciprocating response, it's O.K. to talk about it if you want to, or you may learn in other ways what it means. As for asking about it, you can, in a very accepting way, simply remark that you feel more affectionate than your partner appears to feel, and you would like to know how to interpret that negative response. There is nothing whatever wrong with asking people to clarify the meaning of their behavior.

Other than the merely negative response, you may get signals that are unclear or contradictory. These are most difficult to deal with, and if you are getting such inconsistent messages, you should feel free to ask about these, too—again in an accepting, nonaccusatory way.

The whole seduction process follows this same one-two-three rule: first, reach out; second, notice the reaction; third and last, move forward, stop, or back up, depending on the signals you receive. You can go up the physical-intimacy hierarchy from light inconsequential touching to more affection to more obviously seductive or sexual contact. If you follow the hierarchical approach in mutual seduction, both in talking and in physical contact, neither of you will be jarred or hurt or seriously disappointed. The interaction will progress gracefully, in a spirit of mutual respect and caring. If you are more the receiver than the initiator in this interchange but want to convey acceptance and encouragement, try to respond as positively and enthusiastically as seems reasonable. Even if the particular seductive response that follows is not all that wonderful for you, remember that you are engaging here in a *seduction dialogue*. If the physical approach of your partner is uncomfortable, redirect it or remember to talk about it later. But, to keep the dialogue running smoothly, try to give positive signals clearly when that is congruent with your intention. Besides these positive, reassuring responses to the other's overtures, your taking over any part of the initiation, even a very minor one, will leave no doubt as to your receptivity.

The most important guideline of all is to approach affection, seduction, and sex in each relationship with flexibility, openness to change, and a willingness to learn. Remember, the beauty of sex is in its process of occurring and developing from moment to moment. Respond to it and create it, and you'll be O.K.

WHEN YOU WANT TO SAY NO

One of the reasons women have been thought to be less interested in sex than men is that they have been placed by cultural norms into the stereotyped role of the receptive or rejecting party. Rather than being allowed to act upon their own desires, women have had to wait to have their sexual urges met or to defend their unwillingness to participate. In addition, partly because people change their minds, men have learned to distrust a woman's no and persevere in spite of it. As a result of having been forced into this passive, evaluating, censoring, and defending position, some women have developed a generally negative attitude toward sex. Burdened by the role of saying no, they become burdened by sex itself. On the other hand, a man who is unable to interpret a no and feels threatened by a seeming rejection of his whole person that is not necessarily intended, may be unreasonably persistent in his sexual demands. I can say thankfully that this dual stereotype is not as prevalent as it once was, but in the initial stages of sexual interaction, the role division is still often followed. Sensitive, mutual seduction will, of course, largely eliminate these problems, but it takes two to achieve this, and even then there are junctures at which a no may be necessary.

Increasingly, men are being thrown into the more

passive, evaluative, and defensive role and, having little familiarity with it, they are finding the role difficult. Similarly, a woman who is told no may find it extremely distressing, since she has been educated to believe the nonsense that men are always up for sex. Hence, if her partner is not, she can only conclude that there must be something very wrong with her. What must be understood is that much of the perceived hesitancy of women or readiness of men in sexual encounters is a direct function of the stereotyped roles we have had to play. Women are perceived to be unwilling because they are consistently placed in a position where they must say yes or no rather than "Now." Men are perceived to be willing because, in initiating sex, they are more often responding to their own needs and feelings. As these roles change, so will our stereotypes. As more women begin to say "Now," men will be faced with the need to say yes or no.

If people follow patterns of clear communication and practice gradual and mutual seduction, it is almost impossible for anyone to get into a difficult no-saying situation. The issue will tend to be dealt with far up the intimacy hierarchy where the meaning of limited affection will be clear. The process of gradual and mutual seduction allows the initiator to read early warning signals and save face while it allows the more passive partner to give appropriate signals and say no in a much less pressured context.

Whenever you do get to a point where you need to say no, say it clearly, say it early in the mutual-seduction sequence if you can, say it gently and respectfully if possible, say it persistently if necessary, but say it. When delivering a no, make it clear what your no does and doesn't mean. If the truth is ego-sparing for your partner, so much the better. If you don't wish your no to discourage future dating or a possible sexual relationship in the future, say so; if your no means you are feeling bad about some aspect of your relationship, say so; if it means you're simply tired but would otherwise relish the opportunity for sex, say so; if it means that this relationship has no potential for you as a love-sex relationship, carefully and caringly say so. To hear no when you want to hear yes is frustrating, but it is not nearly as frustrating as receiving unclear, confusing messages that give no guidelines for future behavior. Besides, if you fail to convey the meaning of your no, you may very well be misinterpreted, so it is generally in your own best interest to give some kind of a rationale for your decision. Don't send an unclear message when a clear one will serve everyone so much better. On the other hand, unless you are unsure of your decision and want to be talked out of it, it is generally better not to argue. State your decision and rationale, but don't debate them. Repeat them if you have to, but avoid arguing a judgment based on your feelings.

Two techniques used in the newly popular assertiveness training are especially effective in dealing with those who have not yet learned the wisdom of respecting the negative decisions of others. Although these techniques may seem a bit patronizing, such people often require rather elementary treatment. The first technique, figuratively named *broken record*, involves simply repeating your decision or position again and again, as often as is necessary to make your point register with the other person. You completely avoid getting into arguments about the justification or meaning of your stand. Although it may be constructive for the two of you to discuss your possible sexual relationship and what it may or may not mean, there is no reason why you have to engage in a debate about your sexual willingness. If the other engages in debate, remember you don't have to argue back. You may simply repeat your decision ad nauseam until the other learns you are firm in your position and will not argue it.

The second technique, often useful in conjunction with the broken-record strategy, is acknowledging the concern or argument of the other. This shows the other that you are listening to him or her and that you are holding to your position in spite of his or her argument. The following simulated dialogue will illustrate both of these *negative-assertion* techniques as well as giving examples of clarifying (but not arguing) a position.

Chris: We've been out three times together, Ellen, we know each other pretty well, and I see no reason why we can't sleep together.

Ellen: Yes, we are close enough to be more intimate by many people's standards [acknowledging concern], but I'm not comfortable with that yet [broken record].

Chris: I've never cared about a woman this much or been with her this long and not slept with her. I don't understand this.

Ellen: I know that I may be different from other women you've been with, and I know that must be frustrating and confusing [acknowledging concern]. But I'm just not comfortable about having sex with you yet [broken record].

Chris: We've been sitting here being affectionate for nearly half an hour. You've been leading me on, and now you're leaving me high and dry. You must get some kick out of teasing me.

Ellen: I'm sorry you feel I've led you on [acknowledging concern]; I just liked our being affectionate [clarifying position]. But I'm just not comfortable going any further right now [broken record].

Chris: If you won't sleep with me, it must mean that you really don't care about me. Otherwise you wouldn't treat me this way.

Ellen: I'm sorry that you feel that I don't care about you, especially when I do [acknowledging concern, clarifying position]. But I'm just not comfortable sleeping with you yet [broken record].

Chris: But I feel really close to you and care about you a lot and want to complete that closeness.

Ellen: I'm glad that you care about me. I care about you and I'm sorry you're frustrated [acknowledging concern, clarifying position]. I'm just not ready yet [broken record].

Chris: It still makes me feel that you don't care. How do you really feel about me?

Ellen: Let's talk about that.

At any juncture in this dialogue, Ellen could have easily become defensive or accusatory in standing up for her position. She could have argued her decision in great detail and attacked Chris for misinterpreting her behavior or for expecting her to follow his timetable of feelings and expression rather than her own. But by acknowledging his concerns, clarifying her own position, and restating her decision, Ellen could allow the conversation to proceed to a more important ground concerning her feelings about Chris and the meaning of her decision on intimacy in the context of the relationship. Conflict surrounding sex can, at early as well as later stages in a relationship, be the setting event for important exchanges of openness. Some conflict over sex is natural in any relationship, and I hope I have established that it's best if both partners can make their own sexual desires known and respected from the beginning. To reinforce this, it's important to realize that negative assertion isn't difficult or rejecting or hurtful. It's simply part of living and sometimes requires a little extra skill. When you can say no comfortably and effectively, you acquire a new freedom to act without the fear of being pushed where you don't want to go. And your yes means a lot more. When you're passive, no one knows what you really want.

THE MEANING OF SEX

Single people wonder when sexual intercourse is appropriate for them. They ponder what meaning sex should have for them. They concern themselves with what meaning sex must have in order to be good. These are important questions, but they are questions no one can answer for another. Sex, like life, has whatever meaning one chooses to bring to it. It may have different meanings at different times, either with different people or with the same person. All meanings may be good and wholesome and worthy. At times, sex may feel good to you only as a part of a committed, monogamous, and loving relationship. At other times, or with other people, it may have meaning as a joyful and sensual interchange with someone you find sexually arousing and attractive. At still other times, it will have meanings intermediate between these committed and casual ones. All meanings are good if they are good for you. But, and this is important, it is usually best not to go back on your own requirements for meaning at any given time or with any given person. Generally speaking, if sex does not feel right to you on some particular occasion, don't engage in it. Follow your feelings in sexual matters even if you cannot always specify them completely. If sex feels good to you and you can do it joyfully, albeit with some apprehension, go ahead. If you can't, it is better to wait for another time.

Almost all of us experience some degree of concern about our sexual attractiveness and ability. Particularly on initial encounters, both men and women today worry about how their sexual performance will measure up to the standards of their partner and to their own new standards of experiencing the fullness of sensuality promised by the sexual revolution. Unfortunately, this concern is often the cause of unnecessary problems, and one of the most sensual, liberating, and sensible things you can do for yourself and your sex partners is to believe and get them to believe that, as long as it is not hurtful, whatever happens in sexual interchange is all right. You are not worthless if you happen to come too fast, too slow, too infrequently, or not at all. Your worth does not depend on your sexual prowess. Sex is not an achievement test. In the grand scheme of things, sexual gratification or frustration, particularly on any one occasion, is pretty irrelevant. If you can really accept that and communicate it to your partner, you will be doing a great deal for your relationship.

If you are a man who is concerned about ejaculating before your partner would optimally want you to, or if you worry about the possibility that you will not be able to get or maintain an erection for a sufficient length of time, remember that penil-vaginal intercourse is only one of many ways that men and women can sexually excite and satisfy one another. Remember particularly that you have two good hands with ten long, ever-erect fingers which can probe and often satisfy better than your penis. And you have a lot of other good equipment for sexual gratification for both yourself and your partner if you will but use it, irrespective of what your penis does or doesn't do.

If you are a woman who occasionally, frequently, or always has difficulty in coming to orgasm, or if you never come to orgasm, remember that many sexual activities can be highly enjoyable to you as well as to your partner. Really getting into the experience of sex is what you need to bring sensual joy to yourself and your partner. If you come, fine; if not, also fine. Whether you are a man or a woman, know that many sexual difficulties can be ameliorated and often eliminated by the sex therapy now available to you if you wish to take the time and effort to seek it out and use it well.

The sexual revolution has unfortunately brought with it great expectations of a continuously high level of sexual experience and gratification, instead of the freedom to have as much sex as desired in one's own time and in one's own way. As a result, getting less out of sex than is humanly possible can become just another way of feeling inadequate, guilty, and imperfect. It is absolutely essential for people to realize that their own worth and that of their partner never depends on their ability to be the most sensuous of men or women, and it certainly cannot depend on one's sexual abilities or the height of one's sexual feelings on one single occasion. Separate completely your worth from your ability to be sensual, orgasmic, erect or lubricated, fast, slow, or intermediate, and you will do much to enhance your own sexual enjoyment and that of your partners.

For many who experience these concerns, particularly on the first contact or contacts with a new partner, I have found it useful to suggest that they openly own their concerns before a sexual encounter. For instance, a man may indicate his concern that, with a new and attractive partner, he will become very excited and ejaculate too quickly. Similarly, a woman may indicate that initial sex may make her a little nervous and that she may be unable to come as quickly as she might like, if at all. In instances such as these, signaling such concern to a partner allows you to dismiss it. Not infrequently, getting your concern out in the open like this will enable you to be so much less preoccupied with it that you can turn your attention to getting it on sexually. When you do that, you may find your worry was for naught.

In sex, acceptance—acceptance of yourself and the other person, acceptance of your own and your partner's preferences, difficulties, and sensitivities—is terribly important. Such acceptance allows each of you to relax and enjoy the music of sexuality without the concern that every note must be played according to some predetermined score. Within the broad limits of respecting each other's sensitivities and basic human rights, whatever happens sexually will be all right if you and your partner can only see it that way. Such an approach can free both of you to experience sensuality, experiment with sexuality, and discover each other in the process.

MAKING IT BETTER

Life without music would, indeed, be a mistake, and life can be sweeter if the music is well conceived and adeptly played. After the onslaught of the sensuality books and the emergence of the sex clinics a few years ago, it became fashionable to label the sensuality movement superficial and irrelevant. It is still fashionable but incorrect. As a clinician, I've seen many people whose lives have been significantly marred by remarkably simple and easily remedied sexual problems. People have really suffered and continue to suffer as a result of the unenlightened, narrow, fearful, and moralistic views of sex that often still prevail in this culture. Those who have studied human sexual behavior, those who have treated sexual problems, and those who have responsibly popularized what has been learned have good things to teach anyone who doesn't already know it all. Now it's true that the sensuality movement has gotten a bit out of hand for some, and that keeping sex in perspective has become more of a problem since sensuous became the thing to be. But that reaction is to be expected in a trendy society like ours. It is a small and transitory price to pay for the increased awareness and openness about sex that the sensuality movement has stimulated.

In the rest of this chapter I shall summarize what can be learned from the sex researchers, the sex therapists, and the sensuality writers, making recommendations to you from the totality of my experience. In reading what I or anyone else has to say, however, remember that no one has any absolute answers that apply to all. Nearly all the sensuality books err in putting forward certain rigid expectations for sexual performance. They overgeneralize about the effectiveness or desirability of certain pet prescriptions for sensuality and improved sex. Consider what they have to say and what you read here as suggestions only. Don't allow the tyranny of sexual restraint to be replaced by the tyranny of imperative sensuality.

If you want to make your sexual relationships better, the chances are extremely good that you can. If you experience a serious sexual problem—one involving some specific dysfunction that requires special sex therapy, you may be reassured that success rates of well-trained direct sex therapists are quite good. The results of their treatment for premature ejaculation and erectile-failure problems in men and for inorgasmic problems in women are most encouraging. There is good reason to believe that other, less common sexual problems can also be successfully remedied with direct therapy procedures.

Although it is taking time for these techniques to filter down to practitioners in the helping professions, there is probably a sex-therapy clinic available to everyone who lives in or around a major urban center. If your difficulties are less serious, there are professionally led groups that offer help in achieving a more effective sexual repertoire or enhancing an already adequate sexual relationship. Finally, of course, there is a plethora of new books on sensuality and sexuality, some of which I can recommend to you, provided you remember two things while reading them. First, they contain suggestions, not foolproof solutions. Techniques which work for many may not work for you, and there may be other techniques, not covered in the particular book you choose, that will enhance sex for you or remedy your sexual problem. Second, although some of the techniques suggested for greater sexual enjoyment and competence are extremely simple and often highly effective when administered under active professional guidance, they may be ineffective when applied alone, without knowledgeable supervision. There is usually no harm in trying them without supervision. But if your problem is serious and your self-help sex program doesn't work, this does not mean that you can't be helped. The Masters and Johnson "squeeze" technique for premature ejaculation, for example, is extremely simple to explain and execute, but therapy programs employing it are often far more lengthy and complicated than would be obvious from a simple presentation of the procedure itself. If you try a given technique and it doesn't work for you, don't give up. It may not be the remedy for you or it may be a technique which, for you, requires some professional guidance.

I have found it useful to summarize sexual abilities in three broad categories. They are *sensuality, playfulness,* and *communication.* While any given sex act may be good without these components, sex will be less for you than it can be if you experience a continued inability to appreciate the sensuality of lovemaking, the playfulness of sexual relating, or the intimacy of communicating through or about sex. Although a small portion of the newly recognized sex therapies are devoted to teaching technical skills, most of the therapeutic methods are aimed at enhancing a couple's sensuality, their ability to play, and their capacity to communicate.

Sensuality is the ability to tune into sensory experience and, at least occasionally, be carried away by it. One of the real joys of sex is letting go and giving in to sensual experience, and sex is one of the few activities in which adults allow themselves to indulge their sensuous capabilities. A large part of the treatment for many sexual dysfunctions involves guided experiences, both alone and with a partner, designed solely to heighten the individual's ability to focus on and give in to pleasurable sensations. When done alone, these exercises take the form of examination of one's own body, experimentation with various forms of masturbation, and concentration on the sensual receptivity of the body. In couples, these experiences take the form of guided sessions of massage and other stimulation with no concomitant demand for or expectation of intercourse.

Such sessions, often termed *sensate-focus* or *pleasuring* sessions, teach people to appreciate sensual gratification for itself, demonstrating that a person can find pleasurable stimulation from an infinite variety of sensual experiences. For those who need to learn, such exercises show that foreplay can be a sensual, playful, communicative, and pleasurable activity in itself rather than a necessary step toward the destination of intercourse and orgasm. When couples are given pleasuring exercises, they are asked to alternate so that, for example, the man will caress, kiss, lick, or suck every part of the woman's body in every way that seems desirable to him. The woman may tell him what feels good and what does not, but otherwise she remains passive. Then or in a later session, the man and woman change roles. Not only does this method teach both of them a good deal about where and how to rub, but it also helps them to realize that it is all right and indeed desirable for one partner simply to receive sensual gratification without any immediate responsibility to reciprocate. This is important because it allows the receiving partner to give himself or herself over totally to sensual experience.

Playfulness in sex means the ability to open oneself to different forms of expression just for fun and to remember not to take what happens in a sexual encounter too seriously. What spoils sex for many is the view that it represents a test of something—masculinity, femininity, sensuality, self-worth, sexuality, sexual knowledge, or what have you. Whenever sex represents this kind of test, it is bound to make people a little anxious, and the anxiety can completely destroy the sexual experience. One often does well to forget about his or her sexual repertoire in each sexual encounter and experiment with new, spontaneous, and playful activities. Some experiments will not work very well, of course, and sometimes sex itself will not work well for one or both partners. But this is of little consequence where humor, goodwill, and trust are present. Sex can be good for us, in part because it provides us with the opportunity to abandon ourselves again in childlike play. What better place is there for this than in the arms of a lover?

As for communication, good sex is both a vehicle for communication between lovers and a subject of communication. A sexual encounter provides the opportunity for the expression of acceptance, joy, caring, sensitivity, and a host of other positive emotions. It may also, of course, convey indifference, hostility, selfishness, insensitivity, and disappointment. But, largely because we talk so little about our sexual behavior, the messages we send and receive in this context may be among the most easily confused and misinterpreted. We may be feeling the good things and inadvertently send out the bad. Often we interpret the sexual behavior of others in light of our own idiosyncratic standards, and that can cause a lot of trouble! For example, Eric and Georgia make love and both have a satisfying sexual experience. Afterward, Eric rolls over and goes to sleep. Georgia is crushed; for her, this is a time for the gentle talking and caressing that symbolize the caring relationship between them. The sexual experience itself is diminished and cheapened for her by the absence of what she considers an important and natural part of sex, and Georgia begins to question the whole relationship. She interprets Eric's behavior as a lack of real love and concern for her, although he does care for her very much and is happily sleeping through all this. Georgia's feelings for Eric begin to cool, and their relationship, sexual and otherwise, may never be the same again.

Another example: Don and Carol have a sexual experience in which Don becomes very active and expressive, while Carol is passive and silent and fails to give any noticeable utterance of reaching orgasm. Don assumes that this means Carol is uninterested in him sexually, and his disappointment carries over to other aspects of their relationship. His negative attitudes in other things cause Carol to reevaluate her emerging feelings toward him.

In both of these cases, a simple misunderstanding about the meaning of certain sexually related acts creates disappointment and anger, resulting in difficulties which permeate and threaten to destroy the entire relationship. How much better if you can communicate about sex!

Now that we've defined these three components of sexual ability, see if they are useful in clarifying areas of sexual difficulty which you or a partner may be experiencing. Take sensuality, for example. Are you unable to slow down in a sexual encounter and enjoy caressing and fondling your partner? Are you unable to forget about what your next move will be or to dismiss your concerns about your work or other matters? Are you in a big hurry to have an orgasm and get on with it, rather than being able to find ecstasy in the process of lovemaking? Are you tense or anesthetic to the touch of your partner? Have you never any time for sex? If any of this describes your problem, you have a deficit in sensuality that prevents you from appreciating the physical during sex. You are not a worthless nogoodnik because of this, and you may be quite a good person, respected by yourself and treasured by others, even if you never remedy it. You've got a deficit, that's all. And if you want to remedy it, you probably can.

Similarly, those who have been with the same partner for a long time and are beginning to suffer some of these nonsensuality symptoms can remedy the problem. Long-term sexual relationships are often not as sensually exciting as they were at first or as new ones might be. But their sensuous qualities can usually be improved if both partners are interested enough to make that happen. And, of course, relationships can be quite exciting and positive even when their sensual quality is less than red-hot.

To remedy difficulties in sensuality in yourself, expose yourself in one way or another to the exercises which will help you realize sensual experiences. You may want to look at some of the recommended books in the notes on this chapter. Among the best books providing exercises in sensuality are Alex Comfort's *The Joy of Sex* and *More Joy of Sex*. To these I would add the sensual exercises prescribed in *The Sensuous Woman*. If your partner has difficulty with sensuality, then do whatever you can to see to it that he or she has these sensuous experiences. You may, for example, get your partner to experience a pleasuring session by explaining it to him or her in advance, getting him or her to read about it, or, often more delightfully, just making it happen spontaneously. If you are a woman and concerned about your man's self-pride or his reaction to your asking for some change in his sexual behavior, have a look at the very good book by Lynn Barber entitled *How to Improve Your Man in Bed*. Although Barber's book overemphasizes the subtlety with which you need to change the sexual behavior of any enlightened man, she is correct in asserting that many men are unnecessarily oversensitive about their sexual performance and need special reassurance. Taking extra care of them in this way is certainly warranted sometimes, and Barber's suggestions for gentle, subtle communications about changes in a man's sexual behavior are generally quite good. Whether you are a man or a woman, you may also influence your partner to see the folly of taking his or her sexual performance or attractiveness too seriously. Whatever course you take, it is important to recognize your partner's hang-ups if there are such and, in one way or another, to deal with them carefully. It is, after all, in your own best interest to do so. If you are a man, it will usually be easier to guide your partner to more sensual experience because you are the culturally sanctioned leader in sexual matters, and if you know how to lead her gently, she will often follow.

But you can do only so much to enhance the sensuality of another person. Others may, for reasons quite independent of you, be unable to learn from your most valiant efforts to teach them. In that case, there is very little more you can do about it. Their learning may have to wait for another time, another sex partner, or the guidance of a professional. Simply do the best you can to increase your own sensuality, and that of your partner if that is your wish. If your best is not enough, look elsewhere for more help or give up. Do not blame yourself for being less than perfect as a teacher of sensuality.

Now about playfulness: the ability to be playful in sex is highly related to one's ability to be sensual. I don't honestly know where to draw the line between the two. But you can be a sensuous person and yet not entirely playful about it, if you take sex too seriously. Are you unable to laugh in bed, to have fun when you make love? Do you worry about not doing well enough? Are you unable to experiment with new sexual acts? Does sex not working out on one occasion really disturb you? If you have to answer yes to this general picture, your very human deficit is in playfulness. There are three basic strategies for treating this. First, learn to be playful by practicing it. Even if it seems strange, experiment with new and playful ways of being sexy. In spite of some discomfort with such experimenting, let go. Second, improve your sexual competence so that you can spend less of your energy on concern about your performance and have more of it to devote to getting into sex. Third, change your philosophy so that you begin to see sex in proper perspective—less as a test of your competence as a person, more as a means of expression and a way to have fun.

In regard to the second and third strategies, it is often easier to make sexual behavior more competent than it is to change one's philosophy about sex. Premature ejaculation, for example, is widely considered to be a problem mediated by anxiety about sexual performance. Yet there are a few simple, direct techniques which can retard the ejaculation response. It is not uncommon for a man to require the use of one of these techniques for only a short period while he learns that premature ejaculation is not inevitable for him and that he can control himself if he wants to. Once this is realized and confidence is restored, there is often no more problem and no further need for the retarding technique. Thus, when a sexual problem has become habitual and of great concern, it is often easier to change competence than philosophy.

You would do well, of course, to try all three avenues at once—practice playfulness, improve your competence, and at the same time begin to realize that competence is not the end-all and be-all of sex. Thus, if you are a man with ejaculatory problems or a woman with orgasmic problems, try in spite of this to relax, play, and enjoy your lovemaking. Try to learn whatever you can about the techniques to help you remedy any problems, but remind yourself that your sexual abilities are merely a fact, not an evaluation. On the other hand, while trying to learn to play, don't reproach yourself if playing comes hard to you. And if your partner can't play as well as you would like, reassure him or her that it's O.K., just communicate your own playfulness. If all this takes time, be patient.

Now for communication: Do you ever feel that you don't really know your partner's sexual likes and dislikes? Do you often feel that he or she lacks a good idea of your general preferences? Do you find it hard to talk about these preferences to your partner, or to ask about his or hers? Are you unable to send or receive subtle messages during affectionate or sexual contact? If you have one or more yeses, you have a communication deficit. Your relationship may be good in other areas and may continue to be so if you never remedy this problem. But this deficit is more likely than the others to accompany or produce other difficulties. It may reflect a general communication deficit in your relationship—not just confined to sex—and it may quickly precipitate other problems, as in the two cases mentioned earlier. You can usually remedy such a deficit if you work at it, though ironically, in this most important facet of a sexual relationship, the available sex books are the least helpful.

Consider some of the suggestions I have to offer here which may help you communicate through and about sex. If you have read this far, you have already been introduced to the basic principles involved. The rules for good communication concerning sex are the same as for good communication concerning anything else, but because it's a potentially touchy subject, you may have to be a bit more careful than usual.

First, it's helpful to signal your partner that communication about sex is all right with you, that it can be positive and helpful, and, above all, that it is safe. One of the easiest ways to begin is to signal your partner, during sex, what he or she does that you like. Positive feedback, either verbal or nonverbal, is often the best, and most reassuring, kind of communication. Where sex is concerned, it would be difficult to give too much of it. And the positive feedback and reassurance don't have to be restricted to the sexual encounter itself. Even the most adept sexual partners are not mind readers, and won't know your likes if you don't tell or show them. This positive feedback reassures your partner that he or she is a *good* lover. And people generally live up to their reputations. So, it is in your best interest to let your lover know that he or she pleases you. No matter how bad a lover you've got, he or she must be doing something right. Find it and reinforce it. If carried out sensitively, just this simple, positive communication can enliven and change for the better an otherwise unrewarding sexual relationship. Others may be reluctant to communicate their own likes to you until you begin the process and show them it's O.K.; positive communication is the best way to start.

It's also helpful to signal your lover that sex and communication about it are *safe*. You can do this by projecting your own sane attitudes about sex; both directly and indirectly, you can indicate many of your own healthy attitudes; for example:

Sex is fun.

Sexual abilities are like other abilities that can be learned and improved.

Sex works better sometimes than at other times, and that's O.K.

You don't judge yourself or others on the basis of sexual prowess or knowledge.

You know you have things to learn sexually and you want to learn them.

You will not be destroyed by negative feedback concerning your sexual behavior.

You are respectful of your partner's sensibilities.

Sexual experimentation is good.

Sexual gratification is nice but there are other things which are more important.

It's safe to be intimate, to talk, and to be oneself with you.

You know that blaming another for not satisfying you is a silly waste of time.

If there is a sex problem, you can work to solve it together.

These last two points are especially important. If you blame, you can't be safe. You can be disappointed, wish that things were different, dislike the fact that sex is less than it could be—you can do all this and be safe. But if you blame, you'll cut off communication and greatly diminish the possibility of making anything any better.

Once you have shown yourself and your partner that communication about sex can be good, reassuring, helpful, and safe, you are in an infinitely better position to begin redirecting—to initiate constructive criticism or negative feedback. There are still good reasons to be somewhat cautious, however, about the delivery of such feedback, which during sex can dispel its magic and turn it into an unpleasant encounter for both parties. So, if you need to give redirection or mild negative feedback during a sexual encounter, do it carefully and gently and in the context of a good deal of positive feedback. If this seems indulgent, it is. But that is part of what a caring relationship is all about, and it is in your best interest to encourage rather than discourage your lover. One simple way of doing this is to avoid using words like "No" and "Don't" or other negative injunctions. Rather than "Not so hard," say, "More gently." Rather than "Don't rub there," move his or her hand and say, "Here." Where more major negative feedback is necessary, it is usually wiser to discuss it at a later time, apart from the sexual scene. And, of course, during these discussions, it is wise to let the other know that his or her worth is not at issue and that responsibility for any problem and its solution must be shared. As in every other area of couples problems, you can approach sexual difficulties as an opportunity for joining forces against the problem. You can use it to come closer together rather than allowing it to drive you farther apart.

You can frequently teach your partner what he or she needs to learn by your example. Particularly if the deficits in your partner's sexual activities have to do with his or her ability to appreciate sensual things or to be playful, you can teach these things by showing your

partner how to be playful and sensuous. Mere instructions in being more sensual will usually get you absolutely nowhere. But exposing your partner to sensual
things in the spirit of experimentation and acceptance
and demonstrating your own sensuality can make a
difference. Similarly, if you show your partner how to
be playful, carefree, and nondemanding, he or she can
learn to follow suit. In each of the three ability areas,
example is very often the best and least threatening way
to teach your partner.

Good communication in sex and about sex can almost always make it better. But the communication can
be achieved in many different ways, and the most direct
and verbal method is not always the best. People must
learn about sex, and every sexual encounter presents a
need and an opportunity to learn anew. If you are open
to sensitive, two-way communication during sex, you
make possible a flowing, changing interplay of intimacy
in which mutual satisfaction becomes optimal. And no
one can do better than that.

10
Relationships and Commitments

I'm falling in love again
And if I lose or win
How will I know?
—Willy Nelson

ON READING the first draft of this book, my married friends and colleagues expressed concern that my attitude toward marriage seemed too negative and that the book was more positive about single life than common experience would justify. But some of my single friends and colleagues have complained that the book is not militant enough about being single and that too much of it is devoted to heterosexual dating, sex, and coupling. As long as I kept getting a balance of such concerns, I was reassured. This book is written to help single people with the dilemmas they most often face—the dilemmas of living alone and the dilemmas of living in relationships. The thesis is that mastery of single living is good for living alone and good for getting and staying happily coupled. The fact is that important love relationships of one kind or another are basic in the lives of most single men and women. To master single living, most people need to develop a feeling of confidence in their ability to establish and maintain relationships. And

324

to achieve a meaningful primary relationship, which most single people strive for, it is necessary to experience more than the superficial joining so often associated with dating or sex.

In this chapter, I shall present some principles I have found helpful to my clients in coping with the problems which love relationships inevitably suffer. Then I shall introduce a collection of ideas about communication in relationships which may assist you in understanding and living them a little better.

RELATIONSHIP INEVITABLES

Falling in love is great, right? No doubt about it. But how many passionate lovers have you known who have not also experienced some pretty severe pain in the process? Some of this discomfort is inevitable; some of it is completely unnecessary. Understanding which is which can help immeasurably in dealing with the inevitable and in eliminating the rest.

It is inevitable that a new primary love relationship will cause some trouble because it always demands a significant rearrangement of your life. Whatever your personal adjustment before the beginning of such a relationship, it will be somewhat stressed by the changes required. If you have other lovers, this will, of course, present a problem. If you are alone and much in need of such a relationship, its all-important nature and the associated dependency will be a problem. If you are happily accustomed to being alone, the new accommodations to pairing will present a problem. A new lover will experience the same difficulties, and this can be even more troublesome to you. If you realize that a new love is a mixed blessing for you and your partner, you will be better prepared to deal with what's in store. The required rearrangement of your personal life is only part of the problem. It's also inevitable that you and your partner will progress in commitment to each other at different rates. In any new relationship, there is always one who is more interested in moving the relationship up to the next level of intimacy or commitment. Theoretically, at least, this is always true in any relationship—one partner must be more committed, more in need of the relationship, more aware of what would be lost if it ended.

In addition, your new love will, sooner or later, inevitably be found wanting, just as he or she will find you wanting. *Any* person, no matter how desirable, is going to fall short in some way of your romantic ideals and perfectionistic hopes, just as you are going to fall short in some way of his or hers. How you and your partner respond to this fact of life may very well determine how good your relationship will be and how long it will last.

These are a few of the inevitables. They are much less of a problem if you know they are inevitables and can so remind yourself at the right times. Then, you can devote your energies to figuring out what to do about them rather than wasting your time trying to prevent them.

The human travail which the inevitables usually occasion is not itself inevitable. Let us explore in detail three basic relationship inevitables and illustrate varying ways of responding to them.

Inevitable I. Differences in Commitment and Commitment Timing

Dwayne and Mickie had been dating for about a month when they first talked to me about their relationship problems. Dwayne was a bright, creative twenty-nine-year-old experimental psychologist who had been divorced for about a year. The separation had been his idea, but his adjustment to single life had been less than ideal. He still found the practical aspects of taking care of himself a monumental chore and was still quite uncomfortable with his own company. He had dated actively since separating, but before meeting Mickie had not found anyone who could become very important to him. His social circuit was a narrow one, and he'd met most of his dates in singles bars. There were some serious gaps in his ability to live autonomously. But Mickie found him to be a kind, generous, loving, and lovable person. She said, however, that her interest and caring for him were eroding because he was pushing her toward greater commitment than was comfortable.

Mickie was twenty-five and still single. Unlike Dwayne, she appreciated single life and thrived on it. She had a broad circle of friends, a roommate she enjoyed, and a primary relationship with a man who now lived in another city. She was a graduate student in psychology at another university and was very busily committed to the development of her career.

Dwayne put the problem this way: "I feel like a schoolboy in love, and it's great. This hasn't happened to me since I was in college. I never felt this way about my wife. All I want is to enjoy it and to bring Mickie along with me. If it were up to me, we'd spend every evening and weekend together, but Mickie doesn't want to spend anywhere near that much time with me. I love to tell her I love her, but she tenses up when I say it. And a couple of times I've tried to make some plans for Christmas, even though it's a few months away, but she doesn't want to talk about it. She doesn't care as much about me as I care about her, and that's not the way it's supposed to be. I get extremely jealous of her other friend in San Diego, and it almost kills me when he calls her place when I'm there. I think I will want to marry Mickie sometime in the future, but that's a long way off; that's not what I want now. She doesn't seem to understand that. All I want is for us to be more together than we are, for her to allow me to express my feelings for her, and for her to care about me somewhere near as much as I care about her. Except for this problem, things have been very good between us, but this is beginning to affect us in everything. I get suspicious that Mickie doesn't really care for me at all, even though I know she does. I feel weak because of that, and at her mercy. Sometimes I get angry at her for no reason. I don't like the way it's going, and I see it could end at any time in spite of how good it is."

In a private session, Mickie reported: "Dwayne is a great guy and I like him an awful lot. I might even get to love him if he'd give me a chance, but he's crowding me; he's pushing me. I have other obligations besides him—obligations that go back a long way. I need time to check this relationship out and see how it fits in with the rest of my life. If Dwayne would just cool it, everything would be all right. But he calls every day to ask if we can have dinner and spend the evening together.

I've begun to dread those calls because I hate to say no to him. He tells me that he loves me and I don't know what to say. And he always seems to be pressing me about plans way in the future when I'm not sure where we'll be as a couple. I don't know what I'm going to do about Greg in San Diego. When someone loves you as Greg and Dwayne both love me, you can really hurt them. I can't stand hurting anybody like that. I'm responsible for them because they have committed a part of themselves to me. I've been more attracted to Dwayne than anyone else I've seen in the last two years. But he is getting me down, and I'm really beginning to wonder. I dread his calls; I dread what he's going to say to me when I see him; I dread hurting his feelings; I feel like avoiding him. How can it ever work when I feel like that? I'm beginning to doubt my feelings for Dwayne. I think often of just giving up on it. I feel so burdened."

Now, the difference in commitment timing for Dwayne and Mickie is inevitable. The trouble they're having is not. Both of them are putting interpretations on their own and the other's feelings and behavior that are inaccurate and unnecessarily upsetting. Both are doing things which cause unnecessary pain and failing to do things which could avoid that pain.

For his part, Dwayne has been unfortunate enough to enter this love affair with insufficient resources. He almost naturally depends too much on this budding relationship because, other than his work, he has little else going on in his life, in spite of his varied talents. Although he is dimly aware of the fact that he may be demanding too much of Mickie, he continues to do so and fails to look for other avenues of social outlet. In spite of knowing that his protestations of love, his continual requests for time together, and his "futurizing" about their relationship make Mickie nervous, he fails to restrain himself. He misinterprets her not acting the same way as a lack of caring. He broods unnecessarily about his relative lack of power in the relationship and repeatedly tries to gain additional power in silly, ineffective ways. And he does all this in the name of love.

It is easy to sympathize with Dwayne's position. It is a common one, and his lovestruck behavior is socially sanctioned. For one in love is supposed to be at least a little irrational. People in love often indulge their irrationality; it is one of the ways we know they are in love. Dwayne has every right to do this, and it is very understandable considering his circumstances and social training. But by indulging himself, he is slowly driving Mickie away. It might have been more fortunate had he found and fallen in love with someone who could immediately reciprocate his level of commitment. It certainly would have been easier. But it would not have provided him with such an excellent opportunity to learn that the feelings of another cannot be dictated by his own. If he doesn't learn quickly enough in this relationship, he'll probably have another chance to practice what he'll learn with someone else.

For her part, Mickie is throwing a wet blanket on the whole affair because Dwayne's attentions make her unnecessarily uncomfortable. It is, of course, a hassle to have to refuse repeatedly the invitations of someone you care for, and it would be better for both people involved if this could be avoided. It is hard to deal with unwanted futurizing and difficult to field repeated protestations of love when you are unsure of your own feelings. But that's all it is—a hassle, a difficulty, a problem of communication to be worked out. It is completely unnecessary for her to feel as responsible as she does for the two men in her life. She can afford to allow Dwayne to enjoy his love for her without burdening herself with responsibility. These are his feelings, and he is responsible for them. By punishing their expression, she also punishes the feelings, and, in the long run, this may be exactly the opposite of what she would want to do. She is also overreacting to and overinterpreting their differences in commitment timing. Because of the contrast between her expressions of feeling and those of Dwayne, she is beginning to suspect that she doesn't care for him enough, in spite of many signs to the contrary. The simple, inevitable difference in commitment timing is promoting an avoidable breakdown of the relationship.

Both Dwayne and Mickie first need to know that their difference in commitment timing is a fact of life. To one degree or another, they are going to experience this difference from one side or the other in any relationship they encounter. They can't avoid it, and they can't exert much control over which side they're going to draw. But they can understand both sides a bit more philosophically, and they can handle this situation a lot better. Once Dwayne knows that *all* love affairs experience this problem to one extent or another, he can stop lamenting the fact that his love affair is not "the way it's supposed to be." He can also do some practical things to ease the conflict. In consulting with him, I advised his becoming more involved with other people and activities, so that there would be less need for an excessive dependency on Mickie. I suggested that he consider dating other women and that he begin to become involved in activities such as music and the theater. I suggested that he take Mickie's advice and play it cooler —that he reduce his rate of protestations of love and stop futurizing.

I counseled Mickie about her excessive feelings of responsibility toward Dwayne. I urged her to see his feelings as his own responsibility, to allow him to enjoy these feelings, and to avoid punishing him for them. I urged her to see that Dwayne's feelings were confining to her only to the extent that she allowed them to be.

I proposed to both of them a program that I've used in many cases of this kind: Mickie and Dwayne were asked to alternate in calling each other for making contact or planning time together. Thus, Dwayne could call Mickie once and plan some time with her, but he was not to call again for that or any other purpose until Mickie called him. In this way, their getting in touch for planning time together or for just talking on the telephone would alternate. This would serve to reduce the pressure on Mickie and the number of times she would have to say no to Dwayne. Further, it would give Dwayne appropriate signals for pacing his initiations. Finally, it would give Mickie the opportunity to initiate and, in this way, to show him that she was committed to the relationship. Enthusiastically agreed to by both parties, this maneuver has had the effect of putting more balance in the relationship—taking the pressure off Mickie while reassuring Dwayne. Achieving both a philosophical and practical accommodation to the problem of commitment timing has freed them to experience and evaluate the relationship itself.

Again, by joining together against a problem, any couple can make of their differences a common task which brings them together for mutual support and understanding. This joining together against a common problem is often the most substantial indicator of each person's commitment to the relationship and of the maturity required to make it work. Every relationship will have problems, and each one is a challenge of just how well the partnership can function.

Inevitable II. Mutual Disappointment

There is another inevitable which, in my experience, causes even more difficulty than commitment differences: mutual disappointment. Any person will have shortcomings when measured by any other person's ideals, expectations, hopes, and dreams. Anyone you meet is going to be imperfect in some way, generally in an important way, as you will be for him or her. Success in any relationship may very well depend on whether you accept this fact of life and live happily with it or rage against it and fail to live and love to the fullest. If you are upset about it, brood about it, feel cheated because of it, blame your partner for it, and withhold what you would otherwise give, you will destroy whatever you have. When you blame your partner for his or her failures and withhold, he or she will very likely follow the same unenlightened but human course: to resent your blame and withholding and to start withholding and blaming in return. When this happens, neither of you will *feel like* giving to the other, and the vicious circle of blame and withholding will spiral out of control. Then you will have to adjust to greater disappointment or you will have to reject it all —an unhappily common choice.

Consider Sam and Betty, an unmarried couple who had been together for quite some time. They had dated steadily in college, were separated for a year when Sam went away to business school, lived together for two years after that, were separated again, and now were living together once more. When they came to me for counseling they were on the verge of breaking up. As I talked with them, one central fact of their relationship became abundantly clear. They had never really been separated from this relationship, but neither had they ever been committed to it. Interviews with them both together and alone revealed a strikingly common pattern, different only in specifics. Although they had been very close in their college romance, neither one had been quite ready to settle down with the other after college. But after a lonely year apart, they settled in to live together.

Two years later, Sam had to move to my home city to pursue his career. He had been happy with Betty and wanted her to come along. She did not, partly because she wanted to follow her own career plans, but mostly, she said later, because she wasn't completely committed to the relationship. Among other things, she felt that Sam did not communicate with her openly or well, or give her the emotional support she felt she needed. Sam had been crushed by Betty's decision, but hadn't let her know that. He went off alone to his new life. In spite of the break, they remained closely tied. They tried other relationships again but, as before, relied on each other for their primary comfort, support, and connectedness with another person. After a year, Betty decided to come and join Sam, and they had now been living together for about eighteen months.

When Betty moved in with Sam this time, she made a decision to commit herself to the relationship as much as possible. But Sam never forgot the earlier rejection. He just couldn't seem to regain the level of trust and comfort that he had had before. He had blamed her for their separation, and he was still blaming her. And because he felt this resentment, he withheld. Primarily, he held back from communicating his feelings to her, even though he was now much better able to communicate. This holding back had been bothering Betty for quite a while. In a session alone with me, she admitted to withholding physical affection and sex from Sam because she just didn't *feel like* it anymore. She didn't feel like it because she was blaming him for his withholding. He in turn perceived this and proceeded to withhold more, and in still other ways. Alternately, each began withdrawing more and more from their joint-relationship account. Another withdrawal or two would surely close it completely.

Sam and Betty's problem is the basic relationship problem. One partner blames the other for his inevitable shortcomings and withholds commitment or caring or love. The other resents this withholding, blames the withholder, and withholds in turn. The withdrawals increase until—when the joint account is nearly depleted —the partners sometimes seek out an investment counselor. A superficial approach to solving this problem would be to get each of them to begin giving more of what the other wants. A more fundamental solution would be to get each partner to change the way he or she thinks about and responds to the deficiencies perceived in the other. Each needs to see the stupidity, the shortsightedness, and the destructiveness of this disappointment-blame-withholding cycle. Each needs to realize that, however uncaring the other may be, he or she is not to blame. And then, each needs to begin to act in accordance with that realization.

Both can be helped to live a more comfortable life with themselves and others by learning this premise: at any given moment in time, one does what one must—each of us does the best he or she can. Others are no more to blame for their shortcomings than they are to blame for the color of their eyes. While we can strive to get them to change their behavior in the future, they are as they are in the present, and, at any given moment, they are as they must be.

In this case, Sam must do one of two things to make his life work. He must either accept and love someone who has disappointed him in the past, who continues to disappoint him, and who, like everyone else, will always disappoint him, or he must leave and invest his energies elsewhere. Betty must do the same. Each needs to decide whether the deficits of the other are ones with which he or she can happily settle or whether they are not. Every relationship has its price; every person has his own unique set of problems; every choice carries with it the bitter and the sweet. To want it all for nothing is very human and perfectly sane. But to expect to get it is very stupid, and blaming another for not giving it to you is the height of stupidity. It is easiest for us to see this in Sam's persistent blaming of Betty for something that happened two and a half years earlier. We know that that cannot be changed, and we can more easily appreciate the singularly destructive effect that his withdrawal had on their relationship. But all of this is true for every unfortunate withdrawal from the joint account. Each one has done the best that he or she could at the time. Sam and Betty have the same problem: to decide what they want to do and to do it. If they decide to stay in their relationship, they will do so happily only if each accepts all the other's deficits, even though he or she dislikes them and would prefer to do without them. They will each get the most they can get out of this relationship by giving all they've got and continuing to give it, in spite of whatever withdrawals the other makes. Don't dribble out your love in carefully measured doses: "Shower the people you love with love. Show them the way that you feel. Things are gonna be much better if you only will" (James Taylor).

Inevitable III. Satiation

We tire of each other. However enthralled we may be with another in the beginning of a relationship, there is an inevitable getting used to the satisfaction he or she provides. Like the other inevitables, this one may be mild or profound, but it is, nonetheless, inevitable.

Much of the wonder of falling in love comes from the combination of the novelty of all that a new person can give and the dizzying speed with which it may be given. When two people come together, they usually discover rather quickly what their partner's most important needs are, and they discover the basic ways in which they can be met. The initial pace of this learning is rapid and occurs while the novelty of the other enhances his or her power to be exciting and rewarding. But, then, the pace of learning new ways to satisfy dwindles just as the novelty wears off. This is a powerful one-two punch which has been known to knock out many a budding relationship—a fortunate outcome in many cases, since sheer novelty can be deceptively seductive for a while. To one degree or another, however, the inevitability of satiation occurs in even the most substantial of relationships. Honeymoons end. There are at least two basic things to be done about this fact of life which makes so many couples miserable: to recognize it as a fact of life, and to work at lessening or counteracting it.

I do not enjoy the role of pessimist. I write as one here because I think it is necessary. Romanticism about relationships often destroys them. Reminders of their inherent limitations serve to stop destructive catastrophizing and to preserve not only one's relationships but one's enjoyment of them. If you want to preserve your own relationships and your joy in them, such self-reminders will help. So will self-reminders about the inherent advantages of primary relationships. Thinking through the inevitable losses and realizable gains of relationships will improve them and your adjustment to them.

The inevitability of satiation is more treatable, more avoidable, more open to manipulation than the other inevitables. At the same time, it is so pervasive a problem and its solutions so variable that many books have been devoted to instructing couples on ways to avoid it. I am able here only to list some of these general methods for you and to refer you to other helpful books on the subject in the notes on this chapter.

First, don't isolate your primary relationship from the community that could support it, nor from the *separate* friends and activities that could enrich it. Don't fall into the trap our urban, cubicle culture sets in which men and women couple, withdraw into their cubicles, isolate themselves from the world, and look only to each other for satisfaction. Resist this isolation if you want to be a whole person and have a dynamic relationship. As I have pointed out before, our urban nonculture promotes this isolation, and, unless vigorously avoided, such isolation seriously weakens us and our relationships. Preserving yourself, your relationships, and even your culture depends, I think, on successfully resisting this trap.

Only when primary relationships are not asked to accomplish the impossible can they begin to succeed. Only when primary relationships are placed within a meaningful network of other relationships—within a community—will they be as satisfying as they can be. Only then, I believe, will relationships last and be satisfying. Behind much of my genuine pessimism about primary love relationships is my pessimism about our turning things around as a society. But while the society as a whole may not make these changes, you still can. If you demand that your primary relationship be open to all that a community can provide to each of its members and that, at the same time, it be surrounded and supported by this community, you can make it work.

The second basic approach to remedying the problem of satiation is to promote growth and variation, in both individual and joint activity. We live in a time of incredible personal and social change, and yet in our primary love relationships we often pursue a destructive tendency to define them rigidly, freezing our roles within them. Such rigidity, especially in the context of surrounding rapid change, becomes stifling and frustrating. Throughout this book, I have advocated relationships between men and women whose primary characteristic is that they are fluid, changeable, open to rearrangement of roles and values. A fluid relationship can be most easily maintained by two courageous people who are autonomous adults, strengthened by their community and unhampered by unrealistic expectations. Such couples may be rare, but they won't be bored.

NO-FAULT COMMUNICATION

I have proposed an approach to relationships characterized by acceptance and nonblaming which recognizes that our needs can never dictate what anyone *should* do. When needs mesh in a relationship, that is wonderful; when they don't, no one is to blame. This no-fault philosophy of life and relationships is a basic concept of this book. As we now consider primary relationships and how to live with them, the ideal of *no-fault communication* takes on even greater importance, since conflict is inevitable in all close interpersonal relations. The needs of two people never mesh all the time. No-fault communication establishes exactly what the differences are in a relationship and sets the stage for negotiating about them and joining forces against them. Its principles are practical suggestions for expressing the acceptance of your own needs and those of another.

I-Messages versus You-Messages

Whenever your relationship partner does not behave the way you want, you have a problem. In such situations, there often is no problem apart from your reaction. It doesn't really matter how unfair or reprehensible your partner's action—it's still your problem. For illustration, put yourself in Louise's position. She had been in a primary relationship with Lance for about three months. She found Lance very easy to love, but unfortunately several other women in town felt the same way. And he never seemed to discourage them. He often spent time with his women friends and was usually affectionate with them whenever he saw them. He'd often go to a party with Louise and spend his time with the other women there. All of Louise's friends felt that she had ample grounds for feeling upset, jealous, and angry.

When she talked to me about it, I completely agreed that she had a problem. She had two problems, because she did not initially recognize that her upset was fundamentally her own difficulty. When she had talked to Lance about it, she had communicated her second problem by the way she expressed her concern. When allowed to speak to Lance, I found out about this in detail. After the last party at which he had been particularly attentive to another woman, Louise's reaction went something like this:

"You bastard! How dare you take me to a party and attend to *everyone* but me! You do this every time we go out. You show no consideration or respect or regard for me. You expect to flirt with every other woman in sight all evening and then make love to me. I've had it."

In part because she saw this problems as Lance's, she accused him and demanded that he change. In making these accusations and demands, she set up her own needs as the sole determinant of good, normal, and appropriate behavior for Lance. And what was his obvious response? Defensiveness. In the last confrontation they had had, he simply denied that there was a problem at all and refused to talk about it. The *you-messages* Louise used stressed her philosophical mistake and communicated her blaming of Lance for not acting in accordance with her needs.

In talking with Louise, I attempted to get her to see that it was her reaction—her negative feelings—that created a problem, first for her and then perhaps for Lance. I urged her to talk about her feelings and focus on her reactions to his behavior. After some discussion about this, she was able to go to Lance and present her grievance in *I-messages*, which went something like this:

"I get scared when you spend so much time at parties with other women. I worry that I'm not exciting or intelligent enough for you. I get afraid that you don't find me as attractive as the other women at the party. I fear that you don't respect me when you don't pay at least a little attention to me. I feel one-down. I think that you may not want what I have to offer and may reject me, and then I start thinking about leaving you."

In this kind of presentation of the problem, Louise finally owns her feelings. It is clear from this presentation that the problem results from her reactions to or interpretations of Lance's behavior. The emphasis is on her feelings, not on his behavior. The I-messages in no way challenge Lance's right to do what he's been doing. Rather, they focus on the undesirable effects that his behavior has on Louise. The negative reactions then become Lance's problem to the extent that he cares for Louise and wants to improve their relationship.

The presentation of a problem in I-messages always takes more courage, for this is truly open communication, which reveals one's feelings. But I-messages describe with much greater accuracy what the problem really is, and they open it up for solving. More importantly, this is a communication style which elicits openness, cooperation, and problem solving rather than defensiveness. The I-message says, "I hurt"; the you-message says, "You're a louse." It is obvious which one will better stimulate a helping response.

In attempting to solve this problem, Lance may be willing to give up his flirting at parties or to give more attention to Louise or to include her in his socializing. He may be freed up to look critically at his own behavior or motivations and to clarify what his real feelings are about Louise, their relationship, and his other friends. Whatever the solution, it can be one which speaks directly at least to the initial problem: Louise's needs and feelings. Once this problem is correctly defined, the couple can join to discover any number of solutions. And some may be much better than the simple changes implied by the accusatory you-messages. Whatever the outcome, it should be very favorably influenced by this no-fault communication device, which builds intimacy rather than destroying it. *When we recognize that our needs cannot dictate the correct behavior of others, we are bound to get along with them better.* The language of I-messages expresses that recognition. It allows—indeed, it requires—others to take responsibility for the effects of their own behavior while it recognizes their freedom. You-messages, on the other hand, tend to prescribe what is right and wrong in some absolute sense and thus usurp the freedom of another to determine his own behavior.

Finally, I-messages are almost impossible to argue with. They are statements of fact about one's feelings. Since each individual is the only one privy to his or her feelings, there is no debating about them. Neither can anyone legitimately tell another how he or she should or should not feel. One's feelings simply are. And when you feel bad about the behavior of another and reveal your feelings, he or she can then decide what to do about it. If you use I-messages instead of accusatory you-messages, chances are your partner will want to do something constructive.

Now that you know the distinction between I-messages and you-messages, you can use this knowledge to improve your communication with those with whom you are involved, or you can use it to outmaneuver them. You can criticize others' frequent use of you-messages, correct both their philosophy and their presentation of complaints, increase your likelihood of "winning" arguments, and completely frustrate communication. Just one reminder before you begin your outmaneuvering: becoming thoroughly aware of the feelings, good or bad, of your relationship partner(s) is almost always in your own best interest.

Active Listening

In my clinical practice, I have had occasion to observe many couples in conflict. Those who experience prolonged conflict have one important thing in common. They don't listen. Those who fail either to resolve conflicts or to discover they are unresolvable fail partly because they never hear the problem. People in prolonged conflict are typically so anxious to jump to their own defense or to make counteraccusations that they don't hear the whole story behind their opponents' dissatisfaction. Presuming that someone is surely to blame for any problem that arises, they set out immediately to prove that they are not the one who's guilty. Perhaps the most helpful thing that a counselor can do for couples in conflict is to disrupt the defensive, counteraccusatory reflex of each partner so that each may listen to the distress of the other. When this is done, each partner is helped to discover the content of the other's distressed feelings. Accusations almost naturally decrease and are replaced by I-messages of personal distress. Thus, the best way to get I-messages from your partner is not to give didactic training in communication—especially when the other is upset. Rather, the treatment of choice is respectful and active listening to the other's complaints, no matter how they are phrased.

The basic principle of active listening is to acknowledge in one way or another that you hear what the other has said. In a situation of conflict, you must inhibit your defensive-accusatory reflex by keeping quiet and listening to the other, acknowledging what is said in the simplest ways by nodding your head or by such comments as "I see," "Go on," "Tell me more," "What else?" Although this appears to be extraordinarily simple-minded, the blocking of your defensive-accusatory reaction can have dramatic effects. Continued and responsive listening, expecially by one partner in conflict, is so rare that you need do little more than be attentive to have a dramatically positive effect on the other.

One active-listening skill involves acknowledging the other by a simple *parroting* of his stated concerns. In parroting, you simply say back to the other person what he has said to you. Though this can be rather frustrating if used repeatedly, it is one useful technique among others for acknowledging the concern of the other person and encouraging him to go on. Another technique, which requires more skill and better listening, is *paraphrasing*, restating what the other has said in your own words. Still another technique is *interpreting* what the other means by what he says; this takes the most expertise in listening and requires the most understanding of the other person. Here is a simple illustration of these three different but related ways of acknowledging what another says and encouraging him to go on:

Initial statement. "I'll sure be glad when this week is over."

Parroting response. "You'll be glad when this week is over."

Paraphrasing response. "It will be a relief to be through this week."

Interpreting response. "You're having a rough week at the office."

This isn't as simple as it seems because most of us are so much more inclined to talk than listen, and, when accused, our reflex is to defend and counteraccuse. Psychotherapists in training and marital couples in therapy are often subjected to intensive training in these listening skills. I've taught both groups, and, believe me, it often takes a seeming eternity to get people to become good active listeners. Part of that difficulty comes from a pervasive resistance to learning the basic no-fault philosophy behind the techniques, and part of it comes from the fact that such listening goes against well-established habits of not-listening. If you want to learn to be a good active listener, you probably will have to practice even the simplest skills in nonthreatening situations before you can use them in conflictual settings with your partner. There is plenty of opportunity for practice, since everyone appreciates a good listener, and these skills may be generally applied in all social situations. Then, when in conflict, you can use your knowledge of the different kinds of active listening to order your reactions, and you can remind yourself of these simple strategies for nondefensive listening. When you feel defensive, be quiet, nod, or parrot. Try to listen while inhibiting your defensive-accusatory reflex. Then, when you are less defensive, try the more difficult tasks of paraphrasing and interpreting.

There is one additional active-listening technique which is particularly useful in conflictual situations. It is *negative inquiry.* In negative inquiry, you simply ask for any further criticisms that the other has of you. Since, as

I've noted earlier, it is usually in your best interest to know of the dissatisfaction of your relationship partner, it is most efficient to ask, "What else don't you like about me?"

Now that you know the definitions of the principles, here they are, illustrated in dialogue:

Walter: I'm sorry I'm late, Valerie. A whole bunch of last-minute things came up at the office, topped off by a long-distance call about an important case. I just couldn't get away any sooner.

Valerie: I've about had it with you. This time you're an hour and a half late. I can never depend on you. I'm fed up with you. [you-statements]

Walter: Wow! I didn't expect that. I'm a little overwhelmed. [I-statements] You're really upset. [paraphrasing]

Valerie: You're damn right I am! It's always something. Why can't you show some concern for me? [you-statements]

Walter: You don't think I show concern for you? [parroting]

Valerie: That's right. You're a selfish son of a bitch. You belittle me as if it were the most natural thing in the world. This is just one more example. [you-statements]

Walter: This is just an example of my selfishness and my belittling you? [parroting]

Valerie: Right. You want some other examples? Last Thursday, you were an hour late when I'd asked you over for dinner. And that same night you told me that you were going out with Jane on Friday. A week ago

Sunday you shut me out by going with your friends to play pool all afternoon and most of the evening. You just like to have me around for your convenience. [you-statements]

Walter: I'm scared and surprised by all this. I didn't know these things were bothering you. [I-statements] Is there more about what I've been doing lately that you don't like? [negative inquiry]

Valerie: There's just a lot of little things. I don't like it that you're going out with Jane, but I can handle that. [I-statement] Why can't you just show more consideration for my feelings in handling that part of your life? [you-statement]

Walter: It sounds as though you're unsure of how I feel about you. [interpreting]

Valerie: That's part of it. You seem to want me around only when it's convenient. [you-statement] I feel really one-down because I don't have anybody else and I've been putting out a lot for you. [I-statements]

Walter: I'm sorry for that, Val, because you're very important to me. [I-statement] Is there anything else I do that makes you feel one-down or neglected? [negative inquiry]

Valerie: Yes, I feel neglected and one-down when you and Jerry start talking about the law and law school. I feel left out. [I-statements]

Walter: O.K., let me get this straight. You don't like it when I am late, when I tell you I'm going out with Jane, when I spend time with other friends when you want to be with me, and when I talk law with Jerry. Right? [paraphrasing]

Valerie: That's right.

Walter: O.K., let's try to work these things out. I want things to be good between us. [I-statement]

I made up this dialogue and made Walter the hero. But, except for its smoothness, this interaction sequence is fairly typical of what can occur when one party to a conflict knows enough to use I-messages and active listening. At first, Walter primarily used I-statements to recover after the initial attack and employed the simpler active-listening technique of parroting. Then, as appropriate, he used paraphrasing, interpreting, and negative inquiry to encourage Valerie to continue talking and to expand on her complaint. Prompted by his example and freed by his simple listening, Valerie began to make I-statements of her own and to reveal more about why she was so upset. Walter then summarized by paraphrasing each of her concerns and set the stage for negotiation and problem solving. As the interaction progressed, he could see that his active listening was working because he got responses of recognition, and Valerie kept talking, giving him useful information about her concerns.

If you try active listening yourself, either in conflict or other situations, you can read your effectiveness by noticing the response of the other person. If he or she continues to talk and readily agrees with your paraphrases and interpretations, you are doing very well. If he or she hesitates, stops talking, or repeatedly tells you your paraphrasing and interpreting are off base, you need to listen more carefully. Don't be inhibited by being wrong. An occasional incorrect interpretation, for example, can help the other person clarify for himself or herself what the correct interpretation is. The fact that you conscientiously try to listen and understand is quite good enough. In any conflict, the important thing is to get the needs of each person expressed explicitly, so that negotiation and problem solving can begin with good grounding. That is the next step.

Negotiation

There is only one basic principle to good negotiation: to search for a solution to a problem which meets the needs of both individuals in conflict. This is sometimes impossible, but knowing exactly what the problem is from both points of view makes it far more likely that a solution can be found. Let us pick up this interaction between Valerie and Walter to illustrate this point.

Walter: Well, let's take these one at a time. About my being late—I just had to be late this evening, and that can happen any time. My business is the kind that requires me to be there when I'm needed.

Valerie: I know that. I just want you to call me if you're going to be late, and tell me how late you will be. I don't want you to take my waiting for you for granted. I just want a little respect.

Walter: O.K., O.K., I can do that. If I'm going to be more than, say, a half hour late, I'll call. How's that?

Valerie: That's good enough.

Walter: O.K. But you know I'm not going to stop dating Jane.

Valerie: Yes, I know. I don't want you to stop that unless you want to. But, damn it, I don't want to hear about every time you see her and everything you do. It just makes me feel bad. You don't have to throw it in my face.

Walter: I sure don't want to do that, but neither do

I want to have to censor what I say about what I do. Sometimes I like to talk about the things I do which just happen to be with Jane.

Valerie: I can see that, but it bothers me. Maybe we can't solve this one.

Walter: Maybe not. But I will try to keep it to a minimum and not talk about times with Jane unless there's some purpose to it. How's that?

Valerie: I think that's about as good as we can do. It's not easy for anybody. Now, I don't know what we can do about you and Jerry leaving me out of your law talk.

Walter: Yeah, that's a tough one. Jerry and I just seem to drift into that. It would be awfully hard to stop.

Valerie: Well, actually, I don't always mind it. If there is someone else there to talk to or if it goes on only for a short while, I don't mind it. It's just when it goes on and on, and I have to sit there while you two speak in a foreign language. It makes me feel so unnecessary and so bored.

Walter: Could you signal me when it's beginning to be a bother?

Valerie: Yes, I could if you would check in with me from time to time, too, just to ask me if it's bugging me.

Walter: All right. If I catch myself doing it when you're there, I'll ask if it's O.K., and, if you get tired of hearing lawyer talk, you will tell us.

Valerie: O.K. Agreed.

Walter: About seeing my friends on the weekend; that's something I've been doing for years off and on, and I can't give that up.

Valerie: I just hate saving my weekends for you, and then having you come up with something else to do.

Walter: Well, I must admit that I like your doing that, but I've also wanted the freedom to do other things as well. I guess that is a little selfish, isn't it?

Valerie: Yeah, that's what I thought. Got any proposals?

Walter: What if I took every third weekend for other things and kept all the rest for us as we've been doing?

Valerie: That wouldn't work. They can't be put on a schedule. Two of them travel a lot and they aren't around reliably. It wouldn't work.

Walter: You're right.

Valerie: Maybe I shouldn't save any time for you unless we agree on it ahead of time. Either you invite me for part or all of a weekend, or I'll invite you, and we'll get it all straight ahead of time.

Walter: O.K. I guess I'll have to face up to that. I agree.

Valerie: I think I've just become too dependent on you for where you're at. I'm going to have to plan more things of my own.

Walter: Can you fit me into this weekend?

Valerie: Friday night and Saturday are good, but I do have something else I can do on Sunday, and I'm going to do it.

Walter: Well, I find your independence a little scary, but I know you're right. I agree. Let's talk about all this again in two weeks and see how we're doing.

Valerie: O.K. Now let's make up.

It's possible to be rational about problems when you put them outside yourself a bit and join forces against them. The details of any compromise solution

are not important, but the process by which they're arrived at is. Whenever possible, the solutions should
meet the needs of both people involved. Of course,
sometimes this is impossible, and those are the times
where you must decide whether the conflict is one that
can be lived with or not. This is not a comfortable decision, of course, but it is better made deliberately and
consciously.

Measured Honesty and Persistent Concern

There are two additional guidelines I have found
useful for managing relationships. Both are concerned
with when to communicate information that your partner would find negative or difficult to handle. Many
people seem to choose one of two extreme positions on
how honest to be. Some select a highly passive approach
which dictates that almost nothing of a negative nature
should be shared with a partner, at least not until it becomes an overwhelming problem. Afraid of hurting the
other's feelings, afraid of conflict and a possible breach
in the relationship, these people unwisely pack away
their grievances and often reveal them only in an exploding outburst of hostility. People who behave in this way
are frequently those who, after years of apparent tranquillity, suddenly leave their relationship with a torrent
of pent-up anger. At the other extreme are people who
seem to worship honesty in a relationship. That something is true is the only necessary standard for determining whether it should be expressed. Those involved
in relationships of this kind are often very proud of
their honesty, but in my experience these relationships

often are the most destructive. In my judgment, both of these extreme positions on honesty are unhealthy for most relationships.

As helpful guidelines, I offer the principles of *measured honesty* and *persistent concern*. In communicating negative information, the concept of measured honesty dictates: say only what is *true, timely,* and *necessary*. This principle requires you to ask three questions of any negative information you are about to impart. *Is it true?* Out-and-out lying to avoid hurting another person's feelings is usually not called for and is generally a bad idea. While you need not say everything that is true, it is better if what you do say is true. *Is it timely?* Is the present time and circumstance good for the discussion of what is negative or upsetting? It may be true that your partner is being less than fair about sharing expenses, and to discuss this may be absolutely necessary, but to begin the discussion when you're out to dinner with friends is certainly untimely.

Is it necessary? This is usually the toughest question to answer. Communication of negative or difficult information would be necessary if it were something that the other person would need to know in order to make an informed decision about the relationship, as, for example, one partner's continuing involvement in an important, outside relationship. Similarly, one would usually be well advised to tell a partner about any changeable behavior or characteristic which one does not like, since such communication may lead to an improvement of the relationship.

The principle I call persistent concern, which also helps determine when to share negative information, was introduced by Carl Rogers in his book *Becoming Partners* as follows: "In any continuing relationship, any persistent feeling had better be expressed." If a negative feeling is persistently upsetting, its expression is usually called for. Even if the problem about which you are persistently concerned is not a changeable one, expressing it, bringing it out into the open, can often make it much easier for you to live with. So, in determining when you should share negative information, realize that all things that are true do not necessarily need to be said. When you feel you must communicate negative information, it is best communicated truthfully and at the right time. If it represents a persistent concern, it is likely also to represent a truth that sooner or later must be communicated if the relationship is to survive.

The Modality Check

There is one final principle which is extremely simple to understand and execute and which can assist any couple to achieve a smoother, more helpful communication system. It is illustrated by the following vignette, described to me by Ron and Cathy. A newly married couple, she was a student in medical school and he a graduate student in clinical psychology.

Ron (as Cathy enters at the end of a workday): It looks as if you've had a rough day.
Cathy: Thompson is giving me a hard time again. The same thing happened again today. On rounds, he asked me everything I didn't know, and ignored me when I did know something. He used every opportunity

to pick on me. He directed all his one-upmanship shots at me—as though he has some kind of vendetta.

Ron: I think you should try talking with him about that.

Cathy: I get so upset, I can't talk to him about anything.

Ron: Well, you'll never change this if you can't talk about it.

Cathy: I suppose you're right, but I can't.

Ron: Oh, yes, you can. Let's role-play it. I'll be Thompson, and you come in and talk to me.

Cathy: I don't want to.

Ron: I wish you'd let me help you. Look, I have a book here on assertiveness training I think you should read.

Cathy: God damn it, I know all about that stuff. You think you're so smart. Just leave me alone.

Ron: Well, I was just trying to help. I know some useful things, too, you know.

Cathy: Go help somebody else. I think you're a pain in the ass.

Ron: You're just taking your hostility for Thompson out on me. It's displacement.

Cathy: Fuck off.

What's the problem here? The problem is that Cathy wanted to communicate in the *expressive mode.* She was tired, angry, and defeated, and she wanted support. She merely wanted to complain to Ron about her situation. She knew all the solutions that Ron suggested and at another time might have wanted to discuss them or try them out. But this time she merely wanted to grouse a little to Ron and get his loving support. Ron didn't understand this. Like so many of us, he assumed that a complaint meant something needed to be fixed, and he rushed in to help fix it. He was communicating in the *problem-solving mode*. Cathy found Ron's suggestions demeaning and frustrating, and continuing in the expressive mode, she told him so.

In the course of his training, Ron learned about the concept of the *modality check* and employed it on later, similar occasions. When Cathy complained, Ron would try to remember to ask her whether or not she just wanted to talk about the problem and get it off her chest, or whether she wanted him to help her figure out some solution to it. He tried to avoid offering suggestions until he had Cathy's permission to do so. According to both of them, this simple change improved their relationship considerably. Ron continued to slip up from time to time because his reflex was to solve problems. But, with time and more experience as a clinician, he learned more and more about the value of giving advice only when it's asked for. He learned how extremely important it is just to listen when people complain—that most people prefer to be in charge of solving their own problems.

I recommend this modality check to you for improving your communication, especially in primary relationships. Check out the modality in which your distressed partner is communicating and stay within it. Further, let your partner know when you are communicating in the expressive mode and just want a good listener, and when you're looking for some help in solving a problem. When two people speak the same language, they usually understand each other better.

How Communication Can Help

In relationships today, nothing can be implicit, nothing can be assumed. Increasingly, relationships function according to their own individually negotiated contracts. Expectations, roles, and responsibilities are becoming explicit, and they differ radically from one relationship to the next. Furthermore, the terms of relationship contracts must be open to change as the society changes and as the needs of the partners evolve. One cannot usually succeed in a long-term relationship anymore by entering it with an implicit standard job description and sticking faithfully to it for life. Rather, one must discover what a good job description is in any given relationship and decide whether or not to fill it. And part of the job description for many contemporary relationships will be an acceptance of potential change in the job description itself as the relationship evolves.

It is virtually impossible to do all this without well-developed communication skills. From deciding on the etiquette rules of a first encounter to deciding on whether to have children, people need to be able to talk about their respective needs and to listen to those of their partner in an open and nonblaming way. Good communication cannot make every relationship, but poor communication can certainly break even the best of them.

It is popular to say that relationships end because of failures in communication. This is almost always an oversimplification; more basic is the failure of the relationship to meet the needs of its members—the real conflict which arises when these needs cannot be met. Typically, only as people get farther from their broken relationships do they see much greater complexity in the reasons for their difficulties as a couple—that there were serious and persistent conflicts which were never resolved and which, gradually, eroded their relationship. They often realize that they missed the signs of progressive erosion, perceiving the death of their relationship only after it was too late to be revived. Then they realize that better communication might have achieved a more desirable outcome, either by saving the relationship or ending it on a more constructive basis.

Still, it is important to recognize that not all failures in communication are due to people's not knowing how. Often, people who know how to communicate simply refuse to because they are afraid to listen or afraid to present grievances. Whatever the cause, when there is a breakdown in communication, a breakdown of the relationship begins—a breakdown which good communication would either eliminate or affirm. Whenever we communicate about conflict, we risk learning that the conflict is unresolvable and that our relationship cannot meet mutual needs. Sometimes, that realization will bring an end to the relationship. But, as I have argued from the very beginning of this book, such an ending is infinitely better than the slow and tortured termination of a dead relationship where communication, and thus real relating, has ended and the recognition of death is merely postponed.

In order to have the best relationship with another, we must always be willing not to have it at all. All the communication skill in the world will do us no good if we are unwilling to use it. And, I believe, we will be willing to use it only when we know we cannot lose ourselves by losing another. No-fault communication will be best achieved by an autonomous adult who possesses a no-fault philosophy of life. For such a person, there is little to fear no matter what happens. This is a state of being which may be impossible to realize to the full, but it is, I think, a destination worth the journey.

CONCLUSION

There are no longer established and accepted modes of personal existence. There is no one "right way" to live, endorsed and supported by a unified community. The monogamous-marriage solution has been found wanting in our culture by most who have tried it, despite wholehearted attempts to make it work. People who commit themselves to love another, to marriage, to family, and to the stream of a meaningful life which these commitments usually represent do not forsake them easily. They wish the prescription to be successful, and they have done their best to succeed. But, in spite of this, it has failed again and again. Whether we have tried the prescription personally or not, this fact of our social life must give us pause. In concert with many other developments in our culture, it suggests that we are very much on our own, that we are called upon to *choose* a personal way of life from among those available and try it.

When we do this, life becomes an experiment, and each of us becomes experimenter and subject in the most important and urgent social research. We are all social scientists, selecting an experiment to live and living it as best we can. There are, of course, many gurus and guides and answer books to tell us the way, and most of them claim to have *the* prescription that will work for all. But the catch is that we still have to pick from among them. It is this fact which is so distressing to so many, because it implies that no matter what we choose, we are making up the essence of our life as we go along. This realization can be so frightening that it compels many to search for that safe place where these decisions need never be faced. There is no such place. By incessantly trying to construct it, we miss out on the stream of life, the vitality of new experience, and the joy of personal discovery. Whether we like it or not, we all must determine our own essence and experiment with it.

This confrontation with oneself is usually more apparent for single people because they are more frequently required to make these personal decisions, and they usually feel more freedom to choose among alternatives. With regard to relationships, they must decide whether to remain essentially single or embrace a primary relationship. If they choose the latter, they must decide: Will it be monogamous? Will it mean living together? Will it be marital? Will it involve children? The decisions only begin here and are made considerably more difficult because two experiments in living must join.

No one else can make these decisions for you. You must indeed make up the essence of your life as you go along. You are on your own. But, in making your own decision, consider Don Juan's advice given in Carlos Castenada's *The Teachings of Don Juan:*

> Look at every path closely and deliberately.
> Try it as many times as you think necessary.
> Then ask yourself, and yourself alone, one
> question. . . . Does this path have a heart? If

it does, the path is good; if it doesn't, it is of
no use. . . . One makes for a joyful journey;
as long as you follow it, you are one with it.
The other will make you curse your life. One
makes you strong; the other weakens you.

If you could solve every one of the problems presented in this book, your path with a heart might still not
be apparent to you. You have come to the back of the
book, and the answer to that question is not here. But
solving the problems of living as one—achieving autonomous adulthood—will free you to look for your path and
permit you to follow it just because it's right for you.
Then, as Ram Dass assures, "Whenever you're ready,
you'll hear the next message."

Notes

INTRODUCTION

Page
14 "In 1974, for instance, the divorce rate": Center for Health Statistics, Department of Health, Education, and Welfare. Cited in the *Christian Science Monitor*, March 1975.

1. How to Say Good-bye

36 "How Can I Miss You When You Won't Go Away?" is the title of a song by Dan Hicks.
46 ". . . many contemporary marriages are plagued": Current estimates indicate that from one couple in every four to one couple in every seven are currently unhappy. See Bradburn, N. M., and Caplovitz, D., *Reports on Happiness* (Chicago: Aldine Publishing Co., 1965); Landis, J. T., "Social Correlates of Divorce or Non-divorce Among the Unhappy Married," *Marriage and Family Living*, May 1963, 178–180; Renee, K. S., "Correlates of Dissatisfaction in Marriage," *Journal of Marriage and the Family*, 32 (1970), 54–66; Rollins, B. C., and Feldman, H., "Marital Satisfaction Over the Family Life Cycle," *Journal of Marriage and the Family*, 2 (1970), 20–28.

2. The Emotional Turmoil of Separation and What to Do About It

51 "Recent research has established": Holmes, T. H., and Rahe, R. H., "The Social Adjustment Rating Scale," *Journal of Psychosomatic Research*, 11 (1967), 213–218.

3. Negotiating the Future

93 "Current estimates indicate that women": The U.S. Bureau of the

Census, 1975, indicates that 8.4 percent of the children of divorced parents live with their fathers. The census data reflect a slight increase in paternal custody from 1970 to 1975.

101   "Current estimates indicate that approximately": In Sheresky, N., and Mannes, M., *Uncoupling: The Art of Coming Apart* (New York: Viking Press, Inc., 1972).

4. AUTONOMOUS ADULTHOOD: A JOB DESCRIPTION FOR THE SINGLE ADULT

117   "In this country, 70 percent": U.S. Bureau of the Census figures reported in *Statistical Abstract of the United States*, 1974.

118   "The separated single, the divorced, the widowed": At present, about five sixths of the divorced men and approximately three fourths of the divorced women eventually remarry, according to Paul C. Glick in his presentation to the Seminar on the Single Parent, Center for Policy Research, Cambridge, Massachusetts, April 1974.

118   "In the most recent Roper poll": Reported in *The Los Angeles Times*, October 6, 1974.

120   ". . . single, divorced, and widowed men experience": Gove, W. R., "The Relationship Between Sex Roles, Marital Status, and Mental Illness," *Social Focus*, 51 (1972), 34–44; Gove, W. R., "Sex, Marital Status, and Suicide," *Journal of Health and Social Behavior*, 13 (1972), 204–213; Johnson, S. M., Zeiss, A., and Zeiss, R., *After Divorce: A Study of Readjustment*. In preparation.

121   "In discussing marriage, William Lederer": Lederer, W., and Jackson, D., *The Mirages of Marriage* (New York: W. W. Norton & Co., Inc., 1968).

5. HOW TO CHANGE

149   ". . . there are many helpful books": For basic cookbooks, see the following: Davis, A., *Let's Cook It Right* (New York: Signet Books, 1970); Rombauer, I. S., and Becker, M. R., *The Joy of Cooking*, Vols. 1 and 2 (New York: New American Library, 1974). For a very simple and convenient book for beginners, see Parker, E., *Cooking for One* (New York: Thomas Y. Crowell Company, 1968).

For a good guide to setting up a house, especially for young women on a limited budget, see Krakowski, L., *Starting Out: The Guide I Wish I'd Had When I Left Home* (New York: Stein & Day, 1973).

For advice on financial planning and budgeting, see Porter, S., *Sylvia Porter's Money Book* (New York, Avon Press, 1976). For a simple guide to auto mechanics, see Edmonds, I., and Gonzales, R., *Understanding Your Car* (New York: Harper and Row, 1975; paperback, Canfield Press).

8. GETTING TOGETHER

243 "Our own research suggests": Johnson, S. M., Zeiss, A., and Zeiss, R., *After Divorce: A Study of Readjustment.* In preparation.

9. SENSUALITY AND INTIMACY

310 ". . . there is a plethora of new books": Barber, L., *How to Improve Your Man in Bed* (New York: Pocket Books, 1975); Comfort, A. *The Joy of Sex* (New York: Crown Pubs., Inc., 1972); Comfort, A., *More Joy of Sex* (New York: Crown Pubs., Inc., 1974); Ellis, A., *The Art and Science of Love* (New Hyde Park, N.Y.: Lyle Stuart, Inc., 1960); J., *The Sensuous Woman* (New York: Dell Publishing Co., Inc., 1971); Masters, W., and Johnson, V., *The Pleasure Bond* (Boston: Little, Brown & Co., 1975).

10. RELATIONSHIPS AND COMMITMENTS

339 ". . . other helpful books": See Ellis, A., and Harper, R. A., *A Guide to Successful Marriage* (North Hollywood, Cal.: Wilshire Book Co., 1968); Lederer, W. J., and Jackson, D. D., *The Mirages of Marriage* (New York: W. W. Norton & Co., 1968); O'Neill, N., and O'Neill, G., *Open Marriage* (New York: M. Evans & Co., 1972); Shostom, E., and Kavanaugh, J., *Between Man and Woman* (New York: Bantam Books, 1975).

341 "I-Messages versus You-Messages": Like many of the communication principles introduced in this chapter, this basic concept has been around for a long time, and its specific origin is very difficult to determine. It was Thomas Gordon in his book, *Parent Effectiveness Training* (New York: Peter H. Wyden, Inc., 1970), who labeled this concept in this most helpful way.

354 "Measured Honesty": The concept of measured honesty is introduced by Richard Stewart and William Lederer in their book, *How to Improve a Marriage* (New York: W. W. Norton, Inc., forthcoming).